Digital Character Development:
Theory and Practice

Digital Character Development:
Theory and Practice

Rob O'Neill

Pratt Institute,
Digital Arts Research Laboratory

AMSTERDAM • BOSTON • HEIDELBERG • LONDON
NEW YORK • OXFORD • PARIS • SAN DIEGO
SAN FRANCISCO • SINGAPORE • SYDNEY • TOKYO

Morgan Kaufmann Publishers is an imprint of Elsevier

ELSEVIER

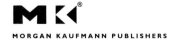

MORGAN KAUFMANN PUBLISHERS

Morgan Kaufmann Publishers is an imprint of Elsevier.
30 Corporate Drive, Suite 400, Burlington, MA 01803, USA

This book is printed on acid-free paper.

Library of Congress Cataloging-in-Publication Data
Application Submitted

ISBN: 978-0-12-372561-5

For information on all Morgan Kaufmann publications,
visit our Web site at *www.mkp.com* or *www.elsevierdirect.com*

Printed in the United States of America
08 09 10 11 12   5 4 3 2 1

Working together to grow
libraries in developing countries

www.elsevier.com | www.bookaid.org | www.sabre.org

ELSEVIER   BOOK AID
International   Sabre Foundation

Contents

v

List of Figures

List of Tables

Foreword

Animation involves breathing life into things. The word *animation* comes from the Proto-Indo-European root *ane-*, meaning "to breathe," via the Latin *anima*, meaning "living spirit." The spirit of animation lies in the characters—entities that people feel are alive (and possibly even sentient) when they engage with them.

Computer animation specifically involves breathing life into things by means of electronic systems that perform millions of calculations each second. Computers have the capability to present complex characters and the intricate worlds they inhabit in ways that draw people in and help us see past the vast arrays of binary digits inside the box. The only challenge is that someone has to tell the computer how to twiddle all those bits.

Breathing life into computer characters is a tricky blend of artistry and technology. The artistic side of this process entails a subtle understanding of both the characters in the animation and the audience to whom those characters are being presented. Great animation requires intuition and finesse, and certain effortlessness that facilitates the audience's suspension of disbelief. Underlying this artistry is an array of fields ranging from graphic design and cinematography all the way to psychology, anatomy, and physics.

Being a skilled computer animator also entails a rigorous understanding of a wide range of arcane technological skills. Terms like "quaternions," "matrices," and "inverse kinematics" are tossed around like grenades. To make the challenge even greater, the hardware and software underlying computer animation change so rapidly that it is hard to keep pace. Thus, computer animation requires a simultaneous grasp on both the esoteric and the cutting-edge.

Rob O'Neill is one among a small group of people in the world who can address both the artistry and technology of animation with equal skill. In this book, Rob provides a comprehensive treatment of several disparate yet interconnected parts, covering the overlap of anatomy, artistry, technology, mathematics, and many other elements that are critical to the creation of digital characters. Rob skillfully illuminates the complex interdependencies among such seemingly distinct aspects of animation and helps the reader understand why it is important to treat all of these issues together. You have chosen a wise guide through the lush jungle of computer animation.

This book is relevant to practicing animators, animation students, researchers, and anyone else who may have interest to know how animation works. It is not just a technical manual and not just a theoretical exploration of the creative process; it is both at once. As such, it gets to the heart of computer animation—an incredibly precise and exacting craft that seeks to produce characters with elegance, subtlety, love, fear, anguish, humor, and compassion.

– **Bill Tomlinson**
University of California, Irvine

Acknowledgments

This book would not be possible without all the hard work, innovation, and creative engineering by those who developed the ideas summarized within. The thoughtful reviews by Bill Tomlinson and TJ Galda added valuable insights and critical thoughts that made this a better book. I can not thank them enough for the time they invested in reviewing rough versions of the manuscript.

I owe a huge debt to all the members, past and present, of the Character Technical Direction Crew at PDI/Dreamworks Animation for their friendship, camaraderie, and ever-present desire to educate at every level. Special thanks to modeler/rigger extraordinaire Lee Wolland for the use of his immaculate human model for the creation of model screen shots and to Mark Snoswell, President of The Computer Graphics Society, for his generous donation of the cgHuman for the creation of muscle images in this book. His model set is an amazing resource for study and use in production.

I owe a huge debt to Dr. Bonnie Gustav of Brooklyn College for getting me hooked on biological anthropology and the evolutionary anatomy that goes with it and to Anezka Sebek of Parsons School of Design for helping me harness that into a career in animation. The support of my colleagues and students in the Department of Digital Arts at Pratt Institute provided much of the inspiration to write this text. In particular, thanks to Provost Peter Barna, Chair Peter Patchen, and Assistant Chair Melissa Barrett Lundquist for their support. Extra special thanks go to my Graduate Research Assistants at the Pratt Digital Arts Research Lab: Paris Mavroidis and George Smaragdis whose hard work is reflected in many of the images in this book and all the other amazing work that has been produced in the Lab.

Thanks to the editorial staff at Morgan Kaufmann past and present for their guidance, support, and patience, in particular: Tim Cox, Jessie Evans, Georgia Kennedy, Laura Lewin, Chris Simpson and Anais Wheeler. Thank you to Claudia Pisano and Beth Millett for the help in securing image rights.

The book was made so much better by the inclusion of interviews with the talented and generous Aaron Holly, Milana Huang, David Hunt, Steve Mann, Paul Marino, Ken Perlin, Nico Scapel, Jason Schleifer, and Todd Taylor. Their views are their own and they in no way endorse any of the other material in the book, but I hope they like it.

As a continual source of inspiration are my partners in the creation of Kickstand Animation Research + Design: Daniel Dawson, Greg Elshoff, and Phil McNagny. Keep an eye on the horizon for some good things in the near future.

Thanks to my parents, grandparents, brother and sister for fostering my sense of imagination and humor, two critical skills for working in animation production. Thanks to the support of my friends, new and old, who keep me sane. Finally my wife, Kate, whose support and enthusiasm for the book really carried me through to the end. From allowing me to take drafts of the manuscript on vacation, to being a great copy editor, she was the backbone of the creation of this book. Words can not express my appreciation for the effort she made.

Epic Games, the Epic Games logo, the Crimson Omen logo and Gears of War are either registered trademarks or trademarks of Epic Games, Inc. in the United States and/or elsewhere.

Introduction

Digital characters are a driving force in the entertainment industry today. Every animated film and video game production spends a large percentage of its resources and time on advancing the quality of the digital characters inhabiting the world that they are creating. We have entered an era when digital characters have reached a level of sophistication that has prompted some critics to question if a digital actor can win an Academy Award for acting. As artificial intelligence and behavioral animation become more integrated with hand-animated entities, we will see a dramatic increase in the realism and interactivity of these characters. Practitioners of the subject will also require a deeper understanding of the underlying conceptual foundation as the complexity of the technology increases. The field of character technology has matured into a topic that spans the realms of anatomy, animation, computer science, performance, and behavioral psychology. The contemporary uses of digital characters are varied and range from purely entertainment to biomedical, industrial simulation, and beyond. This book is an overview of the history, theory, and methods for creating digital characters. Many books cover the step-by-step creation of digital characters using a particular piece of software. This book forgoes existing software and deals with the concepts from a software-agnostic point of view.

Recently, characters such as Gollum from "The Lord of the Rings" series (2001–2004) and Davy Jones from the "Pirates of the Caribbean" series (2006–2007) have both been discussed with regard to earning awards for achievement in acting. Almost more compelling, a recent panel entitled "The Biology of King Kong," part of the 2006 Tribeca Film Festival, included a discussion on how "King Kong" (2005) was incredibly true to life and believable as a real gorilla. Panel member, Roger Fouts, Co-Director of the Chimpanzee and Human Communication Institute, discussed how pleased he was that the rise in technology and artistry has allowed for digital doubles and replacements for roles that were usually reserved for trained animals. While most critics are waiting for a believable human replacement, there is no better compliment for the team that created this digital character and no better indicator for the potential of character technology.

–Rob O'Neill

Part 1

An Introduction to Digital Characters

1

Overview

1.1 **OVERVIEW OF THIS BOOK**

This book is about character technology. Character technology is the merging of character animation and three-dimensional (3D) computer graphics technology into a series of concepts and methodologies resulting in a character able to be animated.

This book is intended to provide an introductory overview of the theory and practice of digital character development, often called character rigging, from a software-agnostic point of view. As a starting-off point for more complicated mathematical discussions and more artistic exploration, the text straddles the line between the arts and sciences that are required for success in the creation of compelling digital characters. As this subject is a moving target, updates, errata, and additional resources are compiled at:

http://www.charactertechnology.com

Starting with the evolution and history of digital characters, which is critical to the understanding of how characters developed alongside the techniques and technologies for creating them, we then begin the process of building characters from the inside out. Character setup starts by defining the anatomical considerations required and how they relate to the

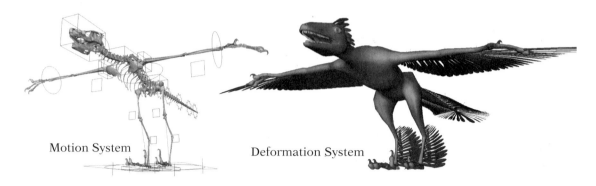

Motion System   Deformation System

■ **FIGURE 1.1** Screen capture of a character motion and deformation system. Character by George Smaragdis and Rob O'Neill.

structure of the character motion system (Figure 1.1) or the mechanical architecture that drives the model. At this point, we will deal with the control structure for the motion system that provides the interface to animation. From there, the look of the character in motion is defined by the deformation system, which is the planning and implementation of techniques that sculpt the character's shape as the motion system drives the manipulation of the model. Much of the life and emotion of a digital character is read through the face, and while facial setup is a mix of motion and deformation systems, the issues intrinsic to this aspect of character development require specific attention. In the areas of motion systems, deformation systems, and facial setup, we cover techniques currently in use by mixing descriptive text with algorithms and graphical representations of code for potential implementation. In the course of this discussion, digital characters created for both games and film are addressed.

Digital characters would be nothing without a means of moving them. In the animation technology section, we cover keyframe strategies and curve interpolation, with an emphasis on performance through traditional techniques. This is followed up by motion capture and how human performers are stepping into the shoes of digital characters. Furthermore, code often also drives motion, so procedural animation, artificial intelligence, and multi-character systems used for crowd simulations are a necessary component of modern character development. Finally, interactive characters are considered with a focus on the setup and limitations for characters created for game and non-game related interactive media.

The future of digital characters is where we conclude with a look into research questions that remain outstanding and some challenges for work beyond them.

1.2 **DEFINING DIGITAL CHARACTERS**

The word "animation" basically means "physically or graphically moving," derived from latin *anima* which refers to living beings, spirit, and feeling and the Greek *anemos* for wind and breath. An animated character could be said to have had the divine wind (animus) breathed into it. A digital character can be defined as an animated entity that has been brought to life using a computer. These characters are often found in films, television, interactive media projects, and most prevalently in video games. The creation of these entities can employ off-the-shelf software or custom programming to attain the desired results. Nomenclature for this digital species is diverse and continually evolving. "Digital actors," "virtual actors," "vactors," and "synthespians" have all been used, but these all imply a connection to acting, and thus humans. The term "avatar" has also been used as a catchall phrase, but this term has evolved into a representation of a player or human inhabitant in an interactive system. For the purposes of this book, we will refer to computer-generated entities as digital characters to encompass all imaginable forms and acting abilities, with an emphasis on 3D animation media. An interesting distinction has been made in the film industry between digital characters and digital creatures [26], the main differentiation being that of performance. Where a digital beast attacking a group of tourists would be described as a digital creature, while a compelling gorilla who falls in love with the film's starlet would be described as a digital character. This distinction comes from the amount of work required in creating the character, the amount of screen-time, and the viewer's connection with the character on screen. This

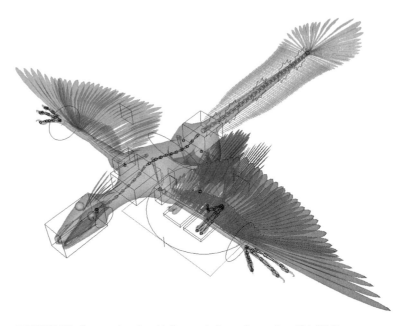

■ **FIGURE 1.2** Character rig and model. Character by George Smaragdis and Rob O'Neill.

book ignores the distinction between digital characters and digital creatures as the underlying functionality and setup is very similar.

Creating a digital character with the ability to produce a rich performance requires the interaction of a number of subjects and pathways of thinking. In a digital space, this process always walks the line between aspects of art and science, using technology as a bridge. This book covers all facets of digital character development but focuses primarily on the realm of what has been traditionally called "character rigging" or "character setup." This is the process of creating the architecture, called "the rig" (Figure 1.2), and methodologies required for animating, by means of user-set keyframes or procedural control, the motion of the character. This is a crucial role that requires knowledge of anatomy, as well as animation. With the increasing complexity of characters needed for various forms of media, a knowledge of programming to reinvent or extend the available tools is crucial.

1.3   **ROLES IN THE CREATION OF DIGITAL CHARACTERS**

There are many tasks when it comes to digital character development. While job titles are constantly evolving and technological growth empowers the individual to accomplish more on their own, it is worthwhile to discuss some of the roles associated with the creation of digital characters. At the start of production, we have the concept artists and character designers who plan the overall look of the characters. Character modelers then take the character designs developed by the art team and build the 3D sculpture based on production specifications for size, proportion, style, and geometric surface type. Once approved, this model is handed off to the position most benefiting from this book, the character technical director. Often called "rigger," "character setup artist," or "creature developer," the character technical director's title at some studios may even be condensed down to something as non-descript as technical director, but the role remains the same. Character technical directors are responsible for taking the 3D model and adding all the "bones" and "muscles" that allow an animator to move the character in a predictable manner and deform those surfaces in a manner consistent with the aesthetics of the production. Character technical directors are charged with designing the motion system which provides the architecture and control structures for how the rig is animated as well as the deformation system which defines how the model is affected by the motion system and the animation that is fed to it. Other components such as dynamic cloth, hair, and accessories associated with the characters are often also the domain of this role.

From here, the character is in the hands of the animators and the technicians responsible for attaching motion to the rig, but the character technical director will continue to oversee the maintenance of the rig until the end of production. At the early stages of production, character technical directors spend time doing research and development on new techniques for improving their character pipeline in addition to the specific challenges of future productions.

1.4 **CONCLUSION**

Digital characters are developed using various techniques, collectively called character technology. This technology is implemented by the character technical director based on the needs of the production. This book serves as an overview of the concepts and the technology behind digital characters to foster the development of innovative techniques and compelling performances.

■ **FURTHER READING**

Tim McLaughlin. Taxonomy of digital creatures: Interpreting character designs as computer graphics techniques. In *SIGGRAPH '05: ACM SIGGRAPH 2005 Courses*, page 1, ACM Press, New York, NY, 2005.

Chapter 2

Contemporary Issues Related to Digital Characters

The challenge of creating a compelling digital character that both looks and behaves in an appealing manner is a tremendous undertaking. Digital characters share the same difficulties inherent in traditional animation, but their trend toward realism presents many additional challenges. In this section, we examine the design decisions that must be acknowledged in the development of a digital character and the pitfalls that can arise along the way. Characters created for live-action integration and those for fully animated productions share the same challenges, and some of the best lessons come from the worlds of illustration and robotics. Also in this section, we will look at how digital characters are being used in important areas, such as education and user survey, where the delicate connection between the character and the human makes all the difference in assessing the successfulness of the project and the intended outcome.

2.1 VIEWER PERCEPTION AND THE "UNCANNY VALLEY"

It's all in the eyes...

The perception of digital characters is determined by the reaction of the viewer to the look and performance of the character on screen. While a poor performance by a human actor may result in laughter or snickering by the audience, the unconvincing performance by a digital character in a live-action film has a much more jarring effect, particulary when that character is supposed to be realistic. Animated characters with a high degree of abstraction or a cartoon-like appearance are generally more accepted by the audience whether they are interacting in an animated or a live-action world. That being said, the stakes are higher for characters, which must be integrated with live human actors.

Writer and comic book theorist Scott McCloud [25] has distilled the distinction between character realism and abstraction. An abstract character with a simplified face has the ability to emote more clearly via the process of amplification through simplification. By eliminating details, we are allowed to focus on the specific details required to create a performance, and thus the expression is amplified (Figure 2.1). We have seen this in the incredible popularity of animated characters, such as Mickey Mouse and Bugs Bunny, that with their simplified design have the ability to captivate a wide range of audiences.

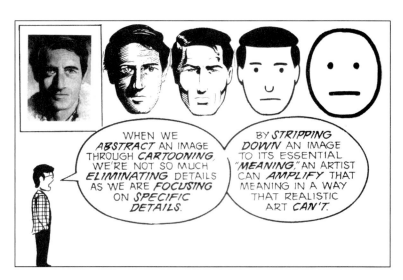

■ **FIGURE 2.1** Abstraction of the human face by Scott McCloud [25]. Copyright © 1993, 1994 Scott McCloud. Reprinted by permission of HarperCollins Publishers.

When it comes to digital characters, much of the discussion with regard to believability and the ability to forge a connection with the human observer is rooted in the study of robotics. Long before digital characters were at a level of sophistication to even address this subject, engineers were experimenting with the visual representation of emotion in real-world robots. Robots share many similarities with digital characters, from the computational aspects of kinematics to their perception by viewers. The connection between them can be encapsulated by the observations of Japanese roboticist Masahiro Mori, who in 1970 raised the idea of the "Uncanny Valley" [28].

Mori's concept states that as we approach a realistic visage of a human, the familiarity level plummets. The drop generally takes place at around the 75% point toward realism, and we experience a drop-off into a familiarity valley where the connection to the entity becomes more akin to how we perceive zombies and prosthetics (Figure 2.2). This is a common issue that, for the most part, cannot be expressed by the viewer but is endemic to digital characters. We, as humans, are naturally accustomed to the nuances and idiosyncrasies of a living

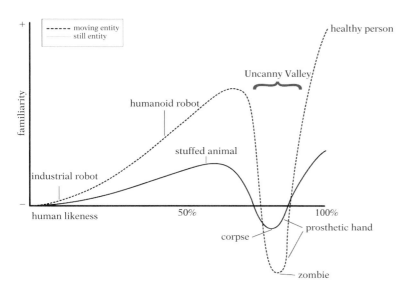

■ **FIGURE 2.2**   The Uncanny Valley as described by Masahiro Mori.

person. What the "Uncanny Valley" describes is how we pick up on the small percentage of "non-humanness" in a character and fixate on that. The other details become irrelevant to us; our senses tell us something is unnatural about what we are seeing. We focus on the lack of skin translucency, the stillness of the eyes, and the slightly robotic motion. The character that was once appealing has given way to an animated corpse and our sense of familiarity plunges.

This small percentage is what animators and roboticists are charged with overcoming when they are in the process of creating something that is supposed to be "alive." This is not a simple feat. At some point, most of us have experienced an "uneasy" feeling when watching a digital character. Perhaps, in watching a film with a character that you were supposed to connect with, you felt as if that character was lifeless, not in a stiff, poorly animated way, but in manner that can only be described as "creepy." Films such as "Final Fantasy" (2001) and "Polar Express" (2004) are the most cited examples of this phenomenon, and one might argue that for "Final Fantasy," this hurt the film's box-office returns. Both films incorporated motion capture, but there were discrepancies in the characters' faces that created the most unease, the so-called "dead-eye syndrome." The real/unreal notion was even discussed by film critic Roger Ebert in his review of the film [10]:

> Not for an instant do we believe that Dr. Aki Ross, the heroine, is a real human. But we concede she is lifelike, which is the whole point. She has an eerie presence that is at once subtly unreal and yet convincing.

The question then remains, how do we combat the lack of subtlety in these characters that causes viewers to have such an unsettled reaction to them? Part of the answer lies in the design of the character and the style of the film. As we have seen, when possible, a more stylized character will communicate easily to its audience. The design of the character is based on the style of the project and is informed by the intended use of the character and the media that it exists in.

The essence of the character generally comes across most easily when stylistic choices are made that accentuate character attributes such as the eyes. The eyes are one of the main conduits of communication to the viewer. A character's expressions should read as well in a still pose as they do in motion. Motion, however, adds a level of complexity as this is where you get into the behavior and the psychology of the character. The animator is responsible for what is going on inside the character's head. This is accomplished solely through the subtle actions of the character. Behavioral clues that trigger a negative response come about from behavior that is categorized as abnormal. In the next sections, we raise questions about how the style and use of a character inform setup in addition to taking a brief look at how we perceive people in day-to-day interactions and the notion of abnormal psychology. To help look at this from the other perspective, we discuss how psychologists are using digital characters in their own research as interview avatars. The psychology of a digital character allows us to think about how we perceive our digital counterparts.

2.2 **HOW DO STYLE AND INTENDED PLATFORM DICTATE CHARACTER SETUP?**

When planning the character setup for a project, the overall style must be analyzed and the manner of motion planned out. While most character setups tend to be complex, for high-resolution digital characters, the requirements of the setup are predicated on the style of motion required of that character for the project. This is especially true for characters that are expected to behave in a more stylized, cartoon-derived manner. Often the difference comes down to the final deformations, which dictate the shape and profile of the character in motion. Such decisions could illustrate the character in either a realistic manner adhering to a realistic anatomy or a cartoon "rubber-hose" style. The rubber-hose style of animation was initiated with Oswald the Lucky Rabbit created by Ub Iwerks and Walt Disney and exemplified by the

Fleischer Brothers' Olive Oyl character in the "Popeye" cartoon series. Other examples of this style of animation include early Mickey Mouse and Bugs Bunny. The difference between cartoon "rubber-hose" animation and that of more realistic motion is the presence or lack of definable visible anatomical structures, such as bones. Certainly, complex digital characters created for integration with live-action feature films often contain an underlying structure that mimics the skeletal and musculature needed if that character existed, no matter how fantastical. For the readers with knowledge of character setup, this discussion of "bones," versus the lack thereof, is referring to the visual anatomical and kinematic representation and not the underlying methodology used to setup the character. While it is assumed that a realistic character with bones and muscles is more complicated than the malleability of a "rubber-hose" digital character, they both have their own unique challenges. These basic questions need to be addressed during pre-production of the project:

1. What is the overall visual style or genre of the character?
2. Is this a realistic character whose anatomy reacts to motion?
3. Do the character's body and limbs need to squash and stretch with motion?
4. Does the style of motion or deformation change throughout the project?

These questions come before the details and issues related to the construction of the actual character rig. Many of these questions can be answered by developing or consulting concept illustrations of the character.

The intended use of a digital character also has a tremendous impact on the design and architecture of how it is built. Certainly, the difference between characters built for games and those for film animation is very different, but there are levels and distinctions within these two uses that will also influence setup. The distinction between lead, secondary, and tertiary characters plays its part as does whether a character in a game is going to be controlled by the player or not. There are limitations to real-time game engines that will influence how the character is developed. Because film characters are not interacted with in their final form, there can be a complexity distinction between what the animator interacts with and what is rendered. Thus, with a careful construction, there is no limitation to what can be built into a film character. Some basic questions can be asked of the production to determine how character use will impact setup:

1. What system will the character be animated in?
2. Is the character intended for rendered animation or a game engine?
3. If the character is to be implemented in a game engine, what types of deformations does it support, and what are the limitations with regard to number of joints?

The challenges that result in answering all these questions are the topic of this book. Beyond form and function, we also need to consider performance and the psychology of digital characters to consider how we relate to them based on how they relate to us.

2.3 CASE STUDIES IN THE PSYCHOLOGY OF DIGITAL CHARACTERS

A number of psychologists have begun to study digital characters with research topics ranging from how they interact with humans to how effective digital characters are as interviewers for survey use. This research is another component as to how artists can transcend the "Uncanny Valley" in the creation of the digital characters. The depth of this subject is too great to go into detail here but worth a brief discussion as it is increasingly informing the way digital characters are designed and animated.

Digital characters are static without the input of motion. We are arguably wired from before birth to instinctively recognize how a human acts down to the smallest details. Any clue that something is not operating as we would expect causes us to assume that there is something out of the ordinary about that individual. This is a steep challenge for the digital character and falls into the category of abnormal psychology. Abnormal psychology can be defined as an area of psychology that studies people who are consistently unable to adapt and function effectively in a variety of conditions. Digital characters are inherently abnormal. It takes a tremendous amount of nuance to overcome the smallest pathology to create a character whose actions do not detract from what would be considered "normal." Character pathology is often discussed with regard to pure character motion where popping knees and an unnatural stance can make something appear injured when in fact it is purely just a poorly animated motion. Pathology at the characters performance level can have a much more damaging effects on the viewers experience as noted above. Viewers often describe the motion and expressions of digital characters as "too perfect." The implication here is that a little bit of idiosyncrasy is actually what makes us human. Striking the balance between character traits and character flaws is a delicate line. A deeper, sustained connection to digital characters is required when it comes to interactive media that strives to teach or collect important information. With this in mind, we can look at situations where digital characters are being tested in the realms of education and automated interview.

Educational software strives to teach lessons through new forms of interaction and connection with its users. The idea that a digital character in the role of a teacher, adviser, or guide could be compelling enough to create a strong connection with a student is a compelling and active subject of research. Preliminary systems are already in place in children's software, agent-based teachers for medical situations, military training, and even at the simple level as help agents for commercial software. Research in education demonstrates that the use of digital characters has many benefits, as discussed by James C. Lester and his group at North Carolina State University [22] where this group describes their work that tries to capitalize on the emotional connection we, in particular children, feel toward digital characters:

Because of the immediate and deep affinity that children seem to develop for these characters, the potential pedagogical benefits they provide are perhaps even exceeded by their motivational benefits. By creating the illusion of life, lifelike computer characters may significantly increase the time that children seek to spend with educational software, and recent advances in affordable graphic hardware are beginning to make the widespread distribution of realtime animation technology a reality. (p. 273)

Lester has, in other experiments [23], demonstrated a phenomenon he termed the "persona effect," which is the positive response and sense of engagement shown by users when interacting with an animated agent. The conjecture is that (in particular for children) animated pedagogical agents will have a higher success rate than similar software without animated agents. It can be hypothesized that children are more accustomed to seeing animated characters. It is also possible that their ability to recognized nuanced behavior is not as tuned as an adult's making them more forgiving of the shortcomings of current digital character and thus able to have more meaningful interaction with them.

Winslow Burleson [4], during his work at Massachusetts Institute of Technology (MIT), used sensors and input devices to look at the subtle non-verbal cues that can make digital characters more adept at social situations. He found that in interactions with pedagogical agents, as in human-human interaction, responsiveness can be enhanced by non-verbal social mirroring, in a sense, the imitation of another's non-verbal cues. By using a four-second delay, the character's mirroring behavior is not consciously detected by users, yet this is a short enough time for the mirroring to have a social effect. Animated agents in education is an ongoing research topic. Similarly, digital characters in the role of interview agents is another application helping us distill the nuanced relationship between digital characters and humans.

Collecting information via human-to-human interview is a time consuming and costly endeavor. The process is also ripe with sources of error and can generally be viewed as inconvenient for the respondent (the person answering the questions). Human interviewers have been shown to result in the higher response rates and improved respondent comprehension over questionnaires. Questionnaires, on the other hand, incur lower costs, increased privacy, and convenience and control for respondents. The hope of using a digital character as an interviewer is that they will actually reap the benefits of both the human interviewer and a questionnaire. The non-judgmental, anonymous aspect of digital characters may also have some benefit. But what are the fallbacks of this forward-thinking technology? Frederick G. Conrad and his group at the University of Michigan are developing digital conversational agents for use in interviewing scenarios. Conrad and Michael Schober [9] of New School University held workshops, entitled "Envisioning the Survey Interview of the Future," intended to expose survey methodologists to upcoming technologies that might be applicable to survey data collection. One of these technologies are video game characters and the associated game engine as a vehicle for survey data collection. To test the hypothesis that animated agents are more successful than live humans, Conrad and his group are conducting exploratory laboratory experiments [8]. Rather than developing the actual agent software, they are simulating animated agents using what they term a Wizard-of-Oz technique, where respondents believe they are interacting with a computer-generated agent when, in fact, they are interacting with an actual interviewer whose image has been rendered graphically in the user interface as if it was computer-generated. The overall goal of the proposed work is to determine when animated agents might help and when they might hurt quality of responses.

A very good overview of a psychological approach to designing game characters is collected by Katherine Isbister [14]. In it, Isbister covers the principles required for game characters to create powerful social and emotional connections with users interacting with current and next-generation gaming environments. By tackling issues of culture and gender alongside the tools we use to communicate, such as the body, face, and voice, Isbister's text challenges us to make conscious decisions about every aspect of designing and animating a digital character.

The research steps outlined in the case studies above may seem small, but the results of them will make our interactions with digital characters more effective, seamless, and dare we say "natural." All of this research is relevant to characters in the entertainment industry. As we put people face-to-face with digital characters and break down our understanding of human behavior into pieces that can be analyzed and recreated individually, it is only a matter of time before this knowledge will make its way into video game and films. The critical topic of behavior will be readdressed when we discuss facial animation, procedural motion, and artificial intelligence later. The historical and evolutionary steps that have occurred are outlined next and will help inform the technical practice of building digital characters.

2.4 **EXERCISE**

Start designing a character you would like to use throughout this book. If it is a human, then think about Mori's Uncanny Valley. What level of stylization will give you the right place on that continuum so as to not present you with the challenge of creating something almost real but not quite? What medium will this character exist in? What aspects of the character's face can you accentuate to make it appealing even if grotesque or evil?

2.1 Start creating a character bible which includes descriptions and sketches of your character. It should also include references for details of the character that you collect over time. These references can be images, quotes, or pieces of fabric that define a texture. Whether these things make their way into your character formally or remain strictly as inspiration is something that only time will tell; so do not hesitate to collect anything that strikes a chord.

2.2 Get feedback from others about the bible. Does the design of the character tell part of its story through the use of details such as period clothing or cultural elements?

2.3 Incorporate the feedback you receive to refine the character bible.

■ **FURTHER READING**

For a solid overview of the psychology behind character design refer to:

Katherine Isbister. *Better Game Characters by Design: A Psychological Approach (The Morgan Kaufmann Series in Interactive 3D Technology)*. Morgan Kaufmann Publishers Inc., San Francisco, CA, 2006.

An interesting panel conversation about Mori's Uncanny Valley took place at Siggraph 2007 in San Diego California. The abstract is below but video transcripts are available:

Thierry Chaminade, Jessica K. Hodgins, Joe Letteri, and Karl F. Mac-Dorman. The uncanny valley of eeriness. In *SIGGRAPH '07: ACM SIGGRAPH 2007 panels*, page 1, ACM Press, New York, NY, 2007.

Scott McCloud's "Understanding Comics" is required reading:

Scott McCloud. *Understanding Comics: The Invisible Art.* Perennial Currents, New York, NY, 1994.

INTERVIEW: MILANA HUANG, CHARACTER TECHNICAL DIRECTION SUPERVISOR, PDI/DREAMWORKS ANIMATION

BIO

Milana Huang is currently the Character TD Supervisor on DreamWorks Animations anticipated fall release, "Madagascar: Escape 2 Africa." Huangs responsibilities include working with the directors, production designers, and animators to interpret the style and movement of characters in a 3D environment.

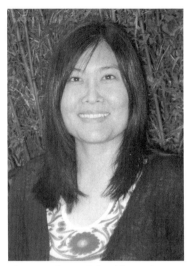

Milana Huang, Character Technical Direction Supervisor, PDI/DreamWorks Animation

Huang joined PDI/DreamWorks in 1999 as a Character TD on the Academy Award-winning animated feature, "Shrek." She was quickly promoted to Senior Character TD on "Shrek 2" and then to her current supervisory role while working on "Madagascar." Prior to joining PDI/DreamWorks, Huang spent three years as a Software Engineer at MultGen Inc., writing functional specifications and implementing deformation tools for the software "Creator," a real-time 3D modeling software package. She also participated as a Virtual Reality Room (VROOM) exhibitor in SIGGRAPH 1994 for her co-development in mathematical visualization and application for rapid prototyping.

Huang received her MS from the University of Illinois in Chicago, writing her thesis on "Untangling Knots with Energy Minimization by Simulated Annealing." She also holds a BS in Art and Computer Science from the University of Wisconsin.

Q&A

Q) *The components of character technology are diverse and span the artistic and technical spectrum. How did you get your start in the industry? Based on where you see the field heading, what experience/training do you recommend people have?*

A) My interest in computer animation started when I was in high school. My Dad would chat with me about what kind of job I might like when I was older. I realized that I enjoyed art and science. We looked around and noticed this thing called computer graphics was starting to happen. It was starting to be used in commercials, movies, and print publications. That kind of work would need artistic and technical skills! At the time I went to college, there were no computer graphic programs, so I majored in art and computer science to learn the basic skills that I hoped to combine. After earning my degree at the University of Wisconsin–Madison, I went to the University of Illinois–Chicago for graduate school. At the university's Electronic Visualization Laboratory, my studies and research involved computer graphics and virtual reality. From there, I soon started working at PDI/DreamWorks as a Character Technical Director.

I recommend that folks interested in this kind of work learn the artistic and technical skills of character setup and animation. I would emphasize learning the technical fundamentals, including computer programming and the mathematics used in computer graphics. These are important tools in one's toolbox of character setup skills so that one can easily innovate on top of evolving software and paradigms.

Q) *Creating compelling digital characters is part art and part science. What is the greatest challenge you encounter on a daily basis? What aspect of character technology keeps you up thinking at night?*

A) Our characters are built to have a large range of motion and to look great when viewed from all angles. Ensuring that the characters are developed and then supported in a manageable way to achieve these goals is a daily exciting challenge.

There are so many interesting character technology issues to think about. An animator may need differing types of controls on the same character depending on the type of acting required. Building a character that allows the animator to easily switch and blend between differing systems is a challenge. Some example systems are forward kinematic verses inverse kinematic control, physical simulation verses hand animated, and bipedal verses quadrupedal movement. Another issue we think about is speed: how can we improve character setup tools so that we can prototype character solutions more quickly, and how can we make the character run faster so animators can work more efficiently.

Q) *What are the ingredients for a successful digital character?*

A) Here are three main ingredients:

- Animator controls that are easy to use
- Beautiful deformations that result in a model that respects the design intent on every frame
- Character setups that run at reasonable speed

Q) *While the industry is competitive, it is ultimately respectful of great work. Outside of the work you have been personally involved in the production of, what animated characters have you been impressed or inspired by? What is the historical high-bar?*

A) "The Lord of the Rings" trilogy comes to mind as an excellent example of pushing the envelope further. The crowd characters created such amazing battle scenes and had impressive abilities to intelligently react to other characters and the environment. Gollum created a wonderful performance.

Q) *Where do you see digital characters in ten years? Where are animated characters for film and games heading?*

A) Visual media that is authored for stereoscopic display will increase to give audiences a more immersive experience. This will affect digital characters as we determine not only which two-dimensional tricks we use no longer apply but also what new tricks we can apply to enhance our characters' performance in a stereoscopic viewing.

There is also a great branching of character development where, on one hand, we see a push for hyper-realism, where it will be difficult to determine if leading characters are real or digital. We also see a push for more cartoony, stylized characters. We will be better able to translate hand-drawn character designs into digital characters that defy the standard three-dimensional physical rules but have their own set of visually stylized rules.

Chapter 3

History of Digital Characters

3.1 INTRODUCTION

This chapter deals with the evolution and history of digital characters. Digital characters developed in response to the projects that they were employed in. By using an evolutionary model to frame the historical development of digital characters, we group innovations into five stages leading us into contemporary projects and hints at what is ahead. The history of digital characters follows and paves the way for the primary concepts in this book.

3.2 THE EVOLUTION OF DIGITAL CHARACTERS

The scale of history for digital characters is not a large one. Digital characters found their start and some might argue greatest success in the realm of interactive video games. The act of arranging pixels into images in the form of characters of some variety goes back to the first days of computer imaging. The moving of these pixels in two dimensions (2D) over time (also known as animation) was not far behind. Alongside developments into character motion came character interactivity, complex imagery, and eventually three-dimensional (3D) graphics. The artistry and the technology tended to advance together, each pushing the other, and they continue to do so today. As graphics hardware provides systems with more power for real-time graphic processing, the level of interactivity and visual complexity available increases. This is a constant give and take and in many ways sets the pace for digital character technology development. Before we look at the historical path of digital characters in various forms of media, it is worth taking a look at the changing technology and methods that have brought digital characters to where they are today and which may give us insight into where they will go in the future.

If we were to frame the development of digital characters, a general framework for our discussion on the history of digital characters may be to look at this history from an evolutionary perspective. Let us use as a springboard the path proposed by artist and animator Matt Elson [11]. Elson's five stages of digital character evolution deal with the technology and methods with which 3D character animation is carried out. Each stage is characterized by a technical advancement inter-related with a paradigm shift regarding motion.

Stage one in Elson's schema is typified by "keyframe animation" or the process of positioning a character every few frames then letting the system interpolate the in-between frames. Animation at this stage is modeled on the work-flow of 20th century cell animation, which included a master animator who drew the keyframes and a more junior "in-betweener" who did what was expected of their title. A primary technical innovation of this phase is programmable expressions, in which technical directors define interactive relationships in the 3D environment. These expressions provide the opportunity for complicated, non-hierarchical relationships within the character to add automatic secondary motion for example. Another example of a programmable expression is the flexing of associated skin or muscles when a joint is bent. Other noteworthy developments of the keyframe animation era include restructured hierarchical objects, 3D paint, and socking and skinning. Critically, keyframe animation is said by Elson to be cumbersome and requiring large crews and complex infrastructures with a high ratio of technical-to-creative talent. Control of the characters is generally achieved at the expense of production efficiency.

Stage two in Elson's schema is "layered animation and single skins." While largely a technical stage, it involves the creation of a re-architected workflow that enables animators, programmers, developers, artists, and technical directors to work on individual modules that address their respective areas of production. These modules are contained and insulated from the larger production until they can be plugged in with the other components. These parallel work flows make it possible for large teams of artists to work simultaneously on a project. This restructuring of pipelines and process happens in part due to improved Application Programming Interfaces (API), which allow third-party developers to write object-oriented system extensions and plug-ins. There is also a move away from straightforward animation production to layerable animation, allowing different motion types to be combined on the same character.

The third stage described by Elson is one he terms "scripted memory and behavior." This stage is typified by the dynamic animation of crowds via scripted actions. As we know, crowd dynamics such as these are already being implemented. Complex animation and the creation of realistic natural phenomenon using tools such as procedural systems for creating hair, fur, cloth, clouds, smoke, and grass are implemented in this stage as are dynamics and physics tools for simulating gravity, motion damping, and wind. On the character technology side, anatomical systems for simulating muscle, bone, fat, and other underlying structures of the body in the form of layered deformations are included. Motion capture will become merely another animation method rather than a last resort. Skeletons will become smarter with built-in functions for pose mirroring and position and motion memories. Animation clips or as Elson calls them "performance blocks" will be kept in a library and reused as needed, for example in crowds.

It is safe to say that we have achieved stage three of Elson's schema. Stages four and five are where Elson's predictions turn toward the slightly more fantastic and futuristic. Keep in mind, as we will find later, the notions encapsulated by these stages are current topics in character technology research and development both in academia and industry.

Elson's fourth stage, "character autonomy," is where true character independence begins. In this particular stage, embedded physics systems in the character will enable it to move about an environment with weight, mass, and improvisational behaviors giving the appearance, though not yet the reality, of intelligence. He provides a note for the fearful animator here: "Animators will still be in great demand to craft all of a character's behaviors, actions, and response" [11].

The fifth and final stage of Elson's evolution of digital characters is "personality." Here, Elson departs from the realm of procedural animation to true AI. Elson describes this stage as characters that have developed emotional and cognitive interior lives. He argues they will begin to "think" and interact with their environment, each other, the animator, and end-user, employing knowledge structures for their basic decision-making. Characters will understand and respond to human speech, so they will be able to translate, perform menial tasks, and sift and sort the digital expanses.

Elson concludes by pointing out that his stages represent an ideal world and that future developments will likely be more mundane. There is no company or facility systematically proceeding from one neat and tidy level to the next because software companies are busy responding to market demands and production companies are busy responding to their clients' visions. All the elements mentioned are in development in various places, though most are in limited use, lacking systematic integration and a compelling economic reason to be pulled together. This book attempts to bring all these stages together, but with an emphasis on the performance imbued by the animator or performer with a lesser emphasis on the application of AI.

This framework is helpful to understand the scope of technologies under the umbrella of digital character technology. However, without historical insights into previous efforts, we are likely to not move forward at the pace that hardware and software are progressing. Our understanding of digital characters in the context of film and interactive media is crucial.

3.3 HISTORY OF DIGITAL CHARACTERS IN FILM

For our discussion of digital characters in film, a differentiation should be made between characters that have been created for full computer graphics (CG) films, such as "Toy Story" (1995) or "Shrek" (2001), and those that have been created in service of visual effects for a live-action production ("The Lord of the Rings" [2001] or "King Kong" [2005]). The difference is mainly stylistic. For characters to be integrated into the environment surrounding them, the design, construction, animation, shading, and texturing of that character must match the rules of the world that they inhabit. Characters for a CG world are inherently easy to integrate as they will share the modeling, shading, and lighting process with the environment as opposed to those created for backplate integration, which need to be built with the real world in mind. Much of this integration lies in the realm of texturing, lighting, and image compositing as even the most stylized character can be integrated with the reality of the scene. Architecturally, in a contemporary production setting, these characters are built and animated in an identical manner utilizing some variety of off-the-shelf or proprietary 3D animation software. It is worth walking through the history of digital characters in film both animation and live action to get a sense of the breath, scope, and explosion of these characters in recent years. This historical overview also serves to illuminate the great strides that have been made in such a short amount of time.

In 1976, "Futureworld" was the first feature film to use 3D computer-generated images (CGI) for an animated hand and face created by Information International Incorporated (III). While it was supposed to be the actor Peter Fonda, the animated hand was actually a digitized version of Edwin Catmull's (co-founder of Pixar) left hand.

"Looker" (1981) featured the first full CGI human character, Cindy, which was made from simulated body scans of actress Susan Dey [16] and created by III. This was also the first use of surface shading as we know it today.

The following year, a major achievement in both the film industry and the world of computer graphics in general, was with the release of "Tron" (1982), which included the polyhedron character, "Bit" (Figure 3.1), built and animated by Digital Effects, Incorporated. This is arguably the first animated digital character, though its basic design and limited animation did not allow for much complexity. The character had two states, one for "Yes" and one for "No."

By the mid-1980s, we start to see digital characters begin to take more compelling forms. The Lucasfilm Computer Graphics short film, "The Adventures of Andre and Wally B" (1985), introduced the idea of incorporating traditional character animation techniques to basic geometric 3D shapes in support of a fully realized short film. Frank Thomas and Ollie Johnston, two of Walt Disney's "nine old men," upon visiting the production of the short saw a convincing demonstration by John Lasseter that animation principles, such as squash and stretch, anticipation, overlap, and follow through, were not alien to computer animation [35].

Created in a similar manner, the Dire Straits "Money for Nothing" music video (1985) featured low-detail but highly engaging animated characters animated by Ian Pearson, Gavin Blair, and David Throssell at the London-based studio, Rushes. That same year, however, the first fully animated, photorealistic digital character in a feature film was a medieval knight that sprang to life from a stained glass window in "Young Sherlock Holmes" (1985). The 30-second sequence took six months to accomplish but was a stunning achievement by the team at the Computer Graphics Division of Lucasfilm, now Pixar, and a huge technical achievement planting the seed for the potential of using computer-generated characters in film as a viable practice.

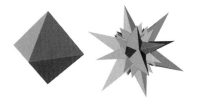

■ **FIGURE 3.1** "Bit" from "Tron" (1982) recreated here was a morphing polyhedron shape, with two states: one for "yes" and the other for "no."

From here, a few small appearances by digital characters emerge including Digital Productions' CG Owl from the opening title sequence in "Labyrinth" (1986), the formidable animation on multiple characters in Pixar's "Luxo Jr." (1986) short, and its follow-up, "Tin Toy" (1988), which featured a somewhat disturbing albeit complex crawling human baby. On the more abstract and procedural animation front, "Stanley and Stella in 'Breaking the Ice'" (1987) featured the implementation of a flocking algorithm by Craig Reynolds [33] along with the Symbolics Graphics Division and Whitney/Demos Productions. This flocking algorithm paved the way for the crowd scenes which are so prevalent today.

With the sale of the Lucasfilm Computer Graphics Group to Steve Jobs and the creation of Pixar, which focused on entirely CG productions and software, the creation of Industrial Light and Magic (ILM) by George Lucas, and the growing presence of Pacific Data Images (PDI), there developed a center of gravity for computer graphics and digital characters in Northern California. The confluence of talent and resources led directly to ILM's creation of the pseudopod in "The Abyss" (1989). The use of realistic lighting algorithms and actor interaction in "The Abyss" took the art of digital character creation and ray traced rendering to a new level by creating a seamless digital character that was perfectly matched to its live-action environment. The pseudopod with its watery tentacle replicated actor Mary Elizabeth Mastrantonio's face and appeared to communicate by movements that resembled facial expressions. See Table 3.1 for more projects employing digital character before 1990.

Continuing in this tradition, "Terminator 2: Judgment Day" (1991), also with effects by ILM, introduced both Hollywood and the public to the large-scale use of CG in feature films. The liquid-metal T-1000 cyborg Terminator, the first computer graphic-generated main character to be used in a film, "morphed" into any person or object and was animated naturally based on human motion. While not a formal digital character, the ILM effects in "Death Becomes Her"(1992) featured photorealistic skin and the first complex human skin replication which linked Meryl Streep's body and head

Table 3.1 Notable Projects Featuring Digital Characters (Pre-1990)

Year	Title	Format	Company
1976	Futureworld	Feature	Information International Inc (III)
1979	Pacman	Video Game	Namco
1981	Donkey Kong	Video Game	Nintendo
1981	Looker	Feature	III
1982	Tron	Feature	III, MAGI/Synthavision, Robert Abel & Associates, Digital Effects
1984	The Adventures of Andre and Wally B.	Short	Lucasfilm
1985	Dire Straits "Money for Nothing" Music Video	Television	Rushes
1985	Tony de Peltrie	Short	Philippe Bergeron, Pierre Lachapelle, Daniel Langlois, Pierre Robiboux
1985	Young Sherlock Holmes	Feature	Pixar
1986	Labyrinth	Feature	Digital Productions
1986	Luxo Jr.	Short	Pixar
1987	Captain Power & the Soldiers Of The Future	TV	ARCCA Animation
1987	Stanley and Stella in Breaking the Ice	Short	Symbolics Graphics Division
1988	Nestor Sextone for President	Short	Kleiser-Walczak Construction Company
1988	Tin Toy	Short	Pixar
1989	Knick Knack	Short	Pixar
1989	Prince Of Persia	Video Game	Brøderbund
1989	The Abyss	Feature	ILM

together with a digital neck during a shockingly magical head-twisting incident. In the same year, "Batman Returns" (1992) featured a flock of digital bats produced by VIFX. The year 1992 also featured hypothesized virtual reality (VR) avatars in "The Lawnmower Man" (1992) with animation by Angel Studios.

ILM's 1993 hallmark, "Jurassic Park" (1993) pushed the limits of photo-realism with their digital dinosaurs. This film raised, if not created, the bar for digital characters in terms of realism, number of characters, and quality of motion. These were the first fully digital characters seen with daytime natural lighting interacting with each other, human actors, and the environment throughout a large portion of the film. Most importantly, "Jurassic Park" broke down the barrier for filmmakers who previously thought it was unfeasible or too expensive to create large-scale digital character animation by proving that it was possible, cost effective, and capable of producing high-quality results. See Table 3.2 for more projects employing digital character from 1990 to 1994.

At this point in the mid-1990s, much attention was focused on creating realistic humans for film effects. In 1995, two examples of the early use of creating digital human stunt people include "Judge Dredd" (1995) and "Batman Forever" (1995). Both films featured digital replacements for stars, the first being Sylvester Stallone, during action sequences. The idea of digital replacement was not new but stemmed directly from synthespians created by Kleiser-Walczak Construction Company (KWCC) in the late 1980s. The term "synthespian" can be attributed to Jeff Kleiser of KWCC, a portmanteau of the words "synthetic," meaning not of natural origin, and "thespian," meaning dramatic actor. Kleiser created the first digital actor for his 1988 short film "Nestor Sextone for President" (1988), which premiered at SIGGRAPH. A year later, Kleiser and Diana Walczak presented their first female synthespian, Dozo, in the music video "Don't Touch Me." KWCC actually produced the digital stunt person in "Judge Dredd" and, as we will see, went on to create a number of big-screen digital actors.

The year 1995 also marked a watershed moment when Pixar released "Toy Story" (1995); their feature-length animated film filled with a cast of digital characters both human and toys. This film established the benchmark for all CG productions, much like "Jurassic Park" (1993) did for live-action

Table 3.2 Notable Projects Featuring Digital Characters (Early 1990s)

Year	Title	Format	Company
1990	Robocop 2	Feature	Kevin Bjorke
1990	Total Recall	Feature	Metrolight Studios
1991	Another World	Video Game	Eric Chahi
1991	Terminator 2: Judgment Day	Feature	ILM
1992	Alone in the Dark	Video Game	Infogrames
1992	Batman Returns	Feature	Video Image
1992	Death Becomes Her	Feature	ILM
1992	Lawnmower Man	Feature	Angel Studios
1992	Wolfenstein 3D	Video Game	id Software
1993	Doom	Video Game	id Software
1993	Flashback	Video Game	Delphine Software
1993	Insektors	TV	Studio Fantome
1993	Jurassic Park	Feature	ILM
1993	VeggieTales	Video	Big Idea Productions
1993	Virtua Fighter	Video Game	Sega-AM2
1994	ReBoot	Television	Mainframe Entertainment
1994	The Mask	Feature	ILM

visual effects. Yet, in the case of "Toy Story," the quality of character acting, personality, and performance became the hallmarks that all digital characters were now expected to achieve.

From this point until the late 1990s, digital characters in film, while not commonplace, were becoming more prevalent with films such as "Caspar" (1995), "Jumanji" (1995), "Dragonheart" (1996), "Starship Troopers" (1997), "Men In Black" (1997), and "Godzilla" (1998), all of which featured digital characters in key roles. Even James Cameron's

"Titanic" (1997) included huge crowds of simulated people. During this time, CG animated films such as PDI's "Antz" (1998) and Blue Sky's short "Bunny" (1998) were giving Pixar and its latest film at the time, "A Bug's Life" (1998), some competition.

By 1999, we see the use of digital characters taking a more important role in live-action feature films. In "Star Wars Episode 1: The Phantom Menace"(1999), a number of highly photorealistic digital characters were created with one in particular, Jar Jar Binks (Figure 3.2), having as much screen time as the human actors. The authenticity of Jar Jar Binks' appearance was in fact so realistic that when the first pictures of him appeared in "Vanity Fair" ([1], see cover) many took him to be a human in makeup. These pictures were of course composited images created by ILM. ILM also flexed their muscles, quite literally, with their work on "The Mummy" (1999), which featured an animated reconstruction of the title character, while in motion, integrating effects and character technology. See Table 3.3 for more projects employing

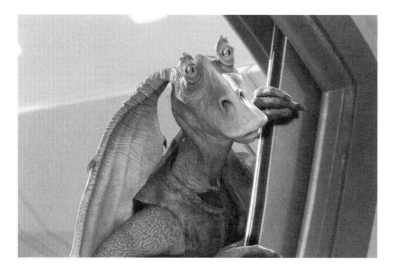

■ **FIGURE 3.2** Jar Jar Binks from "Star Wars Episode I - The Phantom Menace" (1999). Courtesy of Lucasfilm Ltd. "Star Wars Episode I - The Phantom Menace" copyright & trademark by 1999 Lucasfilm Ltd. All rights reserved. Used under authorization. Unauthorized duplication is a violation of applicable law.

Table 3.3 Notable Projects Featuring Digital Characters (Late 1990s)

Year	Title	Format	Company
1995	Babe	Feature	Rhythm & Hues
1995	Batman Forever	Feature	Warner Digital
1995	Casper	Feature	ILM
1995	Fade To Black	Video Game	Delphine Software
1995	Judge Dredd	Feature	Kleiser-Walczak Construction Company
1995	Jumanji	Feature	ILM
1995	La Cite des Enfants Perdus (City of Lost Children)	Feature	BUF
1995	Toy Story	Feature	Pixar
1996	Dragonheart	Feature	ILM
1996	Duke Nukem 3D	Video Game	3D Realms
1996	Tomb Raider	Video Game	Core Deisgn
1997	Alien: Resurrection	Feature	Blue Sky—VIFX
1997	Batman & Robin	Feature	Warner Digital
1997	Geri's Game	Short	Pixar
1997	Mars Attacks!	Feature	ILM
1997	Men in Black	Feature	ILM
1997	Spawn	Feature	ILM
1997	Starship Troopers	Feature	Sony Pictures Imageworks
1997	The Lost World: Jurassic Park 2	Feature	ILM
1997	Titanic	Feature	Digital Domain
1998	A Bugs Life	Feature	Pixar
1998	Antz	Feature	Dreamworks Animation
1998	Bunny	Short	Blue Sky
1998	Godzilla	Feature	Centropolis
1998	Grim Fandango	Video Game	LucasArts

Continued

Table 3.3 *Continued*

Year	Title	Format	Company
1998	Might Joe Young	Feature	Dream Quest, ILM
1998	Small Soldiers	Feature	Dreamworks
1998	Thief: The Dark Project	Video Game	Looking Glass Studios
1999	Outcast	Video Game	Infogrames
1999	Star Wars: Episode I: The Phantom Menace	Feature	ILM
1999	Stuart Little	Feature	Sony Pictures Imageworks
1999	The Matrix	Feature	Manex
1999	The Mummy	Feature	ILM
1999	Toy Story 2	Feature	Pixar

digital character from 1995 to 1999. Taking this anatomical animation a step further was Sony Pictures Imageworks who created the visceral deconstruction and reconstruction of Kevin Bacon's character in "Hollow Man" (2000). Character technology had evolved into a set of techniques capable of reconstructing characters from the inside out and back through anatomically accurate models and rigs.

The first lead role for a computer-generated character occurred in 1999 with "Stuart Little" (1999). This film set a new benchmark for computer-generated characters, like the pseudopod from "The Abyss" (1989) before it, by increasing the amount of actor interaction and adding complex elements, such as fur, to the carefully crafted rendering. In the year 2000, Disney created the film "Dinosaur" (2000), which had the first entirely photorealistic computer-generated cast. This film, unlike others with all animated casts (e.g., Pixar's "Toy Story" [1995]), utilized film shot backgrounds in lieu of an entirely CG environment so that digital characters needed to match the lighting and visual complexity of the extreme settings used in the film.

Entering the 21st century, we encounter a deluge of digital characters. Human and humanoid characters began to take center stage with the release of "Final Fantasy: The Spirits Within" (2001), "Shrek" (2001), and "The Lord of the Rings: Fellowship of the Ring" (2001). While "Final Fantasy" received poor critical response since the characters lack familiarity, "The Lord of the Rings" series brought the role of digital characters to a new level. A major step, "The Lord of the Rings: Fellowship of the Ring" (2001), had digital characters surrounding the main characters with seamless integration even to the point of creating a character, Gollum, that, because of its performance in the later films, posed the question: could a digital character receive an acting award for its performance? Gollum's performance was informed by the performance and motion capture of actor Andy Serkis, but because of the great attention to detail for every aspect of this character, he took on a life greater than any single contributor. See Table 3.4 for more projects employing digital character from 2000 and 2001.

"The Lord of the Rings" series also advanced the role of the digital stunt person with doubles replacing live actors mid-shot. In general, the digital stunt person has evolved into a commonplace role with increasing screen time as evidenced in films based on comic books where superheros such as Spider-man ("Spider-man" series [2002-2007]) and Superman ("Superman Returns" [2006]) are nearly indistinguishable from the actors portraying them. A recent example of a well-integrated digital character is Davy Jones from the "Pirates of the Caribbean: Dead Man's Chest" (2006) and "Pirates of the Caribbean: At World's End" (2007). This character, while informed by the performance of actor Bill Nighy, is one of the most compelling digital characters on film. Capturing the subtle movement of the eyes and face, this character tricked many viewers into thinking that it was created by an elaborate make-up job.

A lot has been accomplished in just 25 years. The art of creating digital characters has grown tremendously, and with this pace, it is likely to continue to incorporate new technologies for some startling results in the future.

Table 3.4 Notable Projects Featuring Digital Characters (2000–2001)

Year	Title	Format	Company
2000	Deus Ex	Video Game	Ion Storm
2000	Dinosaur	Feature	Disney
2000	For The Birds	Short	Pixar
2000	Hitman: Codename 47	Video Game	IO Interactive
2000	Hollow Man	Feature	Tippett Studio
2000	The Operative: No One Lives Forever	Video Game	Monolith Productions
2001	A.I.	Feature	PDI, ILM
2001	Black & White	Video Game	Lionhead
2001	Evolution	Feature	PDI, Tippett Studio
2001	Final Fantasy: The Spirits Within	Feature	Square
2001	Grand Theft Auto III	Video Game	Rockstar Games
2001	Half-Life	Video Game	Valve Software
2001	Halo	Video Game	Bungie Studios
2001	Harry Potter and the Sorcerer's Stone	Feature	MPC, CFC, The Mill, Cinesite, ILM, Sony Pictures Imageworks
2001	Jimmy Neutron: Boy Genius	Feature	Nickelodeon
2001	Jurassic Park III	Feature	ILM
2001	Monsters Inc.	Feature	Pixar
2001	Shrek	Feature	PDI/Dreamworks
2001	The Lord of the Rings: Fellowship of the Ring	Feature	WETA
2001	The Mummy Returns	Feature	ILM

3.4 **OVERVIEW OF DIGITAL CHARACTERS IN INTERACTIVE MEDIA**

As mentioned previously, the process of creating digital characters for film and video games derives from the same root. The imitations of real-time rendering and the impact of interactivity account for the differences. One difference is perception, whereby many video games have the advantage of letting the viewer step into the shoes of that character and interact with its world. This provides a connection that passive media struggles to achieve. As opposed to film, outlined in the previous section, digital characters in games are too voluminous to list as the majority of games have allowed the user to step into the shoes of a digital character. The first characters in commercially created and public accessible games were the famous "Pac-Man" (1979) character and the simple humanoid stick figure in "Berzerk" (1980). Developers realized early on that by attaching images that we could relate to onto a character the users would invest themselves into it. A simply designed character, such as Pac-Man composed of a few pixels, takes on the personality, or at least gameplay tactics, of its user. Despite the simplicity, the ability to control a digital character in video games allows for a connection impossible in film. Tables 3.5, 3.6, and 3.7 include highlights of more projects employing digital character in the late 2000s.

While we find that digital characters in film followed a steady trajectory, characters in games took off in a broad and faster manner. These early characters, such as Pac-Man, were digital cartoons. Other notable video game characters include Mario from the original "Donkey Kong" (1981) and the enduring "Mario Bros" series, Sonic The Hedgehog, Link from the "Legend of Zelda" series, Ratchet and Clank, Pitfall Harry, and Jak and Daxter all of whom have become household names and the stars of their own series of video games. Most digital characters in films have appeared in one, or at most three films, while our interactions with game characters can take many different paths. It is no surprise that games based on animated film characters are top properties. Many of these characters have changed from 2D bitmapped images into 3D geometry-based characters as those found in films and covered by this book. In addition, digital characters in first-person shooters such as those in "Doom," "Quake," "Unreal," "Halo," and "Half-Life" series were some of the first 3D digital characters and continue to be a genre within gaming where much character technology development is done.

The motion of characters in games is typically limited to pre-composed animations that are triggered by user controls or in relation to the environment. Games have become increasingly complex, adding character physics and AI into the mix and triggering animation created through a mix of hand-animated motion and motion capture. Cut scenes and

Table 3.5 Notable Projects Featuring Digital Characters (2002–2004)

Year	Title	Format	Company
2002	Harry Potter and the Chamber of Secrets	Feature	Cinesite, CFC, ILM, MPC, Thousand Monkeys
2002	Ice Age	Feature	Blue Sky
2002	Men In Black II	Feature	PDI, Sony Pictures Imageworks, ILM, Rhythm & Hues
2002	Mikes New Car	Short	Pixar
2002	Minority Report	Feature	ILM
2002	Scooby-Doo	Feature	Rhythm & Hues, Giant Killer Robots
2002	Spider-Man	Feature	Sony Pictures Imageworks
2002	Star Wars: Episode II: Attack of the Clones	Feature	ILM
2002	Stuart Little 2	Feature	Sony Pictures Imageworks
2002	The ChubbChubbs!	Short	Sony Pictures Imageworks
2002	The Lord of the Rings: The Two Towers	Feature	WETA
2002	The Sims	Video Game	Maxis
2003	Boundin	Short	Pixar

Continued

Table 3.5 *Continued*

Year	Title	Format	Company
2003	Elder Scrolls:Morrowind	Video Game	Bethesda Software
2003	Finding Nemo	Feature	Pixar
2003	Star Wars: Knights of the Old Republic	Video Game	Bioware
2003	The Animatrix: Final Flight of the Osiris	Short	Square
2003	The Hulk	Feature	ILM
2003	The Lord of the Rings: Return of the King	Feature	WETA
2003	The Matrix Reloaded	Feature	ESC, Amalgamated Pixels, Animal Logic, BUF, Sony Pictures Imageworks
2003	The Matrix Revolutions	Feature	Tippett Studio, Sony Pictures Imageworks, ESC, CIS, BUF
2004	Garfield: The Movie	Feature	Rhythm & Hues
2004	Gone Nutty	Short	Blue Sky
2004	Grand Theft Auto III: San Andreas	Video Game	Rockstar North
2004	Half-Life 2	Video Game	Valve Software
2004	Harry Potter and the Prisoner of Azkaban	Feature	ILM, Cinesite, CFC, Double Negative
2004	Hellboy	Feature	Tippett Studios
2004	Ninja Gaiden	Video Game	Team Ninja
2004	Shark Tale	Feature	Dreamworks Animation
2004	Shrek 2	Feature	Dreamworks Animation
2004	Spider-Man 2	Feature	Sony Pictures Imageworks
2004	The Incredibles	Feature	Pixar
2004	The Polar Express	Feature	Sony Pictures Imageworks
2004	Van Helsing	Feature	ILM

Table 3.6 Notable Projects Featuring Digital Characters (2005–2006)

Year	Title	Format	Company
2005	Chicken Little	Feature	Walt Disney Feature Animation
2005	Harry Potter and the Goblet of Fire	Feature	Cinesite, ILM, BUF, MPC, Double Negative, The Orphanage, Animal Logic, Rising sun
2005	Hoodwinked	Feature	Blue Yonder Films with Kanbar Entertainment
2005	Jack-Jack Attack	Short	Pixar
2005	King Kong	Feature	WETA
2005	Madagascar	Feature	Dreamworks Animation
2005	One Man Band	Short	Pixar
2005	Psychonauts	Video Game	Double Fine Productions
2005	Shadow Of The Colossus	Video Game	Sony Computer Entertainment
2005	Star Wars: Episode III: Revenge of the Sith	Feature	ILM
2005	The Chronicles of Narnia: The Lion, the Witch and the Wardrobe	Feature	Rhythm & Hues
2005	The Chronicles of Narnia: The Lion, the Witch and the Wardrobe	Feature	ILM, Sony Pictures Imageworks, Rhythm & Hues
2005	The Madagascar Penguins in a Christmas Caper	Short	Dreamworks
2005	Valiant	Feature	Vanguard Animation
2006	Barnyard	Feature	Nickelodeon Movies
2006	Cars	Feature	Pixar
2006	Charlotte's Web	Feature	Iloura, Rising Sun, Fuel
2006	Everyone's Hero	Feature	Dan Krech Productions
2006	First Flight	Short	Dreamworks
2006	Flushed Away	Feature	Dreamworks/Aardman
2006	Happy Feet	Feature	Animal Logic

Continued

Table 3.6 *Continued*

Year	Title	Format	Company
2006	Lifted	Short	Pixar
2006	Mater and the Ghostlight	Short	Pixar
2006	Monster House	Feature	Sony Pictures Imageworks
2006	Open Season	Feature	Sony Pictures Imageworks
2006	Over the Hedge	Feature	Dreamworks Animation
2006	Pan's Labyrinth	Feature	Cafe FX
2006	Pirates of the Caribbean: Dead Mans Chest	Feature	ILM
2006	Superman Returns	Feature	Sony Pictures Imageworks, Rising Sun, The Orphanage, Rhythm & Hues
2006	The Ant Bully	Feature	DNA Productions

cinematic interludes where the player is no longer in control are where characters often lose their believability and sense of familiarity. To a further degree, it is useful to distinguish player-controlled "player characters" and computer-controlled "non-player characters." As the names dictate, player characters are those controlled by the player via the controls supplied, like Pac-Man himself, while non-player characters are those controlled by the system via a level of AI, like Blinky, Pinky, Inky, and Clyde, the ghosts from the "Pac-Man" game. Much research goes into making those non-player characters more life-like and indistinguishable from player characters. The embodiment of the player character by the user has been a key factor in the success of massively multiplayer online role-playing games (MMORPGs). These games, for example, "World of Warcraft," allow users to customize a character and play with other users spread across the world through centralized servers. The idea that you are playing with other humans adds to the realism of the experience and has opened the door for other collaborative virtual environments.

Notions of embodiment and telepresence are no better represented than in the online virtual world of "Second Life" [20] (Figure 3.3). Like a MMORPG, the "Second Life" world is inhabited by users from all over the world via 3D avatars. This has become a functioning community with notions of real estate, commerce, romance, and politics. "Second Life" has also transcended use groups by opening the door to inhabitable digital characters to users who might not typically play games but would be inclined to investigate the social networking and virtual exploration aspects of this environment.

Digital characters in games can also able to be hacked or repurposed because with user control, characters can do things outside of the tasks related to the completion of the game. In this vein, a side branch of gaming is the use of game engines for the purpose of filmmaking, usually termed "machinima." In this situation, filmmakers use and extend the functionality of the selected game engine to compose and produce real-time films. These films usually employ multiple people in a networked environment, controlling characters and playing the roles required. Machinima is also dependant on character customization and ground-up

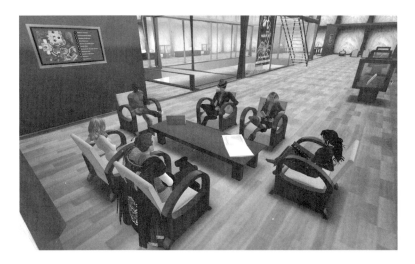

■ **FIGURE 3.3** Characters from "Second Life" by Linden Lab.

Table 3.7 Notable Projects Featuring Digital Characters (2007–2008)

Year	Title	Format	Company
2007	Alvin and the Chipmunks	Feature	Rhythm & Hues
2007	Assassin's Creed	Video Game	Ubisoft Montreal
2007	Bee Movie	Feature	Dreamworks Animation
2007	Beowulf	Feature	Sony Pictures Imageworks
2007	Bioshock	Video Game	2K Boston/ 2K Australia
2007	Crysis	Video Game	Crytek
2007	Elder Scrolls: Oblivion	Video Game	Bethesda Software
2007	Fantastic 4: Rise of the Silver Surfer	Feature	WETA
2007	Ghost Rider	Feature	Sony Imageworks
2007	Golden Compass	Feature	Rhythm & Hues
2007	Harry Potter and the Order of the Phoenix	Feature	ILM, Cinesite, CFC, BUF, Rising Sun, Baseblack, Machine, Double Negative
2007	Mass Effect	Video Game	BioWare
2007	Meet the Robinsons	Feature	Disney
2007	No Time for Nuts	Short	Blue Sky
2007	Pirates of the Caribbean: At Worlds End	Feature	ILM
2007	Ratatouille	Feature	Pixar
2007	Rock Band	Video Game	Harmonix
2007	Shrek the Third	Feature	Dreamworks Animation
2007	Spider-Man 3	Feature	Sony Pictures Imageworks
2007	Surf's Up	Feature	Sony Pictures Imageworks
2007	TMNT	Feature	Imagi Animation Studios
2007	Transformers	Feature	ILM
2007	Your Friend the Rat	Short	Pixar

Continued

Table 3.7 *Continued*

Year	Title	Format	Company
2008	10,000 BC	Feature	MPC, DNeg
2008	Cloverfield	Feature	Tippett Studio, Double Negative, Fugitive Studios
2008	Grand Theft Auto IV	Video Game	Rockstar North
2008	Hellboy II: The Golden Army	Feature	Double Negative
2008	Horton Hears a Who	Feature	Blue Sky
2008	Iron Man	Feature	ILM
2008	Kung-Fu Panda	Feature	Dreamworks Animation
2008	Madagascar 2	Feature	Dreamworks Animation
2008	The Chronicles of Narnia: Prince Caspian	Feature	Moving Picture Company, Framestore CFC
2008	The Incredible Hulk	Feature	Rhythm & Hues
2008	Wall-E	Feature	Pixar

creation, so that unique characters can mix with existing game characters. This process is a great leap for game technology as putting the power of a game engine in the hands of anyone interested in making films opens the doors for low-budget productions in a completely synthetic space with infinite possibilities (Figure 3.4). Users build custom animations to create their performances and in a puppeteering fashion that triggers these animations when needed.

Certainly, the level of character interactivity and complexity being developed for Will Wright's "Spore" (unreleased) is going to be the gold standard by which digital characters in games will be judged. Its mix of procedural character creation and character motion allow the user a great deal of freedom and creativity and thus investment in this world. Later on, we will discuss the technology that lends itself to procedural game characters.

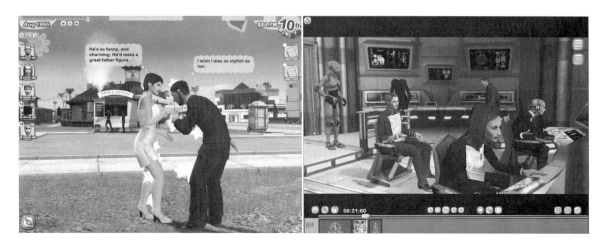

■ **FIGURE 3.4** Commercial machinima software, "The Movies" (2006). Copyright © Lionhead Studios.

The evolution, history, and current state of digital characters leave us in an excellent place to start building our own. There are few limitations to developing what can be imagined by the artist. Through the use of code and new and established techniques, the characters discussed in both games and films will be only the starting point for what comes next.

■ FURTHER READING

Matt Elson. The evolution of digital characters. *Computer Graphics World*, 22(9):23–24, September, 1999.

For a good overview of the industry and the art of animation have a look at:

Isaac V. Kerlow. *The Art of 3D Computer Animation and Effects*, 3rd edition. John Wiley and Sons Inc., Hoboken, NJ, 2004.

Terrance Masson. *CG 101: A Computer Graphics Industry Reference*, 3rd edition. Digital Fauxtography, Williamstown, MA, 2007.

4

Character Technology and Code

4.1 COMMONALITIES BETWEEN SOFTWARE

When it comes to character setup and animation technology, software has come and gone. This book is not about software, but it may be worthwhile to discuss some of the commonalities between contemporary applications with regard to character technology. Most animation packages have a common set of functionalities, which is presented slightly differently in each application. By making clear the fact that there are underlying principles behind this common functionality, this book will teach a crucial lesson to readers who will almost certainly need to adopt several different software packages or other technological tools over the course of their career. All animation software has some notion of the topics covered in this book. While the names may be different, there is an overall trend across software platforms to use the same or similar names for nodes and techniques. Terms such as joints, constraints, deformers, nulls, and groups exist in some form or another, but the real difference is interface. Interface knowledge comes with experience and coming to a new system with a firm understanding of the end goal desired and a road map for the steps needed to get there will ease the transition. This is especially important when learning a system that is specific to a studio and not available commercially.

Many studios invest a lot of time and money into developing proprietary software. This gives them a fully understood framework to develop tools in as opposed to trying to build extensions onto existing third-party platforms where operations are occurring in a "black box." Many studios are in development on films for many years, so the knowledge that they will have full control over the software being used is sometimes a safer bet than relying on the ebb and flow of an external software developer who could stop supporting the software in question mid-production. For character technology, this is particularly important as much of the pipeline for developing a project will be based around the needs of the digital characters. Similarly, the ability to extend existing software is critical, and this will usually require the development of custom code and plug-ins for the existing system. Being able to do this on the fly allows for a system to evolve in response to the needs of production.

4.2 PROGRAMMING AND SCRIPTING

Character technology is a quickly evolving subject and one where no solution is a catchall for every situation. Therefore, it is imperative to have access to the underlying framework of your animation system. This is usually accomplished via a scripting interface or, for more complicated development work, an API, which allows one to access the low-level functionality of the system via a programming language of some flavor.

Programming is the creation and maintenance of code. Whether that code is compiled into a binary executable file or not is the distinction between programming languages and scripting languages. Programming languages are compiled, while scripting languages remain in their original written form and are interpreted each time they are executed. The differences between programming and scripting languages are diminishing and languages such as Python [40] are bridging the gap by being a scripting language that can be executed as-is or compiled. In fact, Python is becoming a commonly used language across commercial and proprietary animation systems.

Programming languages such as C++ are typically used to build new applications or compiled plug-ins for existing software. Scripting is used internally to automate and combine small tasks into macros within the software and externally to interface with the operating system and the data stored on disk. No matter what the situation is, coding is critical to the creation of digital characters. In fact, a general understanding of the concepts behind programming will always complement the other skills required for character setup. Consequently, we can address the software and language-agnostic manner with which we will describe code in the context of this text.

4.3 **ALGORITHM PRESENTATION IN THIS BOOK**

This book is designed to cover the algorithmic thinking behind character technology and to be software-agnostic. Because of this, algorithmic concepts will be presented through graphical flowcharts as opposed to pseudocode or the isolation of one particular language. The concepts can be implemented in any system, and the reader need not be fluent in a specific language or programming in general. For example, an algorithm for a simple joint rotation constraint accumulates weighted rotation values for a series of joints would be illustrated as shown in Figures 4.1 and 4.2.

These images represent the class and an object instance of that class (Figure 4.1), along with the method (Figure 4.2) for a joint rotate constraint. This constraint defines a special control by which a chain of joints has cumulative rotations applied via the control curve offset by a per-joint weight. A class defines the characteristics of an object including its attributes, fields, and properties. An instance of this class is called an object. Objects provide specific data to the fields defined in the class. In our case, each class has a constraint associated with it. In programming parlance, this constraint would be called a method which is equally valid. Methods are the algorithms associated with classes that give them their ability to manipulate the data stored in the object instances. In our example above, the class rotateConstraint defines a list (array) of joints (jointsToRotate), the weight associated with each of those joints (rotateWeight), the value of the

Class	
▬ jointsToRotate:	string array
▬ rotateWeight:	float array
▬ inputValue:	vector
▬ weight:	float

Instance	
▬ jointsToRotate:	neck01
▬ jointsToRotate:	neck02
▬ jointsToRotate:	neck03
▬ jointsToRotate:	neck04
▬ jointsToRotate:	neck05
▬ rotateWeight:	0.2
▬ rotateWeight:	0.3
▬ rotateWeight:	0.4
▬ rotateWeight:	0.5
▬ rotateWeight:	0.6
▬ inputValue:	head.neckRot
▬ weight:	head.neckRot.weight

■ **FIGURE 4.1** Class and data diagram for joint rotate constraint.

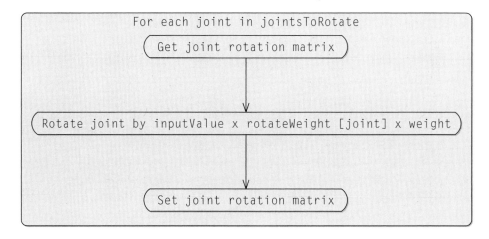

■ **FIGURE 4.2** Method for a joint rotate constraint.

incoming animation control (inputValue), and the overall effect of this instance of the constraint (weight). The instance object of this called neckRot provides the necessary data to create an instantiation of this class. When classes are built, generally they can become the generic building blocks of more complex systems. The actual constraint associated with this class is depicted in the flowchart found in Figure 4.2. All the data defined in the class are utilized and manipulated in the process of curling the joint chain in a user-defined weighted manner. The method cycles through all the joints in jointsToRotate and stores the rotation matrix for each one of them, then for each joint it multiplies inputValue by rotateWeight, and then multiples all of that by weight. While the jointsToRotate and rotateWeight attributes are fixed values which define the properties of the constraint, inputValue and weight are animatable attributes which can be changed over the course of the animation with inputValue being the main interface for the control. Most methods in an animation system have some concept of a weight which allows the character setup artists to minimize or turn off the effects of a tool in the execution of a character. This ability to debug a rig allows an artist to get to the root of the problem quickly.

The sections of code throughout the book are intended to represent simplified versions of what can be complicated tools. Some methods are represented in more verbose terms and others utilize generic method calls for getting and setting vector and matrix values as needed. Where complex operations, like dynamic simulation, are called for, these are internally left as "black box" operations where it would be expected that the character setup artist or animator would turn control over to an established dynamics engine. In general, the code presented is intended to be more representational of the thought process behind constructing a constraint or deformer and not an exact blueprint for developing such tools.

The changing nature of character and animation technology is dependent and predicated in new software tools and techniques developed within those tools. Knowledge of the algorithms underlying currently existing tools also helps a character technical director know the right tool for specific situations by having an intimate familiarity with that tools functionality. While those who work with existing character technology need not be programmers, knowledge of the subject is becoming increasingly important. Further, object-oriented thinking outside of generating code can be a useful mind-set. Creating generic objects (such as regions of a rig) that can be used as modules, and constructed in a reusable manner, to build more complex systems will eliminate the redundancy of building these same blocks again. Whether done with code or modular/procedural thinking, a library of reusable objects is invaluable to any production.

■ FURTHER READING

For a good overview of Python start with the web site:

http://www.python.org/

Some good introductory Python resources include:

Mark Lutz. *Learning Python*, 3rd edition. O'Reilly and Associates, Inc., Cambridge, MA, 2007.

John M. Zelle. *Python Programming: An Introduction to Computer Science*. Franklin Beedle and Associates, Wilsonville, OR, 2003.

For good practical books that are specific to programming and scripting related to animation production, and Autodesk Maya specifically:

Mark R. Wilkins and Chris Kazmier. *MEL Scripting for Maya Animators, (The Morgan Kaufmann Series in Computer Graphics)*, 2nd edition. Morgan Kaufmann Publishers Inc., San Francisco, CA, 2005.

David Gould. *Complete Maya Programming: An Extensive Guide to MEL and the C++ API (Morgan Kaufmann Series in Computer Graphics and Geometric Modeling)*. Morgan Kaufmann Publishers Inc., San Francisco, CA, 2003.

David Gould. *Complete Maya Programming Volume II: An In-depth Guide to 3D Fundamentals, Geometry, and Modeling (Morgan Kaufmann Series in Computer Graphics and Geometric Modeling)*. Morgan Kaufmann Publishers Inc., San Francisco, CA, 2005.

For very hands-on tutorials for advanced rigging in Autodesk Maya, the "The Art of Rigging" series from CG Toolkit are quite thorough [17–19].

Karim Biri, Kiaran Ritchie, and Jake Callery. *The Art of Rigging: Volume I*. CG Toolkit, San Rafael, CA, 2005.

Karim Biri, Kiaran Ritchie, and Oleg Alexander. *The Art of Rigging: Volume II*. CG Toolkit, San Rafael, CA, 2005.

Karim Biri, Kiaran Ritchie, and Oleg Alexander. *The Art of Rigging: Volume III*. CG Toolkit, San Rafael, CA, 2006.

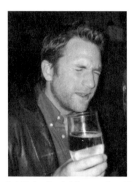

Todd Taylor, Head of Character Setup Technology, Sony Pictures Imageworks

■ INTERVIEW: TODD TAYLOR, HEAD OF CHARACTER SETUP TECHNOLOGY, SONY PICTURES IMAGEWORKS

■ BIO

Todd Taylor is currently Head of Character Setup Technology at Sony Pictures Imageworks in Culver City, California. His film credits include "Shrek 2," "Madagascar," "The Lion, The Witch and the Wardrobe," "Superman Returns," "Beowulf," and soon…"Cloudy with a Chance of Meatballs." He grew up in Andover, Massachusetts and attended Boston College studying both computer science and art.

■ Q&A

Q) *The components of character technology are diverse and span the artistic and technical spectrum. How did you get your start in the industry? Based on where you see the field heading, what experience/training do you recommend people have?*

A) Even though I lived in Massachusetts, my first job in 3D was for a company in Glasgow, Scotland called Digital Animations. I applied randomly through the company's website not expecting a reply, but ten weeks later, I got a call on the phone from a Scottish guy offering me a job. I was hired as an entry-level character animator on the condition that if I was really horrible at animating, I would start programming. Alas, I did a bit of programming (heh-heh), but I actually did mostly animation and rigging. I had graduated from Boston College a couple years earlier with a degree in computer science and concentration (minor) in studio art and art history, but everything I learned about computer animation, I learned on my own. I had always been more of an artist, but the reason I studied computer science was so that I would have a strong technical foundation for my future career in 3D animation. I always assumed that I would be an animator, but all that schooling really gave me an edge on the TD side of things, and I eventually gravitated towards being a technical director.

Obviously, the best experience for getting a job character rigging is doing just that. Nowadays, anybody can learn this stuff on their home computer using the tons of tutorials, example, rigs and scripts that can be found online. Although it is great to know the ins and outs of major packages such as Maya and Softimage, the most important thing is to have demonstrated experience coming up with successful solutions to creative rigging problems, not so much what specific tools you used. Both at PDI/DreamWorks and Sony Imageworks, I walked in the door my first day having no clue how to use the animation software they used in production. Another tremendously helpful skill to have is the ability to program. I have definitely seen people in the past over-engineer things, but by and large, knowing how to write scripts is very empowering for technical directors to get things done that would take forever to do by hand. Right now, I would suggest learning Python because it is widely used and a great scripting language.

Q) *Creating compelling digital characters is part art and part science. What is the greatest challenge you encounter on a daily basis? What aspect of character technology keeps you up thinking at night?*

A) One challenge that I encounter on a daily basis is figuring out when to stop working on a character. Character rigs are never 100% done. If you think you have an absolutely perfect rig, then you probably spent too much time (money to producers) working on it. I have seen so many people (myself included) waste weeks (or even months!) on fancy rigging features that are never used by animators or never seen on screen. Also, animators and directors might keep telling you that you need this or that added or changed. After all, a digital character is a big 3D hack, and sometimes, it makes more sense hack to the model in the specific shot with a corrective shape than to try to make the actual rig behave. Obviously, that kind of solution is not an option for interactive/real-time characters, but I am sure knowing when to quit is still hard for them too.

Hmmm...what keeps me up thinking at night? I am always thinking of ways to do things better and faster than before. We have still got a lot of room for improvement.

Q) *What are the ingredients for a successful digital character?*

A) Hmmm...well the most important ingredients are the same for any kind of character digital or not. I think we all agree that a character can be state of the art technically, but if people do not like him, then nobody is going to care...(cough)JarJar(cough).

Some general character concerns:

- Concept: Is this a good idea for a character? Is it original? Can people relate in some way?
- Look: Is the basic esthetic well designed and appealing?
- Role: Does this character do interesting things?
- Performance: Is the character well played (acting or voice-over and character animation)?

Some specifics to creating these characters in 3D:

- Appealing design with 3rd dimension in mind (can be very cartoony/abstract, but it needs to work in the 3D realm)
- 3D mesh modeled with rigging and texture painting in mind (optimized surface topology with organic flow of span layout)
- Character rigged with animation in mind (useful controls and good deformations)
- Character surfaced with overall look in mind (everything needs to feel like it is in the same world)
- Animation with acting in mind (it is all about the performance)
- Technical animation with character/shot context in mind (hair/cloth/dynamics should not distract)

- Lighting and effects with artistic vision in mind (supporting scene atmosphere, mood, and overall look of film/project).

Q) *While the industry is competitive, it is ultimately respectful of great work. Outside of the work you have been personally involved in the production of, what animated characters have you been impressed or inspired by? What is the historical high-bar?*

A) My favorite 3D animation of all time is actually a music video by Super Furry Animals called "It's Not The End of the World?" I absolutely love how they created a world digitally that appears as though it was created mechanically. The clunky but adorable tin toy characters acting out a very serious sequence of events is mesmerizing. As simple as those characters were, they were unique and perfect for the context. I always think of that when I find myself getting lost in the unimportant details. Search for the video on the web. It is genius.

In recent times, it seems as though Davey Jones from "Pirates of the Caribbean" is a high-bar in this field. I would have to agree because that character had all the right ingredients, and the execution was virtually flawless. I also loved "King Kong." I fell asleep somewhere in the second or third hour of the movie, but I remember being very impressed with the big monkey.

Q) *Where do you see digital characters in ten years? Where are animated characters for film and games heading?*

A) Hmmm...that is a good one. I will answer in the literal sense first. I see them everywhere, generated by almost everyone. I have noticed a huge spike in the last year or so of digital characters appearing in low-budget TV commercials, and it got me thinking that 3D is clearly no longer a niche market of highly skilled artists and techies. Software and computers have been relatively cheap for a while now, but I think the 3D tools have reached a tipping point where the average artist can now generate some good work without being a real expert. Also, character generation applications like Poser will continue to become more and more impressive and used more widely. There is a new game called "SPORE," which allows the player to design and build his own character. I am sure in the future, we will have the ability to do full-color 3D scans of people and turn them into instant avatars and the like very cheaply. As a result, I think we will see a lot more digitally created characters everywhere you can imagine.

I also think that digital characters are going to become smarter and more powerful. No, not like Dr. Manhattan. I mean they will gain more and more animation autonomy. For certain kinds of animation, there will be no more key-framing by hand but something more along the lines of guided simulations. We can already see the beginning of this in current products like Natural Motion's Endorphine, but eventually, we will have the type of character that more or less is "directed" rather than "animated." Of course, there will still be hand key-framed digital characters in the future, just as there are still hand-drawn characters now; however, it is fun to think of a time where key-framed curves and motion capture data are "old-school" techniques.

All in all, I love being involved in digital character creation. Even though the process is technical and can get extremely complex, it is still a very primitive concept at the core. If you think about it, we are doing the same exact thing those cavemen were doing when they painted stick figures of humans and animals on the walls of their caves. We are endlessly fascinated with looking at ourselves, and we are always finding new ways to do it.

Part 2

Character Technology

Introduction to Character Technology

Constructing the architecture of a digital character is one of the most complicated aspects of animation production. Considerations must be made for the mechanical structure as well as the deformation of the character model. In addition, an interface for the animator, motion capture, or a procedural system to control the character is required. All these decisions are based on the type and nature of the production. Requirements for film animation and video games are different, so the limitations and concerns for each medium will be highlighted. This work requires the eye of the artist and the thought process of an engineer.

5.1 NOMENCLATURE

Character technology, and more generally animation technology, is full of terminology, and each software package uses its own terms to describe similar concepts. In the pantheon of computer graphics phrases, the realm of character technology is one of the least standardized with regard to nomenclature. For the purposes of clarity and to propose a uniform language for the discussion of character technology, the following terms are defined:

Motion System The collection of joints, constraints, and controls which provide a control structure and interface for the animator to manipulate the character.

Joint The transformable hierarchical matrix which forms the foundation for the motion system.

Constraint A small program that defines a non-hierarchical relationship between joints. These may include solvers to procedurally place joints.

Control The object, attribute, or interface that an animator manipulates the character motion system through.

Solver A constraint that procedurally determines the relationship of joints through calculation and/or simulation.

Deformation System The collection of methods used to attach and modify the character model via the changing motion system.

Surface An element of the overall geometric character model which is deformed by the deformation system.

Deformer A method for modifying the position of vertices of a surface.

Different studios also use different terminology for these elements, but the above should provide a baseline to carry us through the concepts covered in this book.

5.2 THE PIPELINE FOR DIGITAL CHARACTER CREATION AND MAINTENANCE

In the creation of games and films, the production pipeline is a fundamental concern. The pipeline is the path data travels through the production process. This includes asset management, access to assets by multiple artists, and the workflow from one stage to the next. As can be seen in Figure 5.1, the character technology pipeline starts with the development of the character model. Once the model is completed, it is handed off to the character setup artist who builds the motion and deformation systems. The shading and texturing of the

Character technology pipeline

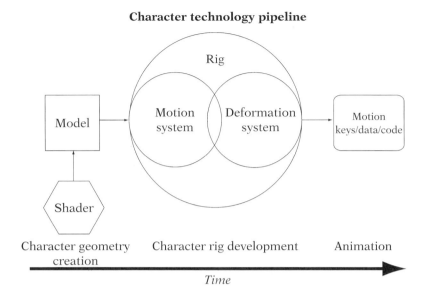

■ **FIGURE 5.1** Character technology pipeline.

character comes into play around the same point as the animation, at the end of the pipeline, but ideally happens as early as the model is completed.

Modularity and efficiency are keys to character pipelines and characters need to be standardized in terms of functionality and element naming. This is essential not only for artists doing the setup and those maintaining characters they did not setup but also for animators who need a consistent and reliable control set. Standardization also allows for the ability to craft "smarter" production tools. With standards come safe assumptions, and by safely assuming certain data, common tasks can be more readily automated. The structure of the production pipeline revolves around the idea of references to assets which have been "published" or "mastered" as opposed to each scene having a static inclusion of the character rig. Similarly, the ability for artists to work on assets insulated from the live working asset is important, and this can be accomplished as easily as artists working in a workshop directory and as complicated as working in "artist trees," which are local versions of the main production tree. Production trees are parallel versions of the production assets that reference the main master production tree. By having access to a personal shadow of the latest production assets, a character setup artist can test solutions without affecting the rest of production. Once the solution is known to fix the problem at hand and can be implemented in a manner that has unforseen circumstances down the line that asset can be "checked in" to the main tree and all other parallel trees can get access to it. Checking a file out through revision control gives that artist the ability to exclusively edit it. Other artists needing to edit that file will have to wait until the owner checks it back in. They then get the latest version of the file and make their edits from there. Often times, multiple files need to be edited to facilitate a change, so associations are made through revision control for grouping files together to define an asset. Similarly, every production has its own standard for managing collections of files which define the revision state of an asset at any time. In the same way that software applications have version numbers, asset states are also numbered for tracking. By integrating production trees with revision control, assets, defined by a collection of files, can always be rolled back to a previous working state.

The evolving state of an asset on the main production tree is ideally seamlessly handled thanks to referencing. Referencing is a means of establishing a symbolic link to an asset stored on the production tree as opposed to storing that asset within each scene. Referencing then allows an artist to have a file "virtually open" in a scene by accessing the reference to it. By including a reference to the asset, the animator, for example, cannot modify original asset which leaves it open for other artists to continue to work on it. Having assets referenced allows for a simultaneous workflow among artists and flexibility to change the design, look, and functionality of an asset across production. Most animation systems include a method for referencing assets and for managing the shot inventory via a referencing system. In proprietary systems, it is possible to handle the shot population and referencing via a production database. In this case, scenes can be a description of assets in the scene with data about their position over time, likely stored as animation curves. When the shot is opened, the database is queried for the latest assets and then connected to the stored animation curves for proper placement and motion. Thus, the shot is built at runtime via scripts which query the database and make the proper connections and not stored as a static collection of assets. This runtime build step is a powerful process where code can be run on the assets and the construction of the shot to implement edits or updates procedurally on a shot-specific or production-wide basis. Once automated by the production pipeline interface, the shot building process is transparent to the user and provides a high level of control in the technical administration of the project.

Maintenance is a critical concern for the character pipeline. Setup artists need access to the character while animation is taking place in an insulated environment so that changes can be made and tested before that character is once again "published" into production. More specifically, setup artists need to be able to make changes that fix problems while maintaining whatever amount of animation has been attached to that character rig. Once fixed or modified, these changes should automatically propagate into the production pipeline so that animators now have access to the latest rig. Referencing makes this possible. Fixes often require adding a new attribute that is a modified version of an existing control. This maintains the current animation, but provides the new control if needed, as opposed to changing the functionality of an existing control and running the risk of changing in-process animation. As animation is produced, it goes through a process of reviews and revisions until it is considered done and "approved" by the animation supervisor and show director(s). As such, it is equally important to have approved final animation remain unchanged by rig updates. Thus, it is sometimes necessary, in extreme cases, to be able to lock versions of rigs and tie that version to the approved animation, leaving them bound together and in a read-only state. Increasingly common is that the geometry deformed by the rig per frame is written out as a geometry cache. As opposed to locking the rig for this shot, the visible output of the rig is stored on disk in the form of a series of models. This "bakes" the animation as geometry and effectively frees the animation from changes to the rig. These models are then read by the renderer at render time, and the rig is never evaluated again for that shot. While managing these per-frame models is a storage issue, the costs are often outweighed by the ability to control the model disconnected from the rig. Shot-specific deformations are often produced by editing the character models after the animation is final. Details like finger contact compression when a character touches something, for example, sell the idea of the character realistically interacting with the environment and other characters in the shot. These shot-specific deformations are rarely included in the ability of the rig, are dependant on animation, and, as such, are enacted on the geometry cache for the scene. While baking character geometry is a method for locking animation from rig changes, it has an increasingly important role in production and has become quite common.

5.3 **GEOMETRY MESH SURFACE TYPES**

Modern digital characters are created by sculpting a 3D surface; this surface is then deformed by the character rig. The surface type of this model is dependent on the strategy and pipeline of the production, but at this point, we typically break down surface types into three categories: polygonal, Bézier-spline-based, and subdivision surfaces (Figure 5.2).

Polygon
Polygons are the most simple surfaces, composed of vertices connected by edges to form polygons which are connected to form polygonal meshes. These are often the only option for video games based on the architecture of most real-time engines. Polygon configurations for production are usually limited to triangles (three sides) and quadrilateral (four sides), with the ideal being quadrilateral polygons as they result in better deformations on character models. In the past, some game engines required polygons to be triangular, but this is not a requirement anymore.

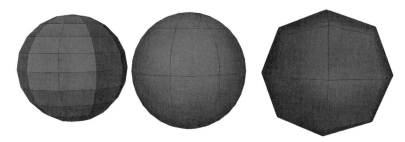

■ **FIGURE 5.2**   Surface type sphere primitives (polygon, NURBS, subdivision surface).

NURBS (Non-Uniform Rational Bézier-Spline)

A NURBS curve is defined by its order, a set of weighted control points, and a knot vector. NURBS curves and surfaces are generalizations of both B-splines and Bézier curves and surfaces, the primary difference being the weighting of the control points, which makes NURBS curves rational (nonrational B-splines are a special case of rational B-splines). Whereas NURBS curves evolve into only one parametric direction usually called "s" or "u," NURBS surfaces evolve into two parametric directions called "s" and "t," or "u" and "v."

Subdivisions

Subdivision surfaces are a method of representing a smooth surface via the specification of a coarser piecewise linear polygon mesh. The smooth surface can be calculated from the coarse mesh as the limit of an iterative process of subdividing each polygonal face into smaller faces that better approximate the smooth surface. Since NURBS have to be created in patches and stitched together to create a seamless surface, subdivision surfaces can achieve the organic qualities of NURBS as a single surface and thus avoiding stitching. Because of this, subdivision surfaces have in many ways replaced NURBS surfaces as the preferred method of modeling character and scene geometry.

No matter the surface type, there are similar guidelines that should be followed for the development of a digital character. Currently, polygons are the preferred surface for character creation, while NURBS are going out of favor and subdivision surfaces are just beginning to find their footing in the industry. Much of the acceptance of these surfaces is based on their access in commercial applications. Studios can write the necessary tools to implement a custom surface type and integrate it into their production pipeline. The independent user does not usually have such a luxury and is subject to the availability in their tool set.

5.4 MODELING CONCERNS FOR ANIMATION

When a character is going to fill a theater screen, it is subject to viewer scrutiny at an unparalleled level. A clean model with a well thought out topology is critical for character deformations. Areas that require extreme deformations require more resolution than areas that have limited motion. The general idea with character modeling is to lay out the topology in such a way as that the areas of articulation have the necessary resolution to bend effectively while maintaining the desired shape. The positioning of the character should be arranged so that the different body parts are far enough from each other to make deformations easier in a relaxed muscular state and ideally at the midpoint of their deformation range. The midpoint of deformation range usually leaves the arms straight out to the side in a "T-Pose" which is directly in-between raising the arm above the head and resting it at its side. Because characters are rarely called to raise their arms over their heads, modelers will often model characters with arms halfway down at the characters side in an "A-Pose" (Figure 5.3). Elbow and knees are also often modeled slightly bent so that the deformation process starts with a shape that is most akin to the extremes that it is responsible for producing. The point of all of this is to make the deformation setup as efficient and quick as possible, and the best way to do this is to not have to correct shapes through deformation before achieving the desired forms.

The humanoid knee and shoulder are examples of where this can be quite straightforward and where it can be the most complex. The human knee (Figure 5.4) is essentially a hinge joint that rotates around one axis and for the most part in one direction around the axis. To preserve the volume of the knee area, two joints are placed, one at the top part of the

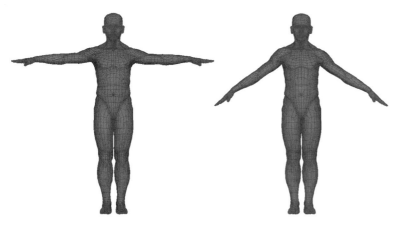

■ **FIGURE 5.3** Character model in T-Pose and A-Pose. Model by Lee Wolland.

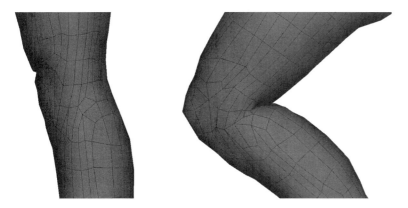

■ **FIGURE 5.4** Knee model straight and flexed. Model by Lee Wolland.

articulation area and another at the bottom of the articulation area, to give the impression of large confluence of bone and muscle that folds when the knee is bent. The topology of the model surface should reflect the understanding of how this region articulates. This relationship means that communication between the character modeler and character setup artist should start early and iterate to reach the optimal result.

Contrary to the relative simplicity of the human knee, the human shoulder is a complex relationship between a ball and socket joint. This allows the upper arm and shoulder region to rotate in many combinations of all three rotation axes and translate, thanks to the shoulder's loose attachment to the axial body via its attachment to the scapula and clavicle (Figure 5.5). This complex region requires well laid-out points to aid in the deformation of the model as it will be affected by a number of joints and is one of the more mobile regions of the body.

Typically for each production, the topology of character models is defined early then used to shape the rest of the characters, when possible, using the original as a base. This consistency allows rigging solutions to be propagated across characters as well speeding up time and efficiency.

With regard to resolution of a film character, there is almost no limitation. Animators require fast feedback with limited processing lag on the execution of a character while they are interacting with it. In many cases, the high-resolution geometry is generated through sculpting, which requires a much higher resolution mesh than can be run interactively (on modern systems). The high-resolution mesh used for final display need only to be processed at the moment of rendering which is a non-interactive event and expected in film to run off-line. This does not mean that the character setup artist

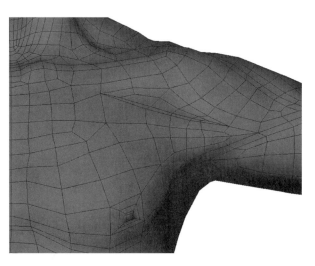 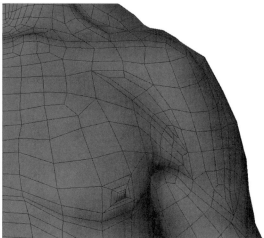

■ **FIGURE 5.5** Shoulder model straight and bent down. Model by Lee Wolland.

should not be thinking about optimization at every step of the way, but there are certain speed allowances that are made in film production that are compensated for with processing power. Character interactivity in an animation system is a sensitive threshold affected by many factors, but true interactivity requires that character response be instantaneous. When an animator moves a control, the element should move in real-time. Sometimes even the deformation of a low polygon mesh is enough to slow down a system, particulary when many characters are in a single scene. As a result, non-deforming proxy models are often what the animator works with as they animate. These are typically simple polygonal primitives that match the initial volume of the character elements and are parented to the appropriate rig elements. They then form a quick-responding approximation of the character. Any lag is a distraction and a time sink, so effort must go into making sure that deforming models, or even stand-in geometry if needed, are fast enough for real-time feedback.

5.5 MODELING CONCERNS FOR VIDEO GAMES AND REAL-TIME ENGINES

While there are almost no limitations for model resolution in film production, this is a huge concern for real-time graphics engines. Before we delve into this, it is worth mentioning that commercials and television series are generally somewhere between the game scenario and the film although constraints for these projects are usually purely based on time and budgets. For games, polygons are exclusively used within most of today's game engines and polygon count, commonly referred to as polycount, is closely monitored. Modelers working in video games must go to great lengths to optimize polycount, and techniques are employed using textures and various other map-based techniques to add details to the model that transcend the surface topology. Files such as bump and normal maps are created to add the appearance of surface details and complexity without increasing the polycount. While graphics hardware constantly pushes up the possibly polygon volume, the general contemporary consensus is that poly-count for game characters in character-based games (such as first-person shooters, role-playing, or adventure games) should be between four thousand and ten thousand polygons. This range will likely be humorous in a few years.

Take for example this character from "Gears of War" (Figure 5.6). The designed character is created at a very high polygon count (in this case, two million polygons) using a mix of modeling and sculpting tools. The high-resolution detail is "baked" into a collection of maps, most notably a normal map, which replaces the surface normal on a low polygon mesh with a multichannel value derived from the high-resolution mesh. This allows the low-resolution mesh to be easily deformed by the engine, but the application of the complexity maps provides all the detail modeled into the high-resolution mesh. Not all map technologies can be utilized by game engines. For example, deformation maps, also called displacement maps, where the surface is changed by the grey scale values of the map are heavily used in animated film and visual effects but not by games at all.

In addition, games often also require characters to be modeled with separate collision geometry which is a very low polygon surface that rides along with the character rig and is used in the processing of collisions in the dynamics engine.

Character setup for game engines puts a number of limitations on the process. The real-time constraint imposed by game engines means that only a small subset of methods available to characters developed for animated films are applicable. Shortcuts and simplifications must be sought wherever possible, leading to a different set of problems and, in their own right, cutting edge solutions. Every tool used in the character setup would have to be interpreted and recreated to run in the real-time engine. For example, default tools such as joints that come in animation software packages have an easily mapped equivalent in most game engines, but other tools used to build a character's motion or deformation system either have to be recreated by the software engineers on

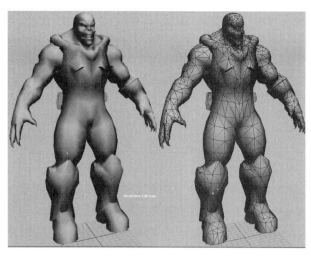

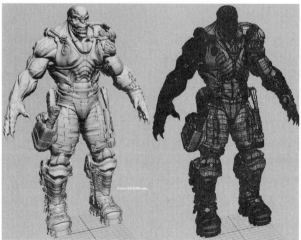

■ **FIGURE 5.6**   Low and high resolution polygon mesh for character from "Gears of War."
Copyright © 2006 Epic Games, Inc.

the game team or ignored and not used in the setup by the character setup team.

Throughout this book, we will be comparing techniques and discussing the limitations and possibilities of game character development as opposed to those for film. As we live in an age of convergence, where films, games, and interactive media intermix and become less and less distinct, we will continue to see less distinctions between characters produced for different media.

5.6   **EXERCISE**

In preparation for taking a character design from 2D sketches and model sheets to 3D model, it is important to take a step back and attempt to bring the 3D form into the real world. The best way to do this is in the form of a posed maquette that harnesses the personality and attitude of the character. This process will give you a better sense of the character proportions and volume and will help immensely as you go into character modeling in your 3D package of choice.

5.1   Begin with making a metal armature. Not only will this help support your clay or plasticine model but it will get you thinking about internal structure and points of articulation.

5.2   To create volumes but keep the weight down, artists often tightly bound aluminium foil to build up areas.

5.3   Once the volumes are right, start covering the armature with the material of your choice to flesh it out.

5.4   Sculpt in minor features in as much details as possible. The more decisions you make at this point, the better off you will be when you go in to digitally model your character.

5.5   Step back and think about the form. Does it work? Does it read from multiple angles? Get feedback and critique from others. Challenge the design to be better and not just done.

5.6   Maintain this test/fix feedback loop until satisfied.

5.7   Harden your maquette in the method associated with the materials you are using.

■ FURTHER READING

There are many software specific books and training videos that cover low and high polygon modeling techniques.

Mario Russo. *Polygonal Modeling: Basic and Advanced Techniques (Worldwide Game and Graphics Library). Wordware Publishing Inc., Plano, TX, 2005.*

Jason Patnode. Character Modeling with Maya and ZBrush. *Focal Press, San Francisco, CA, 2008.*

Eric Keller. Introducing ZBrush. *SYBEX Inc., Alameda, CA, 2008.*

For a more technical procedural overview of models and modeling refer to:

David S. Ebert, F. Kenton Musgrave, Darwyn Peachey, Ken Perlin, and Steven Worley. *Texturing and Modeling: A Procedural Approach.* Morgan Kaufmann Publishers Inc., San Francisco, CA, 2002.

Motion Systems

Motion systems are the mechanical architecture, a collection of joints, controls, and procedures that provide an interface for animation input. Essentially, the motion system has to do with everything outside of the actual deformation of the model. We start with an anatomy overview, including terminology for anatomical direction and motion, followed by a description of the computer graphics concepts required to implement skeletons. This is all brought together with some examples of classes, procedures, and constraints to tie the elements together.

6.1 CHARACTER MOTION SYSTEMS AND ANATOMY

No matter how realistic, fantastic, or stylized a character is, the underlying anatomy must be considered, planned, and implemented in order to achieve the motion and aesthetic required of that character. In this chapter, we look at the relationship between anatomy and the design and architecture of a character motion system. While digital characters do not need to precisely recreate the anatomical structure of the entity they represent, an informed understanding of the underlying structure and the motion it is designed for are crucial for capturing the essence of that character. Once understood, a decision can be made to stray from it as dictated by the style of the production. Building a basic understanding of comparative anatomy requires some adherence to the terminology of biology, so an overview of terms and concepts precedes our overview of anatomical structures and their mechanical properties. Recreating these structures in 3D using matrices and hierarchical transformations follows this discussion and is similarly developed. Starting with a single joint matrix and methods of rotating it, we begin building hierarchies of joints and controlling them with constraints built on relationships between them and custom procedures. This all wraps up with the integration of dynamic simulation and user interface, which provide our initial methods of attaching motion to these systems.

6.2 ANATOMICAL DIRECTION

A "lingua franca" among anatomists is the language of anatomical direction. This is a common and standardized collection of terms that describe anatomical elements based on their position relative to each other. It also happens to be revelent to describing the position of rig elements in relation to each other. Anatomical position is the baseline pose that anatomical direction is based on. For the human body, anatomical position is described as standing erect, the eyes looking forward at the horizon, the arms by the sides, and the palms of the hands and the toes directed forward (Figure 6.1). Keep in mind that this is anatomical position and not the "T" pose that is so often seen in digital characters at their default state. Using the placement of the hands as an example, we can define descriptive terms for the position of elements in relation to each other and the direction of these objects. If hands were to rest palms down on a table, they would be said to face inferiorly. Turn them around, and they face upward or superiorly. Hanging to the sides, naturally they face each other or medially; rotated 180 degrees and they face out or laterally; backwards or posteriorly; forwards or anteriorly. Essentially, three pairs of terms are defined to express the relationship of one structure to another (Table 6.1).

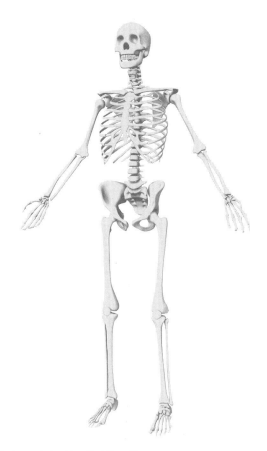

■ **FIGURE 6.1**   Anatomical position. Model by cgHuman.

As most biological structures are generally symmetrical along one dividing plane, these terms are highly effective, and often additional terms such as "left" and "right" are not used except for describing asymmetric details. This symmetry is helpful for the character modeler and setup artist as it allows geometry and rig structures to be mirrored across planes to reduce work and to insure symmetric functionality. Although in a 3D space, these planes are defined by the *xyz* axis that they parallel, biologists have more descriptive terms for them. Once we have an agreed upon natural stance, we can define planes that transect the body splitting it up into regions. The body is divided into two equal halves, a

Table 6.1 Anatomical Direction	
Anterior (in front)	Nearer the front of the body
Posterior (behind)	Nearer the back of the body
Superior (above)	Nearer the top of the head
Inferior (below)	Nearer the bottom of the feet
Medial	Nearer the median plane of the body
Lateral	Away from the median plane of the body

left and a right by the median or midsagittal plane passing through the body at midline. Splitting the body into anterior and posterior halves is the coronal plane which passes through the body perpendicular to the midsagittal plane. Passing through at right angles to the other planes described and dividing the body into upper and lower halves is the transverse plane.

When it comes to describing structures that are local to a limb or relative to an appendage, the part that is closer to the midsagittal plane is the proximal end, while the part that is further away is the distal end. So the feature that lies on the forearm closer the hand is considered distal to the elbow and proximal to the wrist. Combining terms is where the power of this descriptive syntax comes into play.

When we discuss comparative anatomy, we compare the relationship and differences of structures between species, and it is necessary to use a different set of terms which are not related to relative space but to elements of the body. In humans, an orthograde animal, the shoulders lie above the hips, while in a horse, a pronograde animal, they lie in front of the hips (Figure 6.2). With this in mind, their position relative to other parts of the body is the same; thus, speaking from a comparative point of view, it can be said that the shoulders are toward the head, or cranial end of the body, while the hips are toward the tail, or caudal end of the body. These terms are

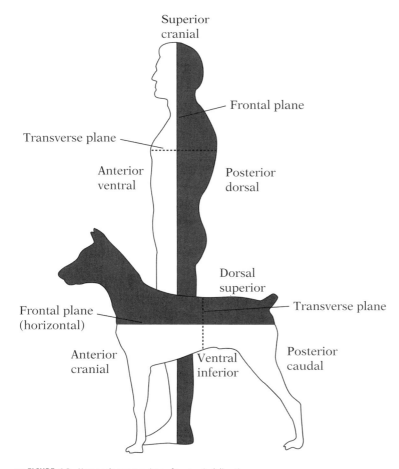

■ **FIGURE 6.2** Human dog comparison of anatomical direction.

applicable to any vertebrate body regardless of its habitual position, bipedal, on two legs, or quadrupedal, on four legs.

- ventral: the belly side of the body
- dorsal: the backside of the body
- cranial or cephalic: toward the head end of the body
- caudal: toward the tail end of the body

6.3 ANATOMICAL TERMS OF MOTION

Body structures are moved by the contraction of muscles. Muscles move parts of the skeleton relative to each other. All

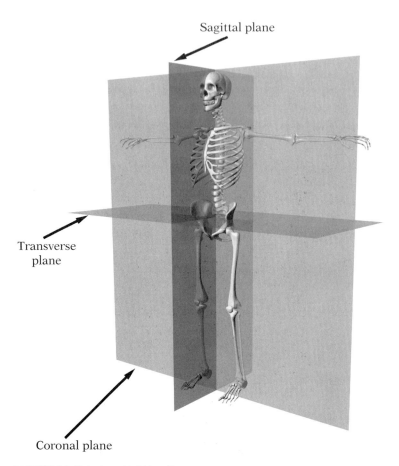

■ **FIGURE 6.3** Body planes. Model by cgHuman.

such movements are classified by the directions in which the affected structures are moved. In human anatomy, all descriptions of position and movement are based on the assumption that the body is in anatomical position (Figure 6.3).

1. Flexion: Movement in the anterior-posterior plane. The angle between two articulating bones is decreased. Flexing the arm brings the hand closer to the shoulder.

2. Extension: The opposite of flexion. The angle between two articulation bones is increased. The continuation of the extension beyond normal anatomical position is referred to as hyperextension.

3. Abduction: Movement of an extremity away from the midline of the body.

4. Adduction: The opposite of abduction. Movement of an extremity toward the body.

5. Rotation: The movement of a bone around its own axis such as rotating your arm at the shoulder.

6. Circumduction: The distal end of an extremity moves in a circle while the proximal end remains stable. Twisting the hand along the axis of the arm.

7. Supination: Rotating the hand so that the palm is superior.

8. Pronation: Rotating the hand so that the palm is inferior.

9. Inversion: Movement at the ankle resulting in the sole of the foot being turned inward.

10. Eversion: Movement at the ankle resulting in the sole of the foot being turned outward.

11. Elevation: Raising a body part such as closing the jaw.

12. Depression: Lowering a body part such as opening the jaw.

13. Protraction: Translating a body part forward such as jutting the jaw out.

14. Retraction: Translating a body part backward such as "clenching" the jaw back.

15. Hyperextension: Body part is extended beyond the straight line formed by normal extension.

16. Plantar flexion: Normal (downward on humans) extension of the foot.

17. Dorsiflexion: Opposite (upward in humans) extension of the foot.

While these terms might have little meaning to animators, they provide an unequivocal vocabulary between character setup artists to describe motion. In most cases, a description such as "when I raise the character's left arm and twist the forearm, I encounter this problem" will suffice, but having access to a common vocabulary has its advantages. As with an understanding of anatomical direction, the terminology for anatomical motion provides a species-independent set of terms to describe character motion.

6.4 JOINT MECHANICS

While skeletal articulations in the natural world are constrained by their function, joints in 3D are, by default, built for articulation within three axes of rotation freedom. With this in mind, it is important to understand the different types of joints common in nature as the implementation of these as constraints allows for a sense of realism in the structure.

There are four principle types of joints based on the kind of movement possible at each location. Gliding or arthrodial joints manage the simplest motion by which two relatively flat articulating surfaces move in a simple sliding action against each other. This motion is created by the translation of one or two surfaces on a single plane. The motion of the articular processes of the vertebrae and between the vertebrae and the ribs is indicative of this surface. This gliding motion can be described as flexion-extension and abduction-adduction.

Angular joints, in which there is an increase or a decrease in the angle between two bones, are broken down into a series of subtypes. A hinge (monoaxial) joint provides rotation of one bone at the point of articulation with another in one degree of rotational freedom. The concave shape of the proximal portion of the human ulna (which is one of the two bones that makes up the human forearm) and the convex shape of the distal portion of the human humerus (the upper arm) provide a perfect example of a hinge joint in this case represented by the human elbow. This type of joint provides the possibility for flexion-extension movements. Ellipsoidal (biaxial) joints allow for motion in two distinct planes of rotation, thus providing more flexibility to the articulating surfaces. The articulation between the carpal bones in the wrist and the distal end of the radius is indicative of a biaxial joint. Biaxial joints are often called universal joints. Flexion-extension and abduction-adduction are possible at this joint type. A saddle (multiaxial) joint, like the ellipsoidal joint, is an angular joint that results in flexion-extension and abduction-adduction motion but allows for three or more degree of rotation freedom. The human thumb, or more specifically the first metacarpal of the thumb and its articulation with the carpels, is a saddle joint.

The third type of joint is a pivot (uniaxial) joint which provides a point of multidirectional rotation around a pivot point. The proximal heads of the radius and ulna in the human forearm articulate via a pivot joint as do the atlas and axis vertebrae that are responsible for much of the rotation of the head.

The fourth and final articulation type is the ball-and-socket, ball, or spheroidal (multiaxial) joint which is most notably located at the human hip and shoulder allowing for complex rotations. Technically, this joint is capable of flexion-extension, abduction-adduction, and rotation.

6.5 **COMPARATIVE ANATOMY**

Comparative anatomy is the study of similarities and differences in the anatomy of organisms. It is closely related to evolutionary biology and phylogeny (the evolution of species) and helps to inform character setup in that it provides a starting point based on what is known about existing organisms and ourselves (Figure 6.4). Two major concepts of comparative anatomy are as follows:

- Homologous structures are structures which are similar in different species because the species have common descent (are evolved from a common ancestor). They may or may not perform the same function. An example is the forelimb structure shared by cats and whales.

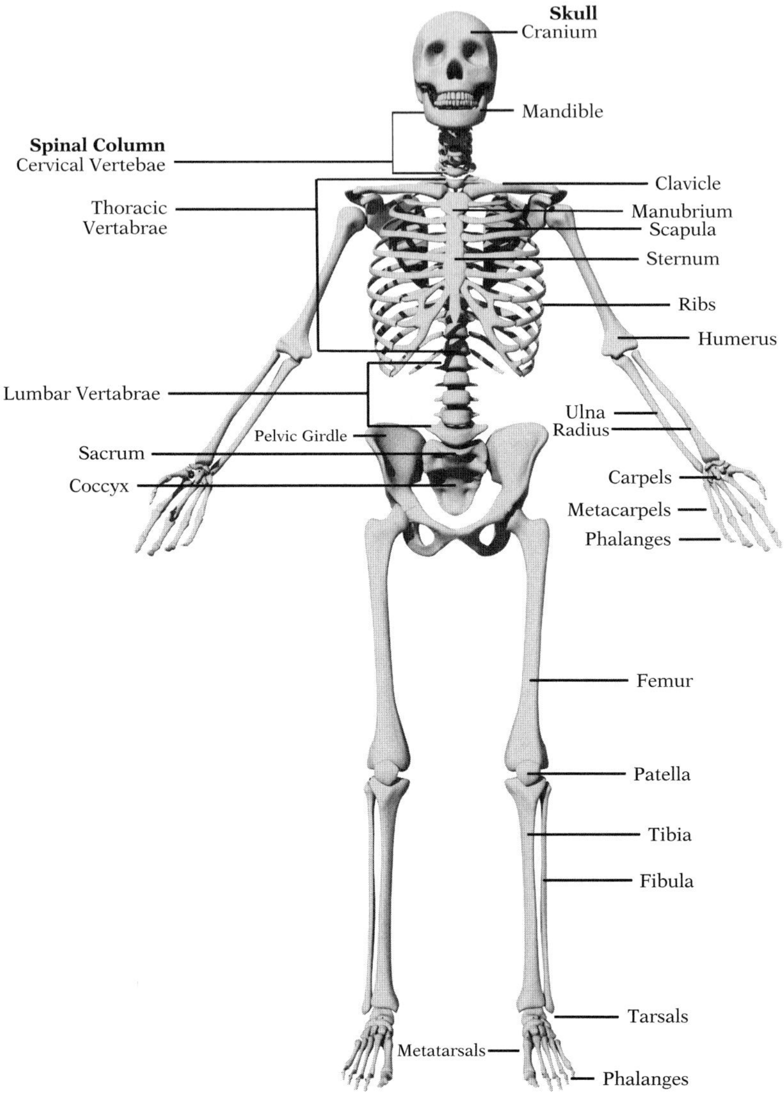

Skull
Cranium

Mandible

Spinal Column
Cervical Vertebae

Thoracic
Vertabrae

Clavicle

Manubrium
Scapula

Sternum

Ribs

Humerus

Lumbar Vertabrae

Ulna
Radius

Sacrum

Pelvic Girdle

Coccyx

Carpels

Metacarpels

Phalanges

Femur

Patella

Tibia

Fibula

Tarsals

Metatarsals

Phalanges

■ **FIGURE 6.4** Basic human skeleton element names. Model by cgHuman.

■ Analogous structures are structures which are similar in different organisms because they evolved in a similar environment (also known as convergent evolution) rather than inherited from a recent common ancestor. They usually serve the same or similar purposes. An example is the torpedo body shape of dolphins and sharks. This shape evolved in a water environment and thus has a hydrodynamic efficiencies, but the animals have different ancestry.

Focusing on mammalian anatomy, we can discuss the commonalities between the limbs as a means of defining the architecture. The architecture of the limbs is primarily designed for motion. The forelimbs and hindlimbs each consist of a series of bones, meeting the trunk of the body at the pectoral (shoulder or forelimb) or pelvic (hip or hindlimb) girdle. The pectoral girdle of most mammals consists of a shoulder blade (scapula) and in many a clavicle. Mammalian pectoral girdles are very much simplified compared with the pectoral regions of their ancestors, which contained a number of additional bones. These bones were either lost or incorporated into the scapula of modern mammals. Monotremes (including the platypus) are an exception; their pectoral girdles include several of these primitive elements. The scapula lies alongside the rib cage and spine sitting in an envelope of muscles and ligaments which connect it to the rib cage and spine rather than being immovably fused to them. The clavicle, if present, runs from the region of the articulation between scapula and forelimb to the anterior part of the sternum. In humans, the clavicle receives forces from the upper extremity and transfers them to the axial skeleton. As the only attachment of the upper extremity to the axial skeleton, excessive force, such as falling on an outstretched arm, causes all forces to be moved into the clavicle. As a result, this is one of the most commonly broken bones in the human body.

The pelvic girdle of mammals is made up of three bones: the ilium, ischium, and pubis. At the junction of these three bones is the socket (acetabulum) for the hind limb. Unlike the pectoral girdle, the pelvic girdle is firmly attached to the spine by a bony fusion between the ilium and the sacral vertebrae.

The forelimb itself consists of a humerus (which meets the scapula), paired radius and ulna, a set of carpals and metacarpals (the wrist and the palm), and five digits, each made up of several phalanges (finger bones). The bones of the hind limb are the femur (articulates with the acetabulum of the pelvis), the tibia and fibula, the tarsals and metatarsals (ankle and foot), and five digits, each made up of two or more several phalanges. The first digit of the forelimb (the thumb of humans) is called the pollex; the first digit of the hindlimb is the hallux. A patella lies over the knee joint (junction of tibia and femur) and functions as a surface for muscle attachment and support. Tarsal and carpal bones are referred to collectively as podials, and metacarpals and metatarsals are metapodials. The calcaneum is a large tarsal bone that extends behind the ankle, forming the heel. It provides an important lever arm for muscles that move the hind foot.

Limbs are drastically modified to different ends in various groups of mammals. Here, we are concerned primarily with modifications that affect how an animal runs. Several terms describe how and where an animal moves.

- Aquatic animals swim.
- Volant animals fly.
- Cursorial animals (cursors) run rapidly and for long distances.
- Scansorial animals are climbers; in the extreme, they are arboreal, spending most of their lives in the trees.
- Saltatorial are hoppers. If they use their hindlimbs only and in a fast succession of hops, they are said to be ricochetal.
- Fossorial forms are diggers, usually living in burrows.

A full cycle of motion of a running or walking mammal is called a stride (Figure 6.5). An animal's speed is the product of its stride length times rate. There are two ways of increasing the speed of running, increasing stride length and increasing stride rate. Some animals are clearly specialized to increase speed through increasing stride length; the giraffe is an extreme example. Others move rapidly by having a very fast stride rate; these would include, for example, shrews and voles.

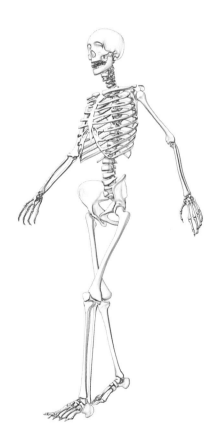

■ **FIGURE 6.5** Human anatomical elements in motion. Model by cgHuman.

Bird versus bat wings

The bird's forelimbs or wings are the key to bird flight. Each wing has a central vane to hit the wind composed of three limb bones: the humerus, ulna, and radius. The hand, or manus, which ancestrally was composed of five digits, is reduced to three digits. The purpose of the hand is to serve as an anchor for the primaries: one of two groups of feathers responsible for the airfoil shape. The other set of flight feathers, which are behind the carpal joint on the ulna, is called the secondaries. The remaining feathers on the wing are known as coverts, of which there are three sets (Figure 6.6).

The wings of bats give their order Chiroptera its name (literally, "hand-wing"). Functional wings and true flight are characteristics of all bats. The origin of bat wings is most clearly revealed by their skeleton. Every element of that skeleton is clearly homologous with structures in the forelimbs of other mammals as bat wings evolved as a result of modifications to the forelimbs of their ancestors. The humerus is long and thin compared with the humerus of other mammals, but its articular surfaces and areas for attachment of muscles are fundamentally like those of most mammals. Attached to the humerus are the radius and ulna. The radius is also long

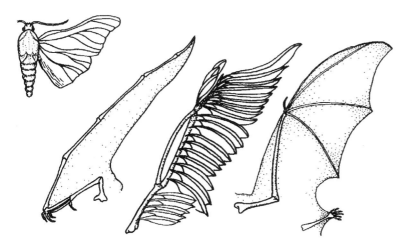

■ **FIGURE 6.6** Comparison of insect, pterosaur, bird, and bat wings.

and thin, but it is a strong bone that supports the wing. The olecranon process of the ulna (at the articulation with the humerus) is the most substantial part of the ulna; the rest is considerably reduced and fused with the radius. The wrist region is very similar to that of other mammals, although less flexible. It is specialized to support the particular motions associated with flying. All bats have a thumb which sits along the leading edge of the wing. It usually has a substantial claw which is used for climbing, food handling, and fighting. The rest of the digits (2–5) support the wing. The wing membrane is an extension of the skin of the body. It is made up of external epidermis and an internal layer of dermis and muscles. These muscles control the curvature of the wing in flight. The membrane is both tough and flexible. Bat wings usually run from the shoulder region to the ankle, or in some cases, to the digits themselves. The wing membrane joins the body along the sides, except in some cases where it arises near the middle of the back.

Tentacles

As we will see, the control and coordination of arm movements in 3D space is a complicated task. This is a challenge to both animation systems and biological organisms. Increasing the number of degrees of freedom of the arm makes this task more complicated, and yet most biological movements involve a large number of degrees of freedom. An extreme case, with especially high degrees of freedom, is provided by systems in which muscles are unattached to any internal or external skeleton whatsoever. These structures are much more flexible than jointed limbs and have virtually unlimited degrees of freedom. Examples of such structures are cephalopod (for example, an octopus) tentacles, some of the vertebrate tongues, and the trunk of an elephant. These structures are composed solely of muscles used to generate movement and provide the necessary skeletal support. These have been termed muscular hydrostats because these are composed of incompressible muscle tissue. The octopus arm is of special interest as a muscular hydrostat because it combines extreme flexibility with a capability for executing various sophisticated motor tasks. An octopus arm can bend at any point and in any direction, and it can elongate, shorten, and twist. The biomechanical principles of movement generation differ in animals with and without a rigid skeleton. Those without a rigid skeleton have what is termed a hydrostatic skeleton, consisting mainly of muscles and fluid, which because they are incompressible support the flexible body. Hydrostatic skeletons are generally of two types. In muscular hydrostats, muscles and other tissues form a solid structure without a separate enclosed fluid volume such as cephalopod tentacles, elephant trunk, and vertebrate tongue. In a second type of hydrostatic skeletons, muscles compose a body wall that surrounds a fluid-filled cavity as seen in sea anemones and worms. The biomechanical mechanism that produces the reaching movement is a stiffening wave of muscle contraction that pushes a bend forward along the arm [13, 41].

While an octopus might not have any formal joints, the rigging of such an entity as a digital character would require the placement of many points of articulation to produce the smooth bending motion that is expected. These points of articulation in the animation world are also called joints and are covered in the next section.

6.6   MATRICES AND JOINTS

A joint in the vernacular of 3D graphics is essentially a 3D matrix in cartesian space often with extra properties that give it special attributes for animation. A matrix is a 2D, rectangular array of values subject to mathematical operations. Each individual value in a matrix is called an element. An understanding of joint properties and the mathematics underlying matrix rotations and hierarchical rotations are crucial to our production of character animation.

Joints are the building blocks of animatable skeletons. Some 3D animation programs are "joint-based" while others

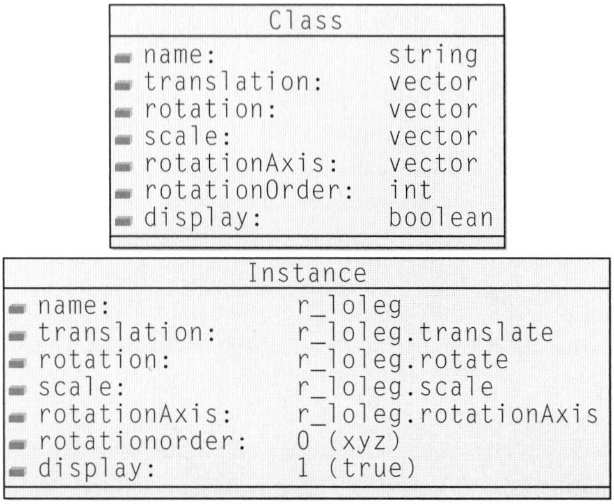

```
                      Class
   ▪ name:              string
   ▪ translation:       vector
   ▪ rotation:          vector
   ▪ scale:             vector
   ▪ rotationAxis:      vector
   ▪ rotationOrder:     int
   ▪ display:           boolean
```

```
                     Instance
   ▪ name:              r_loleg
   ▪ translation:       r_loleg.translate
   ▪ rotation:          r_loleg.rotate
   ▪ scale:             r_loleg.scale
   ▪ rotationAxis:      r_loleg.rotationAxis
   ▪ rotationorder:     0 (xyz)
   ▪ display:           1 (true)
```

■ **FIGURE 6.7** Class and data diagram for joint object.

are "bone-based." Maya, for example, is "joint-based," which means that the bone, or the link, is visualized between two joint nodes. Bones are defined by two joints and serve a visualization purpose only. Other programs, such as 3D Studio Max, are "bone-based" which means that a bone is visualized based on a starting location, direction, and bone length, and a child joint node is not necessary for a bone to be visible. The action of a bone attached to a joint is controlled by the joint's rotation and movement. In both cases, various joint attributes determine how joints behave. Rotation can be limited or restricted along certain planes. For the purposes of this book, we will think about joint hierarchies and skeletons as being joint-based. An example class definition for a joint is illustrated in Figure 6.7.

If we think of each joint as a matrix that stores its position and orientation in 3D space, we have the basics of what is required for developing a skeleton. A matrix is described as having m rows by n columns, or being an $m \times n$ matrix. A row is a horizontal grouping of elements read from left to right, while a column is a vertical, top-to-bottom group.

6.7 **JOINT ROTATIONS**

Joint rotations are the core method of character transformations in an animation system. Rotations around the x, y, and z axes are called principal rotations. Rotation around any axis can be performed by taking a rotation around the x-axis, followed by a rotation around the y-axis, and followed by a rotation around the z-axis. That is to say, any spatial rotation can be decomposed into a combination of principal rotations. In flight dynamics, the principal rotations are known as roll, pitch, and yaw which are mapped to x, y, and z in a z-up coordinate system. Most animation systems work with a y-up coordinate system. The rotation of joints around their local axis, thus transforming their hierarchical children, forms the basis for character motion. Rotation is a rigid transformation, and when considered as a vector, we are rigidly changing its direction around an axis without changing its length. It can be helpful to use the right-hand rule which is a convention for determining the relative directions of vectors (Figure 6.8). First, the hand is held flat and positioned so that the fingers are aligned with axis a. Then, the hand is rotated about the forearm so that the fingers curl to point inward toward axis b. The thumb then indicates axis c.

Rotation matrices around the x-axis, y-axis, and z-axis in a right-handed coordinate system are shown in Figure 6.9. The fourth row is usually reserved for "shear," but character setup artists work hard to avoid accumulating values for shear as it has unpleasant effects on joint rotations and character deformations.

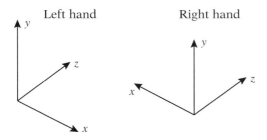

■ **FIGURE 6.8** Left- and right-handed coordinate systems.

$$
\begin{bmatrix} x' \\ y' \\ z' \\ 1 \end{bmatrix} = \begin{bmatrix} 1 & 0 & 0 & 0 \\ 0 & \cos\theta & -\sin\theta & 0 \\ 0 & \sin\theta & \cos\theta & 0 \\ 0 & 0 & 0 & 0 \end{bmatrix} \begin{bmatrix} x \\ y \\ z \\ 1 \end{bmatrix} \tag{1}
$$

$$
\begin{bmatrix} x' \\ y' \\ z' \\ 1 \end{bmatrix} = \begin{bmatrix} \cos\theta & 0 & \sin\theta & 0 \\ 0 & 1 & 0 & 0 \\ -\sin\theta & 0 & \cos\theta & 0 \\ 0 & 0 & 0 & 1 \end{bmatrix} \begin{bmatrix} x \\ y \\ z \\ 1 \end{bmatrix} \tag{2}
$$

$$
\begin{bmatrix} x' \\ y' \\ z' \\ 1 \end{bmatrix} = \begin{bmatrix} \cos\theta & -\sin\theta & 0 & 0 \\ \sin\theta & \cos\theta & 0 & 0 \\ 0 & 0 & 1 & 0 \\ 0 & 0 & 0 & 1 \end{bmatrix} \begin{bmatrix} x \\ y \\ z \\ 1 \end{bmatrix} \tag{3}
$$

■ **FIGURE 6.9** Rotation around the x-, y-, and z-axis.

6.8 ROTATION ORDER

As we mentioned previously, rotations can be broken down into their principle rotations, but the collected rotation is created by an accumulation of rotations in a specified order. This rotation order is typically x, then y, then z, or xyz, but this can be specified in the animation system. Possible rotation orders include xyz, yzx, zxy, xzy, yxz, and zyx. It is important to recognize that an object with a rotation of $x = 45$, $y = 45$, and $z = 45$ will have a different end result depending on the order with which those principle rotations are carried out (Figure 6.10).

6.9 EULER VERSUS QUATERNIONS

There is an important distinction to be made between Euler and quaternion rotations. Euler rotations are the standard, but quaternions provide a more versatile solution for the complex rotations required for character animation. It is increasingly available in animation systems, but Euler angles are the most common rotation implementation.

Euler's (pronounced "oiler") rotation theorem states that any rotation may be described using three angles. The three angles giving the three rotation matrices are called Euler

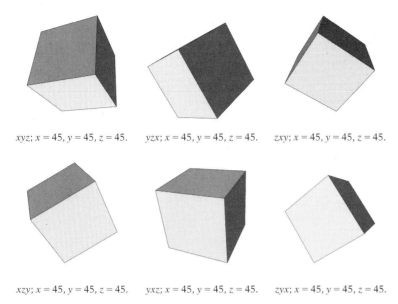

$xyz; x = 45, y = 45, z = 45.$ $yzx; x = 45, y = 45, z = 45.$ $zxy; x = 45, y = 45, z = 45.$

$xzy; x = 45, y = 45, z = 45.$ $yxz; x = 45, y = 45, z = 45.$ $zyx; x = 45, y = 45, z = 45.$

■ **FIGURE 6.10** Rotation orders.

angles. Euler angles have the disadvantage of being susceptible to "Gimbal lock," where attempts to rotate an object fail
to appear as expected due to the order in which the rotations
are performed. Gimbal lock is the phenomenon of two rotational axes of an object pointing in the same direction, thus
appearing to "lose" one degree of rotation. This is a common
problem with IK solvers who attempt to find the position of
middle joints based on two end joints, or combined rotations
over joints, when, as the solution crosses the 180° mark, the
joint position is solved from the reverse angle and flips. This is
a major problem for character animators, and it is the responsibility of the character setup artist to solve this issue in most
situations either by adding controls to counteract this joint
flipping or, if possible, by implementing quaternions.

Quaternions are a solution to this problem. Instead
of rotating an object through a series of successive rotations, quaternions allow the programmer to rotate an object
through an arbitrary rotation axis and angle. The rotation is
still performed using matrix mathematics; however, instead of
multiplying matrices together, quaternions representing the

axes of rotation are multiplied together. The final resulting quaternion is then converted to the desired rotation matrix. Because the rotation axis is specified as a unit direction vector, it may also be calculated through vector mathematics or from spherical coordinates (longitude/latitude). Quaternions offer another advantage in that they may be interpolated. This allows for smooth and predictable rotation effects. This is an admittedly high-level glossing over of a complex subject, but as quaternions are implemented into animation systems, a basic knowledge of their advantages is crucial to character setup artists.

6.10 **JOINT NAMING AND PLACEMENT**

Drawing on our discussion of anatomy, we delve into the placement of matrices in space. By doing so, we define the origin of rotation of joints for the purposes of character articulation. Joint placement on the character model is a tedious process but, of course, a necessary one. Our knowledge of anatomy combined with our understanding of matrix rotation informs our decisions as to where to place our joints.

For realistic characters, once the model is created, the placement of joints starts with the creation of a reference polygonal skeleton that fits the model and represents the underlying anatomy. This reference also acts as a motion reference for the motion system to drive. Once your control system is in place and driving the motion of the bones correctly, the model can be confidently attached to the joints as outlined in the next chapter. For stylized or more cartoon-derived characters, a polygonal reference skeleton may not be needed and the position of joints is based on the ideal point of rotation. In most cases, the reference skeleton is stripped out of the model either way when it is handed off to the animators or exported to the game engine. In an increasing number of cases, the polygonal reference skeleton is used as part of anatomically influenced deformations.

As we have noted, the rotation of joints has a direct connection to the motion of the model and therefore the placement of joints is critical. For example, at the area of the human knee,

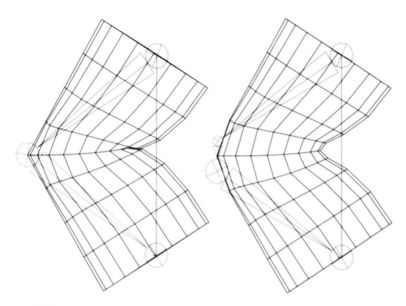

■ **FIGURE 6.11**   Example of articulating one versus two Joints.

the placement of the joint along the side orthogonal plane will determine the amount of pinching that occurs when the leg is flexed. Similarly, for the human knee (Figure 6.11) or any area where the resulting surface is a complex of two articulating surfaces with a bone floating within the connecting tendon (usually called a sesamoid bone) finding the middle area, the optimal solution is to place two joints, one at the bottom of the proximal bone and one at the top of the distal bone. This leaves a surface area about which a volume can be preserved when the leg is bent. Depending on the amount of space between them, the volume of the deforming area will be proportional.

For regions that require smooth and detailed motion along a fairly straight articulating surface, it is best to place the joints procedurally via a curve. The process for this is straightforward. A two-point curve is drawn from where joint placement is supposed to start to the point where the last joint should be placed. This curve is then re-parameterized so that a control point is placed at equally spaced intervals along the curve for the number of joints desired (see Figure 6.12). This

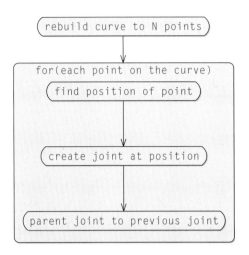

■ **FIGURE 6.12** Method for a curve-based joint placement.

step can be skipped but maintaining a reference curve can be helpful. The joints can then be placed at the locations of these points along a curve with fine resolution. This method is useful for joint hierarchies which are controlled or managed by spline interpolation such as tails, tentacles, and even long necks and spines. Procedural placement of joints can speed the setup and is more accurate in some situations.

Most of the time, joint placement is done in such a way to support overlaying procedural constraints. These often require that joints of a certain number be placed in such a way that the constraint can easily be ported from character to character. This is especially important in a procedural system. From a pipeline point of view, the naming of joints is equally as important as their correct placement. Any number of conventions can be developed as a joint naming strategy, but the most important decision with regard to naming is to decide on one convention and stick to it. Reliable naming provides information about that joint's position and role in the character rig. Consistency across characters also allows other character setup artists to more easily debug a rig that they did not create. A typical structure uses the side of the body as the first naming element, left: "left," "lt," "L," "l"; right: "right," "rt," "R," "r"; middle: "middle," "mid," "M," "m." The descriptive term that follows can be thought of in two different ways; it is

Table 6.2 Naming Convention Variations

Name	Position	Element	Type	Combined
rob	l	uparm	grp	rob_l_uparm_grp
dave	M	back2	JNT	daveMback2JNT
todd	r	hand	IK_CNTRL	todd_r_hand_IKCNTRL
daniel	l	foot	c	daniel_l_foot_c

either the term for the place of placement of the joint or the name of the structure that is moved by transformation of that joint. So the tag "loleg" could mean the lower part of the leg to one person or the knee to another. Production standards and documentation are the only way to enforce consistent naming for a production. The last part of the name is typically an indicator that this is a joint, such as "JNT," "j," or "jnt," so that joints can be queried procedurally and easily. Other suffixes might signify a control ("CNTRL," "cntrl," "CTL," "c"), a group ("grp," "GRP," "g"), or any number of other objects such as locators, curves, etc. Depending on the system and the production pipeline, the character name may be pre-pended to each of these joint names as a means of avoiding name clashing with a scene (see Table 6.2). Personally, my preferred naming convention is characterName_side_element_type resulting in hawkshaw_l_hand_cntrl, but every artist, studio, and production has its own preference or standard.

6.11 **JOINT HIERARCHIES**

Connecting joints to each other with the intention of creating a cohesive hierarchy is the next step. The most basic functionality of our rig comes from the parent-child relationship of the joints and the way that joints rotate around each other. Early digital characters were animated solely on the basis of simple hierarchies, but modern rigs rely on a complex network of joints, even when not directly connected to each other, controlled by constraints.

These ideas go hand-in-hand with joint placement, but hierarchies provide the logic to the connections between joints. All characters require a "root" node that controls their basic transform position in 3D space. The rest of the character is a child of this node as this node acts both as a hierarchical container and as a name space indicator of that character in the scene. All of the elements in a character rig should be thought of as their own modular system that are then connected to each other logically. Where character skeletons have traditionally been composed of a single unified hierarchy of joints, the trend today is to build discrete hierarchies for each element where the joints do not directly connect with each other to associate these modules. These "broken hierarchy" rigs not only provide flexibility by allowing elements to act independently of each other leaving the animator to have more control but they also support the idea of the character rig being a set of modular units that can be improved on individually without impacting other regions of the rig. Single chain joint hierarchies are still used heavily in games and rigs which depend on motion capture, and often times, this simple hierarchy is output from a more complicated non-hierarchical rig.

For rotations between joints to behave as expected, the artist must define the orientation of the axes for their joint chains. Once determined, all the joints for that element should adhere to the convention for expected results. Defining the axis that should point at the child joint and the axes that should be pointing laterally and perpendicular to that will insure that all the joints follow the same directions of rotation. This is particularly important for long chains that define a spine or tail but no less important for joint sparse regions.

For example, to create a joint chain that moves and rotates like the human neck, you would place the desired number of joints to define the neck's articulation then set the degrees of freedom for the joints so that they rotate only within the limit of each joint's range of rotation. The cumulative effect of the rotations for each joint should add up to the desired limits of rotation for the whole neck. Limits are something to be used carefully. Often, character motion must be extreme for the purposes of exaggeration or to cheat a shot. Therefore, the usual practice is to forgo limits or give them a wide range so give the animator the freedom to put the character into an extreme or "broken" pose if even for a few frames. Because joint placement ultimately defines the biomechanics of our digital characters, it is helpful to undertake this process with anatomy in mind.

6.12 ANATOMY DRIVEN HIERARCHIES

An anatomy driven hierarchy is one which recreates the mechanical structure of the natural skeletal anatomy of a character by intricately defining the architecture of the joints (For example see [2, 27, 31]). In this section, we describe the articulation of the human shoulder and implement it in 3D. The human shoulder, or the pectoral girdle, serves as the articulation between the free limb and the torso, or axial skeleton. The girdle is made up of two bones: the clavicle and the scapula, connected by a strong ligament and articulating at a single point. This connection allows for slight motion between the bones. The scapula has no articulation with the axial skeleton; it floats in a complex of muscles. The humerus, or upper arm, connects to the scapula at shallow cup-shaped depression called the glenoid fossa. It is the muscular movement of the scapula and clavicle that moves the shoulders. This motion translates the humerus (and the rest of the arm) producing shrug (shoulders up) and slouch (shoulders down) motions, in addition to being able to rotate the shoulders forward and back.

Taking these articulation points into consideration, the 3D joints can be placed (see Figure 6.13). We would place a joint at the most medial point of the clavicle as the point of rotation for the shoulder complex. All rotation of the shoulder should emanate from this point. The child of this joint should be coincident with the lateral end of the clavicle, thus a 3D bone traverses the length of the skeletal bone. The scapula needs to be able to be controlled by the rotation of the clavicle. It also need its own rotation controls for posing beyond the typical rotation, so a joint is placed on the medial edge of the scapula on the character's back. The child of this joint travels up the back to the point where the clavicle articulates with the scapula. A joint is placed at the center of the head of the humerus, and its child traverses the humerus down to

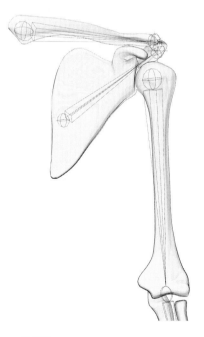

■ **FIGURE 6.13** Human shoulder girdle.

the most distal end. In a basic way, we now have the joints in place for proper articulation.

6.13 CONSTRAINTS AND HIGH-LEVEL CONTROL

Expressive motion requires complex interaction between joints in the motion system. This is the realm of constraints where systems are created to solve the motion of joints by relating them to each other or procedures which manipulate the joint based on factors external to that joint. Joints can be aimed at objects, rotations can be limited, or motion can be offset based on other motion. In essence, the functionality of a complex rig lies in the constraints created by the setup artist, and it is this level of sophistication that often separates a basic rig from one suited for production. In short, constraints are relationships among objects that are maintained automatically by the system [32].

When a character animation pipeline is being developed, a number of constraints need to be implemented to streamline solutions and satisfy animation requirements. Constraints can constrain the position, orientation, or scale of an object to other objects, impose specific limits on objects, and automate animation processes. Basically, joints may need to be able to have their position, orientation, or scale constrained to other objects and potentially their orientation aimed at another object. Other constraints to consider are those that rotate a succession of joints (i.e., curl) and subsets of those constraints that compensate the end node so that end-node orientations (like the head) can be maintained through a rotation.

Position constraints are those which maintain the translation offset (or distance) of an object to that of another object. When a position constraint is created, this offset can be removed (set to 0, 0, 0) so that the constrained object matches the position of the object it is being constrained to, or it can be maintained and the offset value is stored by the constraint. The offset is typically maintained. When the position constraint is activated, the constrained object's translation values are updated to maintain the offset from

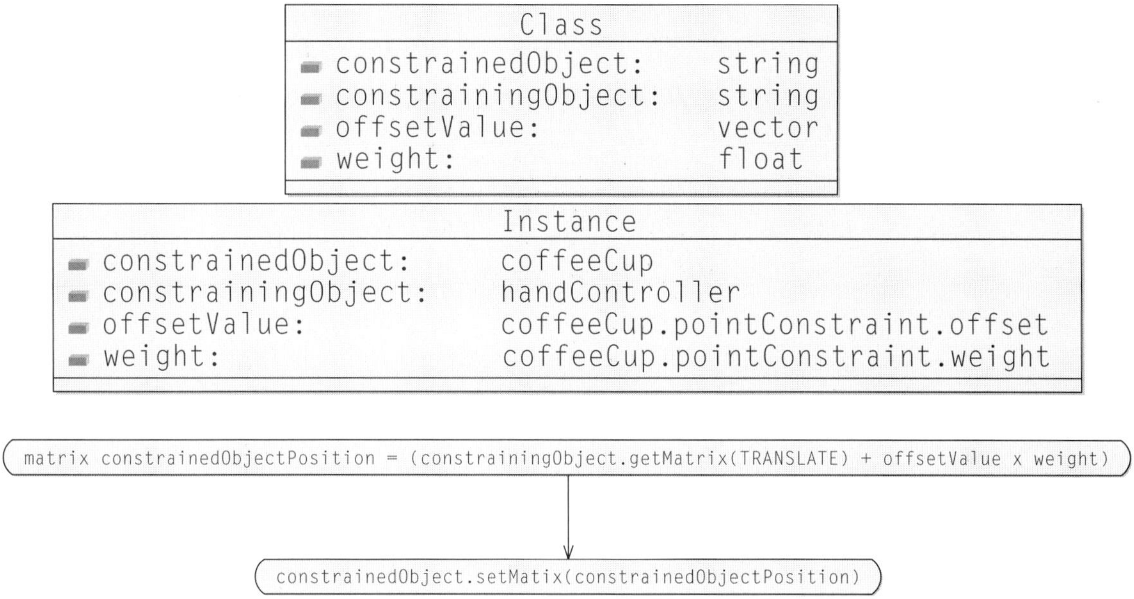

```
                              Class
    ▬ constrainedObject:          string
    ▬ constrainingObject:         string
    ▬ offsetValue:                vector
    ▬ weight:                     float
```

```
                            Instance
  ▬ constrainedObject:      coffeeCup
  ▬ constrainingObject:     handController
  ▬ offsetValue:            coffeeCup.pointConstraint.offset
  ▬ weight:                 coffeeCup.pointConstraint.weight
```

```
matrix constrainedObjectPosition = (constrainingObject.getMatrix(TRANSLATE) + offsetValue x weight)
```

```
constrainedObject.setMatix(constrainedObjectPosition)
```

■ **FIGURE 6.14** Class, data, and method diagram for position constraint.

it and the constraining object, thus moving it relatively to that object (see Figure 6.14). A similar structure is in place for orientation constraint where the offset between the constraining object and the object being constrained is maintained, unless it is removed then the object matches the rotation of the constraining object and rotates exactly as it does. As can be inferred, a scale constraint performs the same function by maintaining a connection with regard to scale between objects. All these transformation constraints add a non-hierarchical connection between objects that simulates a parenting relationship. Combining position and orientation constraints creates a control that mimics a hierarchical parenting situation, which in an animation system is very powerful. Utilizing a constraint instead of a hierarchy integration means that an object can be temporarily connected, in other words, parented to the rig. This is crucial for props and objects that need to be removed from the character. The weight of the constraint can also be blended on and off for a smooth transition because, as with any constraint, making sure that the activation does not "pop" an object into place is an ever-present concern. In animation, nothing breaks the illusion of the moment more than an object linearly popping into place. Even if it happens at a sub-frame interval, objects popping into or out of place may be picked up by the motion blur function of the renderer and be evident.

Combinatory rotation constraints provide a means of rotating multiple joints at once, ideally with a weight attached to each one so that the rotation is not uniform. This is ideal for rotating anatomically similar parts of the body such as torsos and necks. When chains are cumulatively rotated, it is important to have controls that maintain the orientation of the end node (head and/or shoulders). Once important elements like the head have been positioned and the character's line-of-sight with elements on- or off- screen has been established, it is important that rigs allow for animation up the hierarchical chain, not to affect them. In fact, any region can be set to "compensate" for the motion that has been applied to the joints below (see Figures 6.15 and 6.16).

Other constraints go beyond the reference of one transformation to another. Often times, an object will need to be constrained to a geometry surface, thus riding along the surface and maintaining its orientation normal to the surface it is attached to. The real power of these discrete constraints is the combination of them on a joint or joint hierarchy to form high-level animation controls.

The term "high-level control" refers to the ability to control complex systems with single or few attributes or controls. "Low-level control" usually refers to a single control that manipulates a singular discrete piece of an element, like bending a single section of a human digit. Complicated anatomical regions such as human hands and feet are areas which typically have a wide range of intricate motion contained in a compact space and as such are typically controlled via low- and high-level controls. While low-level controls provide the direct access to the individual components, high-level controls allow an animator to post the entire element quickly and with the manipulation of few attributes. Because of the

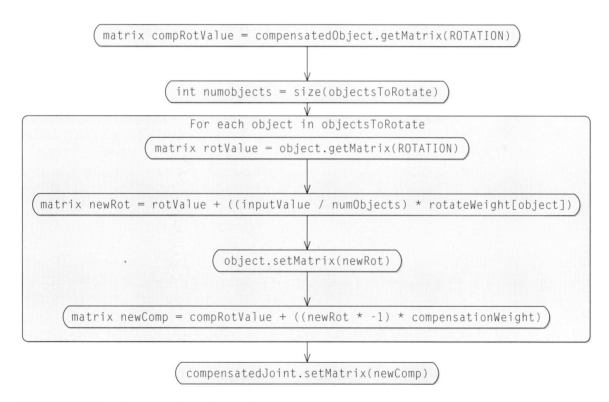

Instance	
objectsToRotate:	neck01
objectsToRotate:	neck02
objectsToRotate:	neck03
objectsToRotate:	neck04
objectsToRotate:	neck05
rotateWeight:	0.20
rotateWeight:	0.30
rotateWeight:	0.40
rotateWeight:	0.50
rotateWeight:	0.60
compensatedObject:	head0
compensationWeight:	head.headNeckComp
inputValue:	head.compNeckRot

Class	
objectsToRotate:	string array
rotateWeight:	float array
compensatedObject:	string
compensationWeight:	float
rotationInputValue:	vector

■ **FIGURE 6.15** Class and data diagram for compensating rotation constraint.

```
matrix compRotValue = compensatedObject.getMatrix(ROTATION)

int numobjects = size(objectsToRotate)

For each object in objectsToRotate
    matrix rotValue = object.getMatrix(ROTATION)

    matrix newRot = rotValue + ((inputValue / numObjects) * rotateWeight[object])

    object.setMatrix(newRot)

    matrix newComp = compRotValue + ((newRot * -1) * compensationWeight)

compensatedJoint.setMatrix(newComp)
```

■ **FIGURE 6.16** Method for a compensating rotation constraint.

many working pieces in a human hand and all of the delicate operations it is called on to undertake, it is a complex system that requires layers of control. As we mentioned previously, low-level controls for the hand give the animator fine control for individually posing sections of the fingers into the desired position. This is a powerful and specific control but leads to a tedious workflow if this is the only control for manipulating the fingers. Higher level controls will give the animator the ability to curl individual fingers from a single attribute; this is essentially an interface for simultaneously manipulating multiple low-level controls. At an even higher level, being able to control all the fingers of the hand through descriptive controls, such as "spread," "splay," and "bend," provides the animator with the ability to quickly pose the hand then offset individual fingers with lower level controls. An even higher level than multi-finger controls are character-specific pose controls which take a character from a default position to a animator defined pose. In the case of a character's hand, a typical attribute driven pose is a fist. The construction is based not only on the final positioning of all the fingers curled with the thumb on top but also the timing of the curl of those fingers so that when animated, the thumb does not cross through the other digits. Controls such as this are usually attributes on a continuum from 0–1 or 0–100, the higher number being the hand in its final fist position. As such, these controls are often composed of animation curves mapped through the attribute value continuum so that as the attribute is manipulated, it is mapped to the proper place on the curve for each finger moving it from a default position to the fist position as coordinated by the animator. In addition, the human foot needs the ability to roll from the heel to the ball of the foot (just before the toes), through the toes, and onto the tip of the foot. This is often programmed as a continuous motion where a single attribute rolls the foot from heel to tiptoe as the character is animated to walk. The three points of articulation of the foot at the heel, ball, and toe are also points where the foot should be able to pivot around all three axes. The ankle and toes also need independent control from this high-level foot rocking system to be able to pose them either on their own or as an offset from the effects of this system. As such, the foot control for a human will be the goal of the IK constraint allowing the motion of the leg to be controlled from the foot and also the interface for all the attributes of the foot pivot system. This high-level system provides a singular interface for all of the foot's control. Other high level actions such as character breathing are often controlled through a single attribute [42].

6.14 **FORWARD AND INVERSE KINEMATICS**

Rotations on a hierarchical set of joints result in a Forward Kinematics (FK) movement where rotations are applied down the joint chain resulting in the final end position of the last joint in the chain. This is counter to the most common constraint in an animation system, IK, in which a joint chain has a root and an end effector and the middle of the chain is solved for based on the position of the end effector (see Figure 6.17).

As we have discussed, FK motion is reminiscent of stop motion puppet manipulation where each joint is positioned and the children are moved relative to the motion of their parents. There is little surprise to FK animation. Each of the rotation values (angles) on the joints in the hierarchy results in the pose of the chain. This allows for very direct manipulation of the joints but also makes it difficult to update or change the animation of a chain controlled by FK. Small changes to joints will place the end joint (say a hand) in a very different place. Very often, FK is reserved for driving animation where the force and energy comes from the top of the chain, like walking or running, as opposed to the end of the chain, like pushing an object.

```
          Class                             Instance
■ rootJoint:      string    ■ rootJoint:      shoulder
■ middleJoint:    string    ■ middleJoint:    elbow
■ endJoint:       string    ■ endJoint:       wrist
■ preferedAxis:   int       ■ preferedAxis:   0
■ goalPosition:   vector    ■ goalPosition:   handGoal.translation
```

■ **FIGURE 6.17** Class and data diagram for simple inverse kinematics constraint.

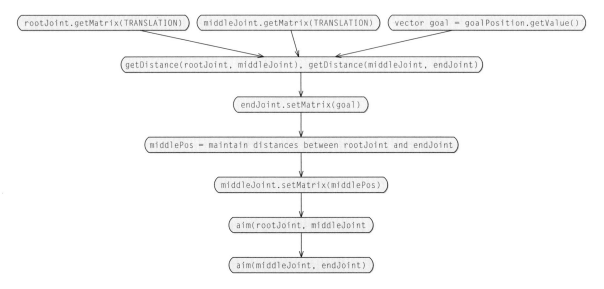

■ **FIGURE 6.18** Method for simple inverse kinematics constraint.

With this in mind, we can briefly describe the difference between FK and IK. In a nutshell, IK controls a hierarchy of joints by solving for the position of the middle joints and determining the angles required based on the position of the root joint and the end effector. The term inverse comes from the joints rotation being solved for from the end joint, up the chain and back to the root node. IK constraints are typically the first constraints learned by animators as they are easy to add to a joint chain in animation systems and provide a lot of functionality. Animators typically find it simpler to express spatial appearance as dictated by the position of the end goal, possibly the hand, rather than joint angles that culminate with the position of that end node based on the nodes above it. They are also overused, and reliance on them in inappropriate settings leads to animation looking weightless and "floaty," which is a common problem for most new animators. There is a definite place for IK in digital character animation; it is an essential constraint for animation systems. Typically, the end effector (often called simply the "IK goal") lives in world space which allows it to be parented to objects that exist outside of the character, and in more complex situations, the IK goal's parent can be dynamically changed so that it can be under the world space or local to the character's shoulders. The resulting "floating" animation is due to the animation curve attached to the IK goal which often leads the goal, and thus the appendage, through a spline-based interpolation that a limb in space, being affected by gravity, would not follow.

There are a variety of IK solutions, and every animation system offers a small variety of solvers for the user to choose from depending on the setup situation or issues that arise. Some IK solvers are designed to be more efficient for a hierarchy of two joints, while others are optimized for many joints. Common differences among implementations are the manner of rotating the system and the level-of-dependance on a plane for orienting and aligning joints. A common accompanying constraint is the pole vector, often described as the knee or elbow goal. The pole vectors of an IK constraint applied to an arm joint chain are constrained to control objects which are placed behind the character, in line with the elbow. Pole vector constraints for leg chain IK are placed in front of the "knee" joint. Because joints controlled by IK can reach an unlimited number of solutions in a circle along the axis, the pole vector defines the reference plane for solving the IK. This leaves the IK solver with two solutions, and the preferred angle which defines the angle at which the joint chain should bend limits which of those two to select. The combination of a preferred angle and a pole vector allows the IK solver to produce a singular solution and thus avoids the joint chain from flipping between multiple valid solutions.

As we discussed above, the method of rigging a long tentacle-like appendage is via a spline-based IK constraint. In this case, the shape of the curve dictates the orientation of the joints in the hierarchy. Each control vertex of the spline curve acts like a goal which, when moved, the joint rotations in the hierarchy are solved to match the shape of the curve. Each vertex should ideally be controlled by a transformation control so that the motion of the spline occurs in a space which is local to the character (see Figure 6.19).

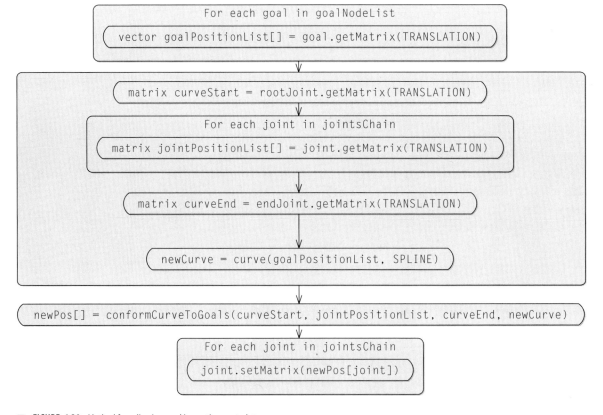

■ **FIGURE 6.19** Class and data diagram for spline inverse kinematics constraint.

■ **FIGURE 6.20** Method for spline inverse kinematics constraint.

6.15 **DYNAMICS AND SIMULATION**

Secondary animation is often produced procedurally by adding a layer of dynamic simulation on top of animatable controls to have the joints react to motion trajectories and forces applied to them. Used sparingly, dynamic joint chain implementations can add a lot of functionality to a rig but must be a complement to the animation and not necessarily a simulation-only component. The application of dynamics could include tails (Figure 6.21), tentacles, clothing accessories such as a feather on a cap, and basically anything that needs to move, but in response to the trajectories of the established character motion. The need for animatable controls for these objects is that simulation is very difficult to art direct, therefore the more animator control there is, the faster it is to reach the desired result. The dynamics on top of animation should compliment that motion.

Dynamics are usually implemented by maintaining coincident chains of joints; one for the animation, the other for the simulation, and often a third which is controlled by the blending of the first two and is the resultant chain that deformations are attached to. Applying ridged body dynamics to a joint chain allows for forces to influence the chain's motion. Forces such as gravity when applied to animated actions cause

```
                      Class
  dynamicRootJoint:      string
  dynamicJointChain:     string array
  gravityValue:          float
  weight:                float
```

```
                    Instance
  dynamicRootJoint:     tail00
  dynamicJointChain:    tail01
  dynamicJointChain:    tail02
  dynamicJointChain:    tail03
  dynamicJointChain:    tail04
  dynamicJointChain:    tail05
  dynamicJointChain:    tail06
  dynamicJointChain:    tail07
  dynamicJointChain:    tail08
  dynamicJointChain:    tail09
  gravityValue:         tail.tailDynamicsConstraint.gravity
  weight:               tail.tailDynamicsConstraint.weight
```

■ FIGURE 6.21   Class and data diagram for tail dynamics constraint.

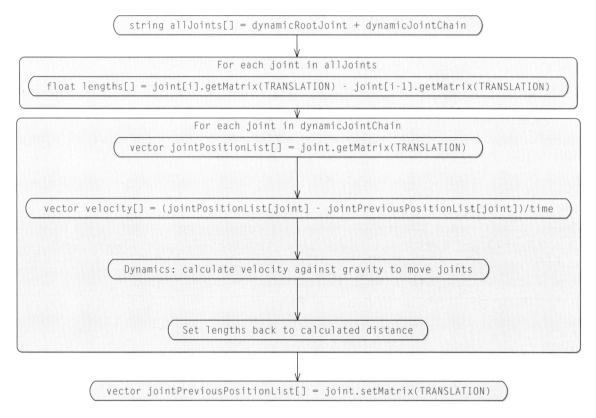

```
string allJoints[] = dynamicRootJoint + dynamicJointChain
```

For each joint in allJoints
```
float lengths[] = joint[i].getMatrix(TRANSLATION) - joint[i-1].getMatrix(TRANSLATION)
```

For each joint in dynamicJointChain
```
vector jointPositionList[] = joint.getMatrix(TRANSLATION)
```

```
vector velocity[] = (jointPositionList[joint] - jointPreviousPositionList[joint])/time
```

```
Dynamics: calculate velocity against gravity to move joints
```

```
Set lengths back to calculated distance
```

```
vector jointPreviousPositionList[] = joint.setMatrix(TRANSLATION)
```

■ **FIGURE 6.22** Method for tail dynamics constraint.

the secondary motion created by the simulation to be ground in the reality of that world. Taking a character tail as an example, we first define the animation control for this structure. The most likely control set for tails is a spline-defined, IK goal-based system. Each animatable node on the hierarchy is controlled by an animation controller, which the animator interacts with to place keys as needed. Once the animated motion is in place, the dynamics profile (the attributes of the system that define its behavior) can be edited to suit the need of the secondary motion. Dynamic simulations are often a matter of trial and error at the offset, but as the animator becomes more familiar with how the attributes affect the final motion, predictable and desired results are achieved faster and with less iteration. Tolerances should be implemented to deal with how much the simulation is able to stray from the keyed position of the controllers. It is important to be able to visualize the simulation (even if in a "debug" mode) on its own without the influence of animator motion. In addition, attributes should be in place to blend between full animator motion (no dynamics) and full simulated dynamic motion (no animator influence) on a temporal basis. This allows the normally blended motion of the two to hand off to full simulated or full animated throughout the course of the shot. This control eases the process of art directing as the motion can be fully controlled by the animator at any time.

6.16 USER INTERFACE AND VISUALIZING THE MOTION SYSTEM

All the constraints imaginable are useless if there is not a means of manipulating the rig. This manipulation is carried out by either an animator, the input of motion capture data, or a procedural system. For an animation system, the goal and challenge is to be truly interactive and allow an animator to produce the performance required by the system, while at the same time, it should have fast user feedback and be an accurate representation of the poses animated. A "control" is a means of manipulating the motion system. This can be interfaced via numerical input or via click-and-drag control of a manipulating object within the 3D environment. These control objects are created, by default, to not be renderable and are often built to be indicative of the motion possible. Utilizing an array of icons, curves, arrows, and symbols, a manipulatable user interface is key to creating a rig, which is reliable and intuitive. Character controls are usually planned in conjunction with the animators, and then that same control set is used across all characters in the production. This even comes down to the individual control icons. Once these have been established, an animator knows what each icon will do by its appearance and no need to learn by trial and error. Each region of the rig needs a special set of controls. In many cases, each region will have a different set of icons depending on what mode the character is in. For example, an arm in FK mode requires a different set of controls, namely those that rotate the shoulder, elbow, and wrist at their point of articulation, than the goal and pole vector (elbow goal) required of the same arm in IK mode. In addition to attaching animation curves to these controls for the animator, these animation interfaces can also be controlled via code in the form of simple expressions or more complicated procedural systems. Actions such as procedurally derived walk-cycles and goal-based pathfinding of appendages can be easily attached to a set of controllers.

When it comes to motion capture and procedurally controlled rigs, the key is having animatable channels free for animation to be attached to. These channels are often on the joints themselves and not the controlling objects so that the motion capture performance is "baked" to the joints. Later we will discuss motion capture and the means for offsetting this data by hand-animated controls to add animator nuance to the base-line motion provided by the motion capture performer.

A key component to consider is that characters are rigged in their default position and all the controls must be free of transformation values. This is often referred to as being "zeroed-out." This allows the animator to get back to a default pose quickly and to tell, numerically, how much the controls have been transformed. It is also important for procedural systems so, in effect, the starting point of a simulation or solved system is zero.

Joints and character controls do not provide enough accuracy for the animator to pose the character within the limits of its shape and proportions. Part of the motion system process is defining a means of visualizing the model surface in a fast and light-weight manner. This often requires turning the model into a collection of broken up polygonal elements that are then parented to the joints that best represent how those parts of the model will move.

These surfaces provide a non-deforming guide to the animator (Figure 6.23). The reference skeleton can also act as a guide but does not represent the volume of the character.

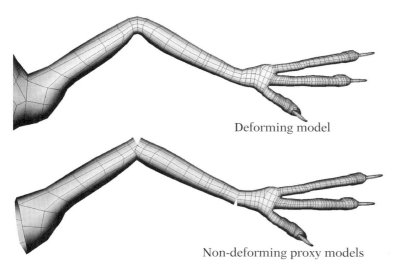

Deforming model

Non-deforming proxy models

■ **FIGURE 6.23**   Deforming model versus non-deforming proxy models.

This volume is an indicator of the deformation of the character model whether implemented or not. A step above this could be a low polygon deforming version of the model that provides a higher level feedback for the end result of the character motion. A character's silhouette is an important aspect of animation and defines the stretch and read of the key poses by stripping away all the details. Being able to read a pose or sequence refers to the clarity of the action despite the amount of complex motion. By providing a fast responding proxy of the character's volume, animators can quickly get a sense of the silhouette. This also requires that the proxy be maintained through model changes to the deforming model so that the two, or more, levels of details match as best as possible. We will discuss this more in the next chapter when we cover character deformations.

6.17 **REAL-TIME ENGINE CONCERNS**

For real-time characters, it is important to keep the number of objects in a rig to a minimum; this includes using as few joints as possible. The fewer the joints that must be stored in memory and calculated in real-time, the faster the responsiveness of the character interaction. As we have mentioned, motion capture provides much of the animation in real-time game engines, so the hierarchy is often tailored to work with the skeleton defined by the capture specification. This is often a simple hierarchical structure that has extra joints added and controlled via constraints. In real-time engines, where deformations (covered in more depth in the next chapter) are controlled by skinning alone, special joints, termed secondary joints, are often added to control deformation-specific functions. Actions such as flexing muscles are controlled by the motion of these joints, which are driven by constraints. As game engines are able to process more and more data, the number of joints allowable increases, but it is still best to keep this number to a minimum. There is always a trade-off in game production with regard to processing power. For example, if you wanted to add a new feature to the calculation of the environment, then character joint count or other feature might be affected or vice versa.

6.18 CONCLUSION

Motion systems form the mechanical architecture for digital characters. They rely on knowledge of anatomy paired with an understanding of computer graphics principles to recreate the mechanics of articulation and motion. The combination of joint hierarchies, constraints, and user interface forms the motion system. By providing an intuitive interface, complex operations can be hidden from the animators, allowing them to focus on the performance of the character in the scene.

Integrating this motion system with the character model is the role of deformation systems, which is covered in the next chapter.

6.19 EXERCISE

In this exercise, we go through the conceptual and technical process of creating a character motion system. Split into groups of two or more. One of you is the animator, the other team members are the character setup artists. Follow the steps below.

6.1 Draw a character using nature as a guide (or use one you created in a previous exercise or from your own portfolio). Think about appendages and how they relate to locomotion. The characters' mechanics should be physically plausible even if they are outlandishly designed.

6.2 Based on the design, the project you think this character will be a part of, and the animator's specifications, determine this character's motion and needed actions.

6.3 Design its skeleton on the model sheet. Design the skeleton by drawing the joints in the place appropriate for the needed points of articulation and rotation.

6.4 Build the skeleton either in an animation system or procedurally.

6.5 With the help and feedback of the animator, design an interface for it.

6.6 The animator should generate ten poses for the character using the low polygon (non-deforming) stand-ins as a guide.

6.7 Based on these poses, supply the setup artists with feedback to be addressed.

6.8 Maintain this test/fix feedback loop until satisfied.

■ FURTHER READING

Some good anatomy references include:

Tim D. White. *Human Osteology*. Academic Press, New York, NY, 2000.

Kenneth Kardong. *Vertebrates: Comparative Anatomy, Function, Evolution*, 4th edition. McGraw-Hill Science, New York, NY, 2005.

Susan Standring. *Gray's Anatomy: The Anatomical Basis of Clinical Practice*. Churchill Livingstone, New York, NY, 2004.

There are a few technical resources that every character technical director should have on their bookshelf. The first is a text which provides a solid base-line understanding of the principles of computer graphics:

Michael O'Rourke. *Principles of Three-Dimensional Computer Animation: Modeling, Rendering, and Animating with 3d Computer Graphics.* W. W. Norton and Co., Inc., New York, NY, 1998.

The second is a solid implementation of those principles as applied to animation.

Rick Parent. *Computer Animation, Second Edition: Algorithms and Techniques (The Morgan Kaufmann Series in Computer Graphics).* Morgan Kaufmann Publishers Inc., San Francisco, CA, 2007.

The third reference to own is a math text for when you want to bend the rules or get into deep water when developing a constraint:

James Van Verth and Lars Bishop. *Essential Mathematics for Games and Interactive Applications: A Programmer's Guide.* Morgan Kaufmann Publishers Inc., San Francisco, CA, 2004.

INTERVIEW: AARON HOLLY, LEAD CHARACTER TECHNICAL DIRECTOR, WALT DISNEY ANIMATION

BIO

Aaron Holly has over ten years of production experience in video games, visual effects, and feature animation studios.

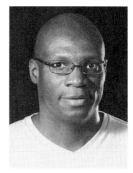

Aaron Holly, Lead Character Technical Director, Walt Disney Animation

Aaron first began taking 2D animation classes while getting his Bachelors Degree at UCLA. He then continued his studies at the Academy of Art College where he earned an MFA in Computer Arts and later, while working in visual effects, returned to teach Graduate and Undergraduate classes.

Aaron has worked at Tippett Studio, Industrial Light + Magic, ESC Entertainment, DreamWorks Animation, and currently, Disney Feature Animation. He has worked on various projects including "The Haunting," "Hollow Man," "Mummy Returns," "Time Machine," "Matrix Reloaded," "Shark Tale," "Meet The Robinsons," and "Speed Racer." He is now working as a Lead Character TD on an upcoming feature animated movie directed by Glen Keane and Dean Wellins at Walt Disney Animation.

www.fahrenheitdigital.com

Q&A

Q) *The components of character technology are diverse and span the artistic and technical spectrum. How did you get your start in the industry? Based on where you see the field heading what experience/training do you recommend people have?*

A) When I completed school, the discipline of Character TD did not exist in most studios. I was amazed when I started working at Tippett Studio that they had just then decided they needed a group of people dedicated to rigging characters and this was after "Starship Troopers!"

In school, I always enjoyed modeling more so than animation. I liked animation and was decent at it, but I found myself drawn to modeling, and students who focused on animation needed things to work with, so I would gladly build rigs in order to see my creations moving. It all worked out perfectly!

I first started working in video games and cinematics. I was required to do it all. Maya 1.0 was still in beta, and I convinced the studio I was working at to give it a try. The deal was that since I was the evangelist, I was responsible for learning it, training others, and rigging the characters in the cinematic we were working on. I have been working as a Character TD since then.

For those studying now, I have to first say how lucky you are to have so many resources available to you. What attracted me to rigging is that it was a great combination of multiple disciplines: modeling, animation, scripting, and an understanding of anatomy and physiology. I also liked that rigging tends to exist between multiple departments, so we need to interface with a number of disciplines.

I think you will find people who love creative and technical problem solving, as well as an understanding of esthetics and motion drawn to this discipline. And we Character TDs tend to be mellow people due to the fact that we have to effectively communicate with others and are constantly problem-solving.

My BA was in Philosophy. Sounds completely unrelated to what I do now, but to the contrary, it is directly applicable! One of the main skills I learned in that major was how to strip away the ancillary elements of a complex problem and delve down to the root arguments and issues. This is exactly what we does in rigging. Looking at very complex systems and figuring out the simplest way to achieve a goal or to solve a problem. It is called Occam's Razor in philosophy.

I would recommend aspiring and existing Character TDs to study their tools (i.e., Maya, XSI, etc.) as well as the work of others. Just seeing what someone is doing usually sparks ideas in creative minds. Scripting is also essential. For Maya, I recommend MEL and Python more and more. I am even working to build my Python skills right now.

And never be afraid to try something, and if it does not work out, back all the way up and move forward on a new path; you will have learned a lot regardless. And, it is better to rebuild a new, more solid foundation than to try to spend a lot of time down the road patching over the problems left in a rig early on.

Study anatomy and the motion of humans and animals. The complexity is amazing and beautiful but quite difficult to replicate reliably and efficiently in CG. The first step is understanding the motion and mechanics driving it.

Lastly, I cannot stress building communication skills.

Q) *Creating compelling digital characters is part art and part science. What is the greatest challenge you encounter on a daily basis? What aspect of character technology keeps you up thinking at night?*

A) First, clearly identifying the needs of those relying on my work is the first task. Animators, art Directors, the Directors, all have needs of the characters that I need to identify and meet.

Next, when developing a rigging system and tools, it is a fun challenge figuring out the most effective and efficient way to get to the end game. The more complex the system, the more difficult it is to troubleshoot and to allow for intuitive controls for the animators.

In essence, a Character TD is the mechanic building the car and the animator is the driver of that car. They don't want to be concerned with the inner workings of the engine, they have enough to worry about just getting it around the track as best as possible. So, we need to build complex but fast cars that are easy and intuitive to drive.

Q) *What are the ingredients for a successful digital character?*

A) The model topology is quite important. It is not uncommon to get a model, do some preliminary rigging, and then have to make changes to get better deformations. The flow of the edges, the amount of polygons on the model, where the inevitable 5-corner polygons are placed all impact deformations.

Next, clear and constant communications with animators and the director and/or art director are essential. You are not building the rig for yourself, you are building it to allow animation to put the vision of the director on screen. Knowing what they want and why they want these things is the starting point for our jobs. Without this interaction, we are stumbling around in the dark or worse, handcuffing our animators.

Q) *While the industry is competitive, it is ultimately respectful of great work. Outside of the work you have been personally involved in the production of, what animated characters have you been impressed or inspired by? What is the historical high-bar?*

A) Of course, Gollum and King Kong. The level of subtle and believable expressiveness was amazing. I never doubted that they "existed" in those movies. I could see what was going on in their minds.

I am loving where the feature animation industry is going in general with characters, both in terms of design and the balance between caricatured motion and realism.

Q) *Where do you see digital characters in ten years? Where are animated characters for film and games heading?*

A) That is such a difficult question. I know there is a push to create digital characters which are completely indistinguishable from living people. I won't even go into the "why" of this. But having worked on projects with this goal in mind, I think we still have a long way to go.

All the data we put into a character is filtered, sampled down. Not only can we not capture the full range of subtlety using current motion capture technology, but for bandwidth reasons, we tend to down sample the data we do capture. The same is true for lighting and texture information.

And a part of me wonders if there are subtle aspects of the human face which are so deep in our subconscious that we are not even aware that they are a part of what our mind's need to know a human is real. The human face is likely the first thing we lock onto as we enter the world. We know the smallest details of the face without being aware of this intimate knowledge.

I think is it not a surprise that the most successful digital characters (in my opinion, Gollum and King Kong) are NOT human, but humanoid.

Video game art is growing by leaps and bounds! The games are looking more and more amazing. I am still skeptical on the convergence of video game and film. They are two different mediums. One is an interactive experience driven by the end user, while the other is a completely passive experience. You are being told a story.

Imagine someone telling you the most amazing story. You are completely on the edge of your seat throughout. The storyteller gets to the end, you are holding your breath waiting to hear what they have to say then they stop and say, "So, how do you want my story to end?"

I think there is a lot of potential for technical and content crossover, of course. And, I hope I am proven completely wrong when I talk about how different the mediums are.

7

Deformation Systems

Deformation systems are responsible for how the model is impacted by the actions of the motion system. Deformations can be abstractly thought of as the muscles that stretch and bend skin in response to the motion of the body. In actuality, for animals, the muscles drive the skeleton, but for the purposes of animation, the inverse is true. Deformations can be as simple as a per-vertex connection to the joints that drive them and as complex as an anatomically-based layered muscle system that drives successive layers of geometry. This chapter discusses the physiology of muscles in addition to the physical attributes of skin and the relationship between skin, muscle, and bone. An overview of deformation methods, including skinning, spring meshes, and shape interpolation, and taking into account the theory, code, and best practices for study and implementation, put these anatomical concepts into practice.

7.1 PHYSIOLOGY OF MUSCLES

Muscles can be thought of as motors which actively generate force and produce movement through the process of contraction. Skeletal muscle comprises one of the largest single organs of the human body (with skin being the largest). It is highly compartmentalized, and we often think of each compartment as a separate entity, such as the biceps muscle. Each of these individual muscles is composed of single cells or fibers embedded in a matrix of collagen. At either end of the muscle belly in skeletal muscle, this matrix becomes the tendon that connects the muscle to bone.

The basic action of any muscle is contraction. For example, when you think about bending your arm, your brain sends a signal down a nerve cell telling your biceps muscle to contract. The amount of force that the muscle creates varies. In effect, the muscle can contract a little or a lot depending on the signal that the nerve sends. All that any muscle can do is create a contraction force. As that contraction force dissipates, the biceps muscle (Figure 7.1) relaxes, and in the case of the arm, the triceps muscle at the back of the upper arm contracts and acts to extend the arm. The biceps and triceps are a good example of working pairs of skeletal muscle that works together to perform the actions needed for that range of articulation. These working pairs are also classified as antagonistic pairs.

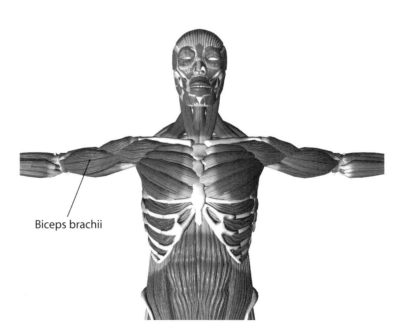

Biceps brachii

■ **FIGURE 7.1** Biceps muscle. Model by cgHuman.

Digital characters for use in visual effects often include complex muscle systems as a means of creating complex deformations for realistic characters. Studios and projects differ as to how anatomically realistic a muscle system needs to be (Figure 7.2). The common belief is that the visualization of

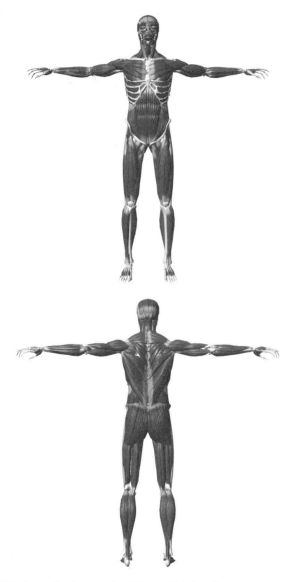

■ **FIGURE 7.2** Front and back of a muscle model setup. Model by cgHuman.

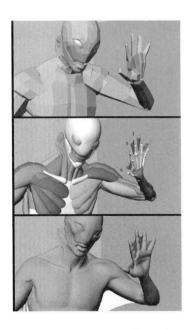

■ **FIGURE 7.3** Abe sapien muscle setup from "Hellboy." Hellboy images copyright © 2004 Columbia Pictures. All rights reserved. Photo Credit: Tippett Studio.

structures moving under the skin is critical to the creation of complex characters. This leads many studios to create abstract surfaces and deformers that look like muscles (Figure 7.3), thus creating a more simplified setup that achieves the visual results desired [3].

Something to keep in mind is that in nature, the brain fires a signal, which triggers a muscle to act which, in turn, manipulates a bone. For digital characters, the muscles are implemented for a visual result and not a kinematic one whereby the bone is moved and the muscles trigger to produce the desired look. There is biomechanical research that is going into creating a simulated neuron to muscle relationship, but at this point, this is still not feasible for production.

7.2 THE POLYGONAL MODEL AS SKIN

The manner in which skin slides over skeletal and muscular structures is intrinsic to its mechanical properties. When the deformation of the model surface, in this case our character skin, reveals an anatomical structure moving under the surface, we are clued into its structure and the complexity of the character. The topology of our model defines the anatomy of our character. The shape of muscles is reflected in the surface of the model (Figure 7.4). The way in which polygonal edges flow and loop over the character defines the first level of how the character should deform when in motion. Therefore, character modelers with a strong sense of anatomy and character deformations are key to developing complex characters.

The model is the initial manifestation of all the design and planning for the character. Proportions, points of articulation, and musculature are all contained in the layout of the vertices (Figure 7.5). This is the starting off point for the character setup artist whose first task for a new character is to provide feedback on the model to the modeler. This feedback usually includes issues with resolution of regions—too much or too little, general flow of the edges with regard to how they will deform, and adherence to surface naming, scale, or position conventions that may be standard for the production. Obviously, catching character model issues early can save a

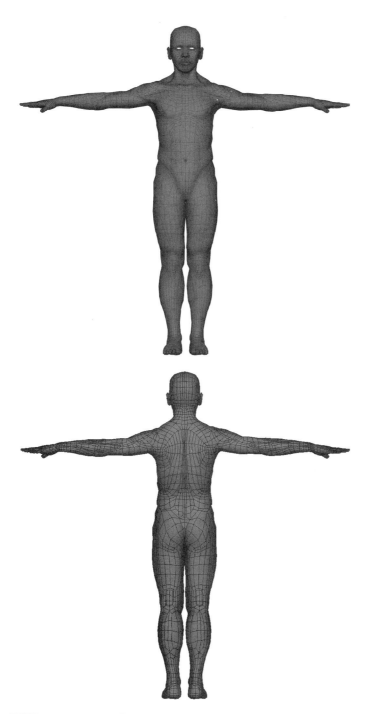

■ **FIGURE 7.4** Front and back of a character model with defined muscles. Model by Lee Wolland.

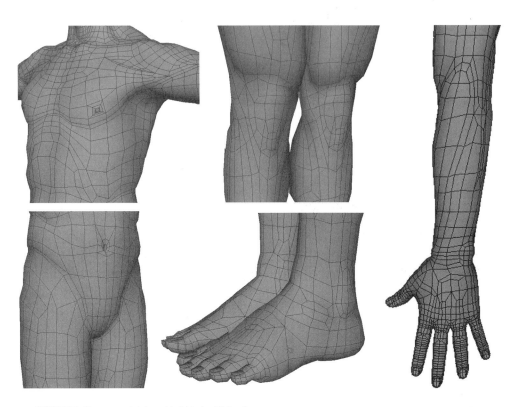

■ **FIGURE 7.5**   Close-up model views. Model by Lee Wolland.

lot of time later. Once the model is approved, motion systems and basic deformations can be applied. Model changes, from a design perspective, happen often, so there are many times that motion systems will need to be updated while the model is in flux. It is best to hold deformation system development until these changes are complete, but it is not unheard of for character design changes to be drastic enough to require reworking of a portion of a completed deformation system.

7.3   DEFORMATION

For digital characters, deformations are implemented to reach the desired shapes of the regions being moved. Once a motion system is developed for a character, and taking the notion of skin dynamics into consideration, a plan is put into place for how that system will deform the model it was built to fit.

Depending on the final output, there are a number of options available for methods of deformation. Game engines rely on joint-based manipulation, often termed "skinning," of the model, while animation systems used for film and non-real-time production have a few more options at their disposal; these include skinning, layered deformations, spring mesh, and shape interpolations. But before a method is chosen for a character, there needs to be an understanding of exactly what mesh deformation is and the type of variation that can be achieved depending on the type of character you are developing. For purpose of clarity, our discussion of geometric deformation will be limited to polygonal surfaces.

The elements of creatures such as robots and other mechanical characters can usually be implemented with rigid non-deforming parts that are constrained to the most logical joint. For situations such as this, each part is transformed by its joint matrix independently. Thus, parts of the character are parented to exactly one matrix as defined in $v\prime = v \cdot W$, where v is defined in the joint's local space. These transformations, while sometimes all that is required to attach a model to a motion system, are not technically a deformation.

In the most generic terms, deformation is the modification of a geometric surface shape from any previous state. Deformation is typically a combination of bending, stretching, and shearing a mesh of polygons (Figure 7.6) in relation to the methods enacted on them. Bending the vertices of a polygonal mesh involves the rotation of those points about the axis

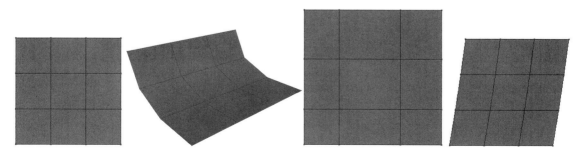

■ **FIGURE 7.6** Undeformed, bent, stretched, and sheared polygon plane.

of the joint that they are weighted to follow. Stretching the vertices is a way to describe the motion of points away from other points that are static or moving in an opposing direction. This will cause the the polygonal faces to grow in size as they move apart or shrink as the vertices move towards each other. Shearing is the motion of vertices moving in opposite parallel directions from each other, possibly due to twisting rotational forces.

There are numerous methods for deformations and many more being developed. The challenge is the development of methods that are stable, reusable, and efficient in terms of user setup and calculation speed. As computation speeds increase, we are able to calculate methods which would have seemed incomprehensible only a few years ago.

7.4 **SKINNING AND ENVELOPING**

If we think about deformations from the simplest solution, where the points of a polygonal mesh are uniformly (non-weighted) constrained to a joint matrix in motion, we get what is often referred to as rigid skinning. Similar to the rigid transformation described above, the motion of each individual vertex is constrained to a single joint. Now every vertex of a continuous mesh is individually moved by the transformation of the joints as they are moved by the motion system. This "rigid skinning" approach is used extensively in games.

The maintenance of offsets between the vertexes of a surface and the default position of joints is the simplest form of deformation system. Typically called "skinning" or "enveloping," this basic form of deforming the model is effective for film animation and necessary for the implementation of deforming characters in games. The term "enveloping" comes from the idea that the model is enveloping the joint set that controls it. The use of the word "skinning" is contrary to the traditional usage, in that it refers to the attachment of the model, or skin, to the joints. In modern animation systems, the influence of joints can be defined as uniform, with each point having one parent, or weighted, where points on the surface share influence from multiple joints. The careful adjustment of skin weights to associated joints creates the appearance of general skin sliding, where the model seems to be moving as a whole with the motion of the body, as skin would naturally respond. This is contrary to uniform or rigid skin weights where each vertex on the model is associated with one joint which tends to have a more localized deformation appearance. Weighted skinning allows for a falloff from the joint's influence so that joints appear to have a gradation effect on the skin, which, in effect, is a simulation of the falloff from the mechanical elasticity of skin (Figure 7.7).

However, because of the elastic properties of skin, we realize that the motion of a point on the surface should actually be controlled by multiple joint matrices at the same time. This "smooth skinning" is a weighted mapping between a surface vertex and a series of joint matrices where adjustable weights control how much each joint affects it. The speed limitations of these operations are proportional to the number of vertices and the number of influences acting on them as each vertex is transformed for each influence and the results are averaged to find the ending position for a vertex. The resulting vertex weight is a normalized value with all the weights of the influences adding to 1.

$$v\prime = w_1(v \cdot M_1) + w_2(v \cdot M_2) + \cdots + w_N(v \cdot M_n)$$

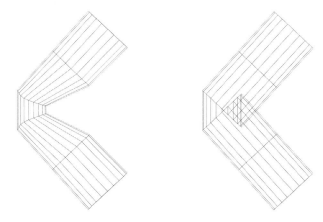

■ **FIGURE 7.7**   Smooth (weighted) versus rigid (uniform) skinning.

or

$$v' = \sum w_i(v \cdot M_i),$$

where

$$\sum w_i = 1$$

With rigid parts or rigid skinning, v can be defined locally to the joint that it is constrained to. For smooth skin, several joint matrices transform a vertex, but the vertex cannot be defined locally to all the joint matrices; so they must first be transformed to be local to the joint that will then transform it to the world. To do this, we use a binding matrix B for each joint that defines where the joint was when the skin was attached and premultiply its inverse with the world matrix.

$$M_i = B_i^{-1} \cdot W_i.$$

For each frame of the animation, after executing the motion system, the deformed vertex position is calculated as a weighted average of all the influences of the joints that the vertex is attached to:

$$v' = \sum w_i v \cdot B_i^{-1} \cdot W_i$$

W is a joint's world matrix and B is a joint's binding matrix that describes where its world matrix was when it was initially attached to the skin model. This is often referred to as the bind pose position. In some animation systems, this position must be returned to in order for the skinning to be edited, but this is becoming less and less common. Skinning is always tested by posing the character in various extreme positions and watching how the skin responds. When moved, each joint transforms the vertex as if it were rigidly attached, and then those results are blended based on user-specified weights. The normalized weights, as mentioned earlier, must add up to 1:

$$\sum w_i = 1$$

When coupled with creative motion systems, smooth skinning can often be the final solution for character deformation setup. The weighted influence often provides enough smoothness to create appealing results, particulary for less detailed characters. For cartoon-derived characters, the realization of sliding skin is not a crucial issue, but for realistic ones, it is a critical component of deformation setup. The alternative is that cartoon-styled characters generally need to be able to squash and stretch, maintaining volume as they extend and compress through extreme motions. This squash and stretch is essentially a scaling of the joints or deformation influences in the regions that are being effected (Figure 7.8).

Realistic characters should avoid stretching joints, but this is often handy to cheat shots. These characters require a more

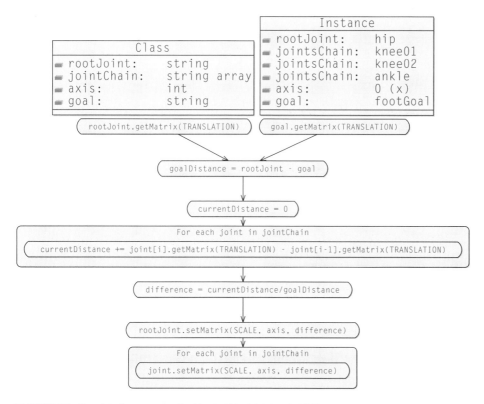

■ **FIGURE 7.8** Class, data diagram, and method for stretching joints in a straight line.

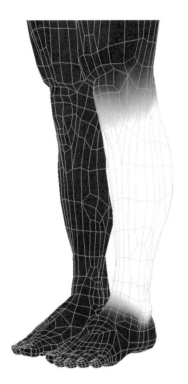

■ FIGURE 7.9 Painting interface for editing skin weights for the left knee joint.

subtle reaction to underlying surfaces that include wrinkling and the motion of structures under the skin as we will discuss ahead. Weights associated with character skinning are usually adjusted through a painting interface (Figure 7.9), that creates weighted maps, where values are associated with vertices per joint matrix based on a gray-scale map. This map will display black for the points that are unaffected by the joint selected and white for a point fully weighted to that joint. Gray values in between illustrate a value between 0 and 1 for that joint. Artists should avoid making areas a muddy region of various character weights; therefore, it is best to paint the area based on the most direct influence then add others as needed. Joint falloff is usually smooth and seamlessly overlapping with the next joint influence. Methods and best practices vary based on the artist's preference and style, but it is usually agreed upon that painting weights should happen from the middle out (for example, down the arm or down the leg) and that for most characters, extreme bending should avoid resulting in the surfaces intersecting.

Since skinning is based on weight maps for each joint, these maps can be exported and stored on disk. This can be done to backup character skin weights, to transfer them to another character with identical or similar topology, or to export them before a major change that may require unbinding the character model from the skin. Once a deformation system change is complete, the weight maps can be reimported and changes can be addressed as needed, but the original state of character skinning is intact. Character skinning can, for feature characters, often take weeks to perfect, so whenever possible that hard, and tedious, work is preserved as disk-based weight maps. Similarly, the amount of detailed weight painting incorporated into the character should be taken into account when exporting maps. Since these maps are generated procedurally, the user can set the resolution for output. There is no harm in exporting at a higher resolution to retain the small details that a lower resolution map may not retain in an effort to save disk space (See [15] for a comparison of linear skinning techniques).

7.5 **THE DEFORMATION RIG AND PIPELINE**

Since the motion system and the deformation system for a digital character are essentially two interconnected systems, it is often helpful to consider them as two different rigs. At some studios, the two systems are individual tasks carried out by potentially two different artists; this is especially true with regard to complex "hero" characters. In the end, the idea is that the deformation system "hangs" on the motion system. The deformation is the interface between the animation applied to the motion system and the response of the model surface that is rendered in the final image. Often times, the deformation system is a complete hierarchical rig that has all the procedural controls designed to manipulate the surfaces associated with the deformations.

The set of joints associated with the deformations should be denoted with a special string in their name, such as "def," as these will be the only ones used for skinning or whatever method used to attach the model to the rig. These are also often referred to as "secondary joints." Joints can be placed with procedural control to recreate muscles or just to create smooth transitions to certain regions. For example, in the human forearm, we can bend our hand at the wrist and we can move our hand from side to side at the wrist, but the twisting motion, such as turning your hand over, is produced by the rotation of the radius bone around the ulna. This motion starts just below the elbow and works its way down to the wrist. As such, the deformations for the twisting motion of the human forearm should be weighted from wrist to mid-forearm. In the deformation rig, this can be accomplished by a series of joints that start with full rotation weighted at the wrist then fade down to no rotation as you get closer to the elbow. The joints in between will have a logic falloff depending on the number of joints.

When in place, the deformation rig adds a layer of abstraction between the motion and the model. Deformation rigs can be updated on the fly, without impacting the animation already produced. This is a critical point because as we previously stated, the deformation system is responsible for the look of the model topology that is handed to the renderer. Therefore, it is very possible, and unfortunately very common, that once animation is finished for a shot, the deformations may need to be tweaked to achieve the desired look for the character. This harkens back to traditional animation where no matter what a character did, it was critical that they always "stay on model" and appear familiar. The distinction between the motion system and the deformation system allows a character technical director to work on character deformations without impacting the functionality of the motion system and risk altering approved animation.

Studios also must take into consideration the fact that deformation systems need to be calculated and that the calculation of the deformation system is dependant on many factors. The smallest change to any of these factors can result in different model results. In the same way that character motion is approved, character deformation can be approved. These approved deformations for a particular shot are often preserved on disk so that changes to the deformation system down the line do not effect them. Deformation system changes are intended to be non-destructive, but when a lighting team is art directing the placement of light and shadow in a shot, a small change to the curvature of a surface can have major effects. To preserve character deformations, the deformations are executed per-frame and the models for each frame of the animation are stored to disk. This cache of models is then associated with the shot and loaded, instead of the full character rig when the shot goes to the lighting. This is also a valuable time-saving device for the rendering of frames. If the renderer just needs to the load the appropriate model and not execute the motion and deformation systems, valuable time can be shaved off the computation of that frame. As the cost of hard drive space decreases, this solution is becoming more and more viable for smaller studios as well.

As we will see later, other systems can piggyback onto the deformation system as well. Since the deformation is responsible for the final form of the model, systems responsible for character clothing, for example, could be run on the resultant models. Character clothing can be simply attached to the models via skinning or can be simulated. Simulated clothing requires that the resultant character model surface be used as a collision surface against which the clothing surfaces would be collided against over the course of the animation. More commonly, because it is extremely more efficient, a low polygon single surface collision proxy model will be attached to the deformation rig and used as the collision surface. The collision proxy model is usually smoothed out to not have any extra creases where clothing simulations may get caught. The artist who sets up the character's main deformation setup is usually also responsible for binding this collision proxy and making sure that it ends up in a very similar position as the character model surface. One can imagine the computational difference between colliding against a production quality character model and a simplified surface that merely represents the volume of the character needed for clothing to react to.

Character texturing and shading is another important aspect playing into the depiction of the model on screen. In many ways, the approval of the model is in the hands of the character shading artists and the character technical directors. Changes to the model once, either of these teams have started their work, can be time-consuming.

The character deformation pipeline is responsible for the motion of all the character surface points throughout the entire project, from creation to motion and rendering. This is a huge amount of data to keep track of, and therefore, a clear plan and architecture is a critical component of production planning and technical pipeline design.

7.6 **DEFORMERS**

Animation systems are continually adding new deformation methods and stand-alone deformation tools. These are usually push button functions that are applied to an object. The user is then given attributes to tune the influence and relationship between objects. Free-form deformations (FFD), for example, are usually defined as a rectangular 3D lattice of points that surrounds an object (Figure 7.10) [34]. When transformed, the points of the lattice apply a weighted local transformation to the points of the affected surface. FFD can be applied to regions of the character that need special localized deformation. They are often used for muscle bulges, to twist or untwist regions of a limb, or even to smooth out unwanted creases at points of articulation. The points of the lattice can be animated and controlled based on properties of the rig.

Shrink wrap deformers are another important tool for character setup. Often just called "wrap" deformers, this method attaches one surface to another regardless of the resolution. In many ways, a wrap deformer acts like a lattice, but where a lattice is geometrically cubic, a wrap deformer can be any polygonal surface. Implementations have been developed for NURBS and subdivision surfaces as well, but as stated previously, for the purpose of clarity, we are restricting our discussion to polygons. Wrap deformers connect to other surfaces by generating a weighted relationship between all the points in the target mesh and all the points on the wrap surface. This surface connection proves valuable when a high-resolution mesh is to be controlled by a low-resolution mesh. This relationship between high- and low-resolution

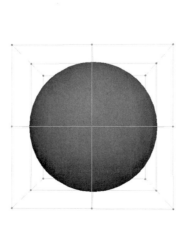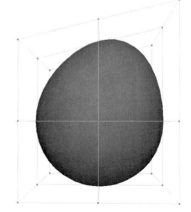

■ **FIGURE 7.10** Sphere modified by a lattice.

meshes also opens the door for the low-resolution mesh to be the control source for complicated solutions such as dynamics. As we will discuss later, methods such as dynamics and spring meshes can be effective and powerful tools to generate secondary motion on deforming surfaces. The ability to carry out these computationally expensive operations on a low-resolution mesh is one of the only ways to make such methods feasible for production.

Algorithms can also be applied to surfaces in the form of deformers. Functions that curve a surface or warp it (in some manner) are often used for the quick deformation of props and objects in a scene without the use of complex joint setups and controllers. Often termed "non-linear deformers," these functions are typically volumes of influence with defined regions, such as top and bottom, that modify the position of vertices of a model based on the parameters supplied to it. For example, a deformer programmed to bend a surface will define a curve that travels through the defined deformation volume. When the bend value is modified, the curve is bent, visualizing the amount of bend requested by the user, and the points associated with the curve bending are rotated to match the curve. Compression-based methods, such as squash and stretch, have also been implemented. These create a curve or volume of a particular length and the model is constrained to it. As the curve or volume is stretched or squashed, the compression value applied is used to deform the surface in a volume preserving manner. Squash and stretch, as we have discussed, is the idea that when something elongates, it thins out, and when compressed, it expands in the direction perpendicular to the compression. An elastic container filled with water, such as a water balloon, is a perfect representation of squash and stretch in the real world.

7.7 LAYERED DEFORMATION METHODS

Our understanding of weighted skinning can be extrapolated such that a series of underlying skinned models would produce the appearance of surfaces sliding under each other. This not only visually provides the sense of bones and muscles but also allows for more control over the final model deformations. The style and design of a project dictates the level of abstraction for the anatomical model required (Figure 7.11). Animation systems allow for the layering of surfaces, and the resultant underlying surfaces drive the visible skin of the character. The visible effect of surfaces moving under the surface of the skin adds a layer of visual complexity that is required for creating realistic characters (Figure 7.12).

Layering underlying structures is easier said than done, and there are a number of techniques for attaching surfaces to each other. These methods range from UV surface attachment, where the vertices of more complex surfaces are mapped to the UV coordinates of simpler deforming surfaces, to collision-driven layers. None of these solutions, at this point, can run in real-time and most rely on simulation and solving. Often times, the surface connection is done through what is conventionally called a "wrap" deformer (discussed above), in which the vertices of a driven mesh are controlled by the deformation of a driving mesh based on a falloff value. These types of deformers are difficult to edit and are usually

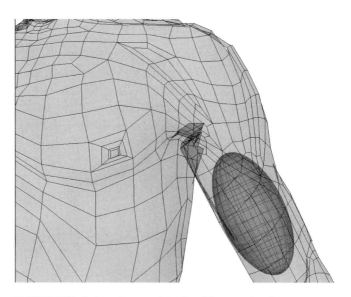

■ **FIGURE 7.11** Surface acting as an abstraction of biceps muscle surface.

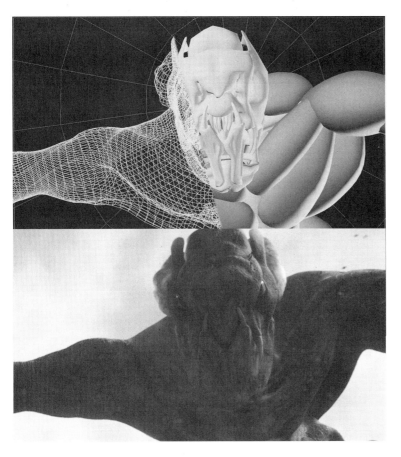

■ **FIGURE 7.12** Layered deformation setup from "Cloverfield" (2008) by Tippett Studios. Cloverfield images copyright © 2008 Bad Robot. All rights reserved. Photo Credit: Tippett Studio.

used for push-button solutions where a low-resolution mesh controls the deformation of its high-definition counterpart. A more efficient means to work with surface-to-surface attachments is on a regional basis where course deformations on low polygon models propagate up to more and more refined surfaces. The higher surfaces deform by maintaining the established offset, leaving only the lower ones to be manipulated. The point is that the fewer the points that need to be hand-weighted, the faster and more comprehensible the process is. It is inefficient (and painful) to craft deformations on extremely high-resolution surfaces.

If an anatomical setup is required for the production, then we take our cues from nature. The layers to be considered for an anatomical model include bone, muscle, fat, and skin. These are made up of geometry and potentially particles. A skeleton model set is created and parented to joints so that all the actions of the motion system translate to realistic articulations. The skeleton model need not be accurate down to each realistic anatomical feature, but the proportions and general shape should be enough for attaching muscle surfaces where needed.

Muscles have points of origin, where they start, and insertion, where they end. Muscle surfaces are defined as influences on the model surface layer above them. They are attached to the bones and often have procedural controls and callbacks to define the motion expected of them in various situations. For example, as the arm bends, the biceps muscle is supposed to flex and bulge. This can be set up through a triggered shape deformation (Figure 7.13), triggered procedural code to change the surface, or even as simply as procedurally moving a set of joints to deform the muscle surface. The process to

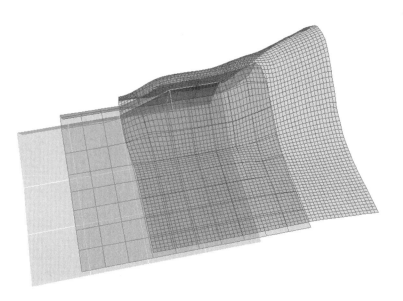

■ **FIGURE 7.13** One low-resolution surface controlling two subsequently high-resolution surfaces.

set up these muscles is time-consuming and tedious, so the effort must be justified by the end result. Many production studios are developing simplified abstract muscle structures for characters that are fewer in number, lower resolution, faster to calculate, and have a very similar visual result to more complex setups.

The fat layer is typically a modeled surface or even dynamic particles that form a regionalized implicit surface. This layer is simulated once animation is carried out to shift the loose connective tissue found just below the skin. As will be seen later, the dynamic jiggle associated with this layer can be represented at the skin layer as a spring-based deformer, but the notion of a layer-based solution is worth noting.

The skin layer is the character model itself. While this rendered surface in layered deformations is, most of the time, just the result of the deformers acting on it, there are opportunities to apply callbacks directly to this surface. These callbacks should be applied to the lowest resolution representation of this model when possible as the highest resolution could be prohibitively large for procedural control.

7.8 SHAPE INTERPOLATION

Shape interpolation is the transformation of a set of vertices from one state to another. Usually termed "morphing," the technique is heavily used in computer graphics and will be covered again with regard to face setup in the next part. The common terms associated with the creation of a series of models that are stored as a library and called as needed in the animation system is "blend shapes" or "morph target." These shapes are sculpted by the artist, based on copies of the original model, into the configuration required. When called, these shapes are blended via normalized weights from 0 to 1: zero being the default mode, one being the target blend shape. The transition between states is typically linear, meaning that points move in a straight line from default to target shape. As stated, blend shapes are an effective technique for character face setup, but they are also increasingly helpful for character body deformations. When combined with triggered events, surface interpolations can be combined with particular character motion. These pose-based deformations, or pose-space deformations (PSD), are often used for simulating the effects of body rotations on cloth to create wrinkles (Figures 7.14 and 7.15). For example, as the character's body twists, the diagonal wrinkles that would appear naturally on clothing are created as a blend shape and triggered based on the rotation values of the spine joint matrices. Thus, a PSD is a deformation that is created within the context of a character pose. This is a common replacement for dynamic clothing. Wrinkles in clothing provide the visual richness and sense of material weight associated with natural fabrics. Computer-generated clothing without wrinkles will often have the appearance of stretchy, form-fitting neoprene used in wet suits for surfing or diving.

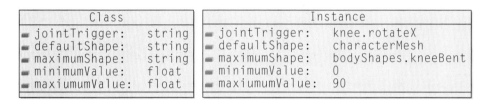

Class			Instance	
▬ jointTrigger:	string	▬ jointTrigger:	knee.rotateX	
▬ defaultShape:	string	▬ defaultShape:	characterMesh	
▬ maximumShape:	string	▬ maximumShape:	bodyShapes.kneeBent	
▬ minimumValue:	float	▬ minimumValue:	0	
▬ maxiumumValue:	float	▬ maxiumumValue:	90	

■ **FIGURE 7.14** Class and data diagram for pose space interpolation.

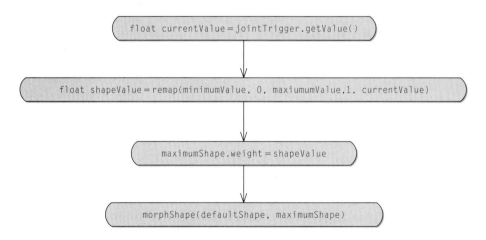

```
float currentValue = jointTrigger.getValue()
```

```
float shapeValue = remap(minimumValue, 0, maxiumumValue,1, currentValue)
```

```
maximumShape.weight = shapeValue
```

```
morphShape(defaultShape, maximumShape)
```

■ **FIGURE 7.15** Method for a pose-space interpolation.

Further, PSD have a more general application in the deformations of the body. Take, for example, the human knee which rotates along one axis and has a very distinctive appearance when both flexed and extended due to the motion of the floating knee cap (patella bone). In this case, the rotation of the knee joint can trigger and blend a shape from one state to another depending on the rotation.

This pose-based deformer is essentially a "blend shape" that is activated on the mesh when triggered by the rotation of a trigger joint. The benefit of such a solution is that the resulting shape is reliable and art-directed. The shape desired can be achieved at the desired time and is not based on an accumulation of deformation processes. The downside is that creating blend shapes to fix body deformation is a slippery slope. Their use can lead to the need to create and apply corrective shapes depending on the state of the trigger joint and the other influences on the model surface. These can be difficult to keep track of, so it is best if this method is either used as a last step to fix an area not controllable by other means or planned from the start. In areas of complex articulation, such as the human shoulder, the amount of shapes required and multiple joints might make this solution inefficient. On the other hand, it would be difficult to get the shapes desired from the knee or elbow region without a sculpted model solution. Shape interpolation and PSD are a useful addition to the options in the deformation system toolkit.

7.9 DYNAMICS AND SIMULATION

The elastic properties of skin allow for the stretching and local motion caused by the reaction of the movements of the character. Looking at any high-speed film footage of athletes in action, it is clear that our skin reacts to all the small and large motions produced by the body. Even the leanest runner's skin reacts to the extreme forces applied to the body during vigourous motion. These reactions range from small vibrations to large ripples and are magnified depending on the amount of body fat present. The jiggle of muscle and skin adds a necessary secondary motion to the animation of realistic characters. Large characters, in particular, benefit from the perceived weight that comes along with skin rippling in reaction to heavy motion. In fact, for animals with column-like legs such as elephants and sauropod dinosaurs, the reaction of the skin to the impact results in the skin rotating around the muscles. This rotational inertia is crucial to characters who are bearing a large amount of weight and appear large on screen. This motion is often carried out by callbacks within the deformation setup. For example, a point jiggle deformer applied to the mesh can provide a slight secondary motion to a subset of the mesh points based on the motion of the rig (see Figures 7.16 and 7.17). Dynamic simulation adds the real-world effects that are impossible to hand-animate at the surface level. The foremost of these is gravity which acts on the skin in relation to the motion of the body action.

Callbacks such as these work as a post-animation dynamic deformation stage. They are run after the animator has completed the shot and are tuned to the appropriate values for the motion of the shot. These values often must be animated as extreme motion may require that dynamic motion be damped to maintain a stable solution. This method is a surface-based approach where the effect is computed based on per-vertex motion surface. A spring-based solution can also be implemented, where each vertex is connected to adjacent vertices by springs. These springs create a similar result to a jiggle deformer, but per-spring attributes, such as stiffness and damping, provide the user with more control. In methods such as these, each vertex can be visualized having a weight

Class		Instance	
▬ inputSurface:	string	▬ inputSurface:	face_GEO
▬ magnitude:	float	▬ magnitude:	jiggleMesh.magnitude
▬ damping:	float	▬ damping:	jiggleMesh.damping
▬ gravity:	float	▬ gravity:	jiggleMesh.gravity
▬ weight:	float	▬ weight:	jiggleMesh.weight

■ **FIGURE 7.16** Class and data diagram for jiggle deformer.

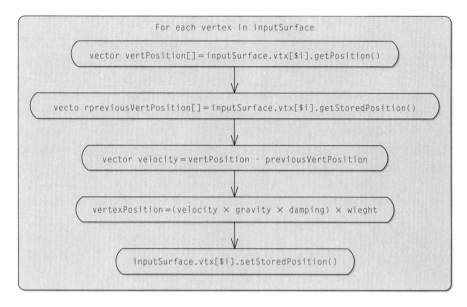

For each vertex in inputSurface

```
vector vertPosition[] = inputSurface.vtx[$i].getPosition()
```

```
vecto rpreviousVertPosition[] = inputSurface.vtx[$i].getStoredPosition()
```

```
vector velocity = vertPosition - previousVertPosition
```

```
vertexPosition = (velocity × gravity × damping) × wieght
```

```
inputSurface.vtx[$i].setStoredPosition()
```

■ **FIGURE 7.17** Method for a jiggle deformer.

attached to them. Each weight has its own mass and the connections between each of them have an elastic property. As the motion system is executed, the mesh is moved by the skinning deformer to follow the rig. After skinning is executed, the dynamics pass is run to compare the previous position against the current one. Often, it is compared to multiple frames in the history to calculate more accurate, albeit slower to compute, simulations. The points are then moved relative to their mass and gravity in the scene, the spring connections to other vertices, and the velocity and direction of motion.

7.10 **SPRING MESH DEFORMATION METHODS**

As joints rotate, they move the deformation surfaces, like muscles, and pull the skin across them. There exists in humans an elasticity to the skin which stretches and pulls to meet the demands of the underlying movement. In an animation system, the skin layer can be represented by a spring-mesh surface composed on a low-resolution mesh with its vertices connected by springs. These springs can be uni or bidirectional.

They can also be rigid to represent areas where skin does not slide. The purpose of such a system is to provide smooth regional motion falloff as the rig is articulated. Skinning alone is a time-consuming and tedious process. The addition of a relaxation step makes basic skinning all that is necessary. The application of a relaxation step after a joint-based deformation smooths out the surface and dissipates the influence of the articulated region. Relaxation methods are iterative, meaning that they are run successively for a defined number of times. The more times a relaxation is run, the smoother the final result will be, but keep in mind that the surface also stabilizes and cannot relax any further after a certain number of steps, depending on the algorithm. Thus, finding the balance between the final visual result and the number of iterative relaxation steps is critical to final deformation efficiency.

When combined with a spring mesh, relaxation methods are powerful. Spring meshes, as we mentioned earlier, are surfaces where each vertex is connected to adjoining vertices by a spring. As an initialization step, the springs determine a tension that will balance them against the others surrounding it to maintain the surface in its initial position. Once surface balance has been reached and mapped to the initial settings, the system is ready to run. The implementation of this system is done based on a copy of the input mesh. The duplicate mesh is created with the balanced springs and the true character mesh is shrink-wrapped to this mesh. The spring mesh has per-vertex attributes related to the point's status. Points can be defined as mobile, or floating, by the system or rigidly attached, or fixed, to the joints. The edges between the vertices have attributes related to the springs between the points, namely the elastic value that defines the tension of that spring. A vertex connected to a series of loose springs will be very active during motion, while one attached to very rigid springs will have limited secondary motion during relaxation. A point with three loose spring attachments and one rigid spring will be pulled toward the vertex from which the rigid spring originates. This allows certain points and regions of points to have more influence, and literally "pull," over other regions. Assigning certain regions to contain fixed points means that they will have limited to no stretch. On the human face, the bridge of the nose has limited motion during expressions and talking, so those points would be more likely fixed, while areas around the nostril and the forehead and brows are very active and inherit a lot of motion. The purpose of all this is to cause small motion in one region to have logical smooth motion in adjacent regions. Think about the human back and how the skin stretches to accommodate the raising and lowering of the arm. The motion is centered around the shoulder but also shows up down the middle of the back. Results using this method are very similar to what you would expect from skin. The little nuances like this add the visual complexity we are accustomed to seeing in humans and strive to recreate in digital characters (See [5] for a technical resource for deformations and dynamics).

7.11 **DEFORMATION ORDER**

The order in which deformation methods are executed has a bearing on the end result. If each is thought of, and designed as, a discrete function that is called one after the other, then each deformation method begins with the topology of the model resulting from the previous method. If each method is discreet and specific to its task, the user can expect predictable results, and its effect can be readily seen when it is deactivated (Figure 7.18). One of the best examples of this is in the interplay between joint-based skin weights and blend-shape deformers on, for example, the character's head. In every case, you would need to run the skin weights operation first to put the head geometry into the right place, then run the blend shapes to modify the point's local position from there. Running these in reverse will often result in the head

Deformation order
1. Rigid skinning
2. Pose-space deformer
3. Spring mesh relaxation

■ **FIGURE 7.18** Sample deformation order.

moving back to the origin when the blend shapes are enacted. In animation systems, this ordering can be a simple change to the order of inputs on a surface. On a procedural system, programmed deformation steps are run in the execution loop of the character and can be reordered, but the interplay between methods can take some tuning. Ideally, if each method returns a reference or handle to the deformed surface, then this handle can be passed down the line efficiently.

Switching between functional deformation orders mid-production can often result in slightly different output meshes at the end. Even if the result is generally the same, one can expect subtle variations between results. Changing deformation order should be done carefully and only if absolutely required by the production.

7.12 **REAL-TIME ENGINE CONCERNS**

In games, and depending on the engine in use, animation is generally baked out to the joints, and similarly, all deformations ultimately fall under the category of skinning. All deformers created for a particular character are not carried over. This drastically changes how the character setup is conceived and executed. A number of techniques have been developed to overcome this limitation. One solution is to bake complex deformations to joints, so the motion of the surface mesh is baked to a set of joints, one for each vertex. This is a joint heavy solution, but the baked motion of these joints carries a lot of information. This technique allows the results of methods like pose-space deformers and muscle and cloth simulations to be maintained in the character deformations in a format that is game engine-compliant.

For real-time characters, it is important to restrict the number of objects in a rig to a minimum as these things must be executed at every frame. One way to do this includes using as few joints as possible. This includes primary joints for the motion system and secondary joints for the deformation system when they are available. So a balance between character execution speed and realistic deformation must always be struck. In recent years, character execution speed has always won over character deformations, but thanks to fast processors, we are starting to see a shift toward richer character deformations. Limiting the number of vertices in the skin is given for real-time engines. While the "polycount" limits are rising with each hardware and engine iteration, there are ways of faking detail on a low-resolution model. A highly effective way to do this is the use of normal maps, which are a form of bump mapping that store the normal information of a higher resolution mesh. This allows the detail of a high-resolution mesh to be applied to that of a lower resolution at the shader level, taking the responsibility off the deformation system. These normal maps can also be triggered in the same manner as PSD where instead of a mesh being swapped out, a different normal map is blended into place.

The amount of joint weights per vertex used during skinning is another concern for real-time engines. As described earlier, the position of a vertex needs to be solved for the number of joints associated with it. Thus, four joint weights require that vertex to calculate its weighted position based on the result of the influence of each of those joints. The lesser the joints a vertex must solve its position against, the faster it finds its position per frame. Many practitioners suggest not using more than four joint weights per vertex when skinning.

7.13 **CONCLUSION**

Deformation systems manipulate the character model as initially influenced by the motion system to result in the final posed mesh. Digital characters for film rarely rely on a single method to achieve the desired deformations. As new techniques emerge, it is likely that they will be integrated into the character deformation pipeline and not revolutionize it immediately. It is the intelligent combination of techniques that has found the greatest success. In many ways, this is akin to the way that living organisms work and multiple systems work together.

On the horizon, we can expect new techniques for elastic deformations and even deformations produced without the influence of joints. These shape-filling algorithms are an alternative, albeit a costly one, to deforming a model based on the standard character technology conventions. In this method, multiview video streams are used to create a volume. This volume is analyzed and the digital character model is deformed to fill the volume, maintaining the initial proportions of the character. Techniques such as this might have a major impact on our work flow in the future. The immediate challenge ahead is the integration of complex deformations into real-time engines.

Integrating motion and deformation system concepts into expressive faces is the next hurdle in the successful setup of a digital character.

7.14 **EXERCISE**

In this exercise, we go through the conceptual and technical process of creating a character deformation system. Split into groups of two or more. One of you is the art director, the other team members are the character setup artists. Follow the steps below.

7.1 Starting with the character you developed in the last section, design the manner with which the character deformations should behave. Should the character bend with smooth cartoon-inspired motion or be more realistic and detailed?

7.2 Determine the methods you need to implement the deformation design and list out the order of deformations.

7.3 Implement the deformations using the motion system and animation poses developed in the previous section.

7.4 The art director should provide feedback on the look of the character and how "on model" the character remains while in extreme poses.

7.5 Maintain this review/fix feedback loop until satisfied.

■ FURTHER READING

Christopher Evans of Crytek has a great collection of resources that relate muscle anatomy to rigging ranging from technical papers to practical implementations:

http://chrisevans3d.com/

A good physics introduction:

David M. Bourg. *Physics for Game Developers*. O'Reilly Media, Inc., 2001.

Some Technical References on Deformations:

Ferdi Scheepers, Richard E. Parent, Wayne E. Carlson, and Stephen F. May. Anatomy-based modeling of the human musculature. In *SIGGRAPH '97: Proceedings of the 24th Annual Conference on Computer Graphics and Interactive Techniques*, pages 163–172, ACM Press/Addison-Wesley Publishing Co., New York, NY, 1997.

Luciana P. Nedel and Daniel Thalmann. Real time muscle deformations using mass-spring systems. In *CGI '98: Proceedings of the Computer Graphics International 1998*, page 156, IEEE Computer Society, Washington, DC, 1998.

John P. Lewis, Matt Cordner, and Nickson Fong. Pose space deformations: A unified approach to shape interpolation and skeleton-driven deformation. In Kurt Akeley, editor, *Siggraph 2000, Computer Graphics Proceedings*, pages 165–172, ACM Press/ACM SIGGRAPH/Addison-Wesley Longman, 2000. Longman.

Alla Sheffer and Vladislav Kraevoy. Pyramid coordinates for morphing and deformation. In *3DPVT '04: Proceedings of the 3D Data Processing, Visualization, and Transmission, 2nd International Symposium*, pages 68–75, IEEE Computer Society, Washington, DC, 2004.

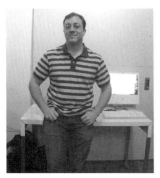

Stephen Mann, Senior Character Technical Director,
Charlex

■ INTERVIEW: STEPHEN MANN, SENIOR CHARACTER TECHNICAL DIRECTOR, CHARLEX

■ BIO

Stephen started his career working for a small Burlington, Vermont studio as an editor and VFX creator while getting a Bachelors of Studio Art at the University of Vermont. He then attended USC Film School to get a degree in Digital Art and Animation. While in Los Angeles, he worked for several small studios and for Sony Imageworks on the production of "Stuart Little." Upon returning to the east coast, Stephen worked for Klieser-Walczak serving as a 3D artist on commercials, ride films, and on the feature films "X-Men" and "The One," along with teaching at New York's School of Visual Arts. He then served as CG supervisor for Hornet Inc for a year, before working as a Character Rigger for Blue Sky Studios on "Robots." He is now the lead Character TD and Pipeline TD for the post production studio Charlex in New York City.

■ Q&A

Q) *The components of character technology are diverse and span the artistic and technical spectrum. How did you get your start in the industry? Based on where you see the field heading, what experience/training do you recommend people have?*

A) While I was still in school at USC's Film School studying animation, I got the chance to work at Sony Pictures on "Stuart Little." I was hired as an student on site trainer (SOST). Maya was not even out yet, and my job was to learn as much about using Maya and then turn around and teach it to various artists at Sony. I had done some really simple character animation with Power Animator, and so I was totally blown away by the animation done by the Sony artists. I was mostly impressed by their sculpting, painting, and animation skills. A lot of animation directors had stop motion backgrounds and most of the animators were either traditional (hand drawn) or stop motion artists. Previously, I had worked freelance, and before school, I worked for a really small place creating educational videos, but this experience at Sony really sparked me to push myself and focus as a character artist and not just a 3D user.

I think the same skills that were needed 30 years ago are still the same skills needed now and will be in the future. The computer is just an expensive pencil and unfortunately, one that has its own brain; it tries to do things for you. Solid figure drawing, sculpting, photography, acting, and story telling are always going to be what makes someone stand out. Technology changes too fast to keep up with, and you can learn most of what you need in a couple weeks. It is honing the traditional crafts that take time and then taking the brain away from the computer and forcing it to create your vision. One thing on the computer side I have found useful, however, is learning how to type. I know it sounds weird, but I think it helped me to learn how to script and helps to keep your fingers in touch with the keyboard.

Q) *Creating compelling digital characters is part art and part science. What is the greatest challenge you encounter on a daily basis? What aspect of character technology keeps you up thinking at night?*

A) Good character design that works well in animation is probably one of the biggest challenges. Frequently, you do not get enough time to fully develop a character until it goes into production. What makes this difficult is being able to change things on-the-fly and have everything still work, and look like you want it to. Time is the greatest killer; right now, everyone is trying to figure out ways to make the process faster. The ones that are doing it right are taking the time to do it. Technology wise, what I think about most is creating new and interesting ways to move and pose the character, to give as much control to the animator. Muscles, fur, and cloth are still going to be the larger hurdles, but even those are getting easier due to the new technologies out there.

On one side, I love all the technology going into creating characters, but I also hate what some of it is doing. I think mocap is a super cool technology, but I do not consider it animation. It is getting better, but it is always going to remain "the devils rotoscope" to me. I think the programmed rotoscope can attest to that. There is a short called "Snack And Drink" (directed by Bob Sabiston) that is all hand rotoscoped, and the artists were not harnessed to any computer or boundaries, which is what makes it so interesting. The same director went on to make other "rotoscoped" films but did it using more computer assistance, which I think took away everything that can be interesting about rotoscope.

Q) *What are the ingredients for a successful digital character?*

A) Wow, that is a tough one. I suppose it is true of what is successful in any animated character: "life" or the illusion of life? Ok that is cheesy, but I think that all the old adages are relevant. The character must be appealing, have a soul, have meaning behind its actions and emotions. On the technical side, you must have arcs, weight, overlapping action, and GREAT posing. I think this is why mocap will always be mocap for digital doubles, games, and HyperReal live-action animation. We as humans do not move like animated characters, and when we try, we look goofy. Look at Jar Jar (from "Star Wars"). Extremely great work, but the movement was based on a guy in a suit. I think that is why Weta's work on Gollum is so impressive. They really brought so much life using Andy Serkis' movements and their own animation on top of that. Developing character models and rigs that allow for traditional style animation is probably the biggest hurdle on that front. You have to have a rig and model that behaves to allow the animator to work and not have to counter animate or think too much about how something moves.

Q) *While the industry is competitive, it is ultimately respectful of great work. Outside of the work you have been personally involved in the production of what animated characters have you been impressed or inspired by? What is the historical high-bar?*

A) I am still very impressed by the Scrat character from Blue Sky Studios "Ice Age." His animation is phenomenal. He is a well-designed character, and he is pushed really far. I do not think they were trying to mimic anything that was already done, but more developing a new character, and I think that is what makes him work so well. I must admit, I have not seen the movie, but the parts of the evil character in "Meet the Robinsons" I also found to be very good. I like the direction they were headed, in giving him all sorts of curved squash and stretch to his movements. And, of course, you cannot deny Pixar's animation. For various reasons, I really like "The Incredibles." They have terrific animation, and the story is fantastic. On the technical side, I recently saw some facial work being done for games that blew me away on the hyper-real front. I believe it was mocap, but it was really impressive stuff.

Q) *Where do you see digital characters in ten years? Where are animated characters for film and games heading?*

A) Just like traditional animation, you have different styles of non-realistic animation, and from FX work, you have all sorts of realistic techniques merging with animation. Live action requires digital doubles, which in films like "Beowulf" are beginning to have speaking rolls. Then, you have what can be referred to as "cartoon," which is more like what Pixar, Blue Sky, and Disney are all doing, and then you also have people starting to work with digital characters in ways harking back to UPA and other pioneers of animation that did not stick to traditional guidelines. As far as games versus film, it feels like a swap is happening. Due to a number of factors, a lot of "hyper-real" CG human development has come out of games with the integration of mocap and real-time interaction to make realistic characters. Now, you are finding that really well-animated characters that are more "toon" like emerge in games, while live-action directors, like Zemekis, are forging ahead on the "hyper-real" human path. I feel like we are going to have less specific divisions of digital characters out there. I would think there would be a giant merge of games and movies as entertainment goes, we will always need a separation of the two, but the techniques will become more and more alike. We are just going to see more refinement in the acting of "hyper-real" characters and more "tooning" of cartoon characters. Lately, I have been seeing the "clay stop motion" look being developed in 3D. I love this not only because of how hard it is but that it forces us even more to be creative about a look. How do you really define that look and repeat it but also make it worth doing in 3D. The best thing is that technology is coming down in price dramatically, allowing individuals to make shorts and movies on their own. I cannot wait till full-length films are being filmed in basements and animated on laptops and still find their way to the big screen.

Chapter 8

Face Setup

8.1 **INTRODUCTION**

Our faces serve to visually communicate emotion and are also a vehicle for spoken language. Digital character development of the face requires a setup which is capable of creating the shapes associated with emotional expressions, in tandem with the shapes needed to visualize the sounds required for lip-sync. Lip-sync is the process of animating the character's face to match the voice or sounds present in the character's voice-over audio track. By incorporating the anatomy and psychology of faces into our setups, we gain the ability to create compelling, emotive characters no matter how fantastic they are.

8.2 **ANATOMY**

As humans arguably have the most range of expression known in any organism, we will focus our discussion of face anatomy on ourselves, while at the same time maintaining a generality of terms and concepts to be able to port these ideas to characters of any design. The complexity of the human face starts with the skull and the muscles attached to it. The only moving part of the cranium is the jaw, which attaches with the two temporal bones on the skull just in front of the ear. The jaw has the ability to rotate from this temporomandibular (the point at which the temporal bones on the skull articulates with the mandible) joint allowing for the opening and closing action. Translation is also possible, thanks to the articular disk, which allows the jaw to slide forward, back, and side-to-side. The jaw is a critical rigid object that defines much of the look and feel of the face, so it must be incorporated in some manner, whether through a modeled geometry surface or just a carefully weighted joint. The articulation point where it attaches to the neck is toward the back of the skull around the foramen magnum where the spinal cord enters the skull and connects with the brain, which leaves the head weighted toward the face and free to rotate about from this posterior position. The skull also contains the eyes, a critical piece of the human expression puzzle, as we will discuss ahead.

Fifty-three muscles are responsible for the wide range of expressions and face shapes available to humans. These muscles fire in patterns to produce the conceived result. Human expressions cross cultural, regional, and linguistic boundaries. Emotion and the ability to classify emotions is a debated subject. There is a categorical model which defines a number of discrete emotional states, and there is a dimensional model which maps a range of emotional phenomena onto an explicitly dimensioned space. References for these approaches are listed at the end of this chapter. Looking at emotions categorically, we all express happiness, sadness, anger, fear, surprise, and disgust, the so-called six basic emotions, in addition to all the more complex emotional reactions the same way. Facial muscles function similarly to skeletal muscles in the rest of the body. Below is a list of muscles which may be a relevant starting point for a muscle-based facial setup (Figure 8.1).

Major facial muscles and the motions they are responsible for:

1. Epicranius: frontalis and occipitalis, control eyebrows and scalp
2. Orbicularis oris: closes lips
3. Zygomaticus: raises the corners of the mouth when a person smiles
4. Levator labii superioris: elevates upper lip

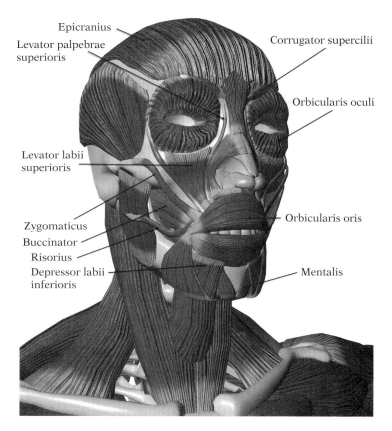

Epicranius

Levator palpebrae superioris

Corrugator supercilii

Orbicularis oculi

Levator labii superioris

Zygomaticus

Buccinator

Risorius

Depressor labii inferioris

Orbicularis oris

Mentalis

■ **FIGURE 8.1** Major face muscles responsible for motion (platysma not shown). Model by cgHuman.

5. Depressor labii inferioris: depress the lower lip
6. Buccinator: compresses the cheeks against the teeth
7. Mentalis: elevates and wrinkles skin of chin, protrudes lower lip
8. Platysma: draws down the lower lip and angle of the mouth by lowering the corners
9. Risorius: draws back mouth angle
10. Orbicularis oculi: closes eyelids
11. Corrugator supercilli: moves eyebrow downward and medially, vertically wrinkles forehead
12. Levator palpebrae superioris: elevates eyelid

As we will see later, there has been research to develop tools that attempt to quantify and describe the association between the action of a muscle and the facial motion that it results in. While character setup artists should be versed in musculoskeletal anatomy and have a general sense of the muscles responsible for the motion of different regions of the face, what is more important is a working knowledge of the general regions of the face and the motion possible for each. For example, the list below contains the major muscles responsible for facial expressions and the regions they effect.

8.3 PSYCHOLOGY BEHIND FACIAL EXPRESSIONS

Facial expressions are a window to the mind of the character. Our discussion of the Uncanny Valley in Section 2.1 illustrated that the subtle motion of the eyes and the face are one of the keys to a convincing performance by a digital character.

Emotion and emotional responses are a highly debated and controversial subject in fields ranging from anthropology to psychology and philosophy. The fact remains that a big part of our emotional response to the world is communicated by our faces and the subtle interplay of regional muscles. Further, the same is true for successful digital characters where the emotional response is reflected across the face and not limited to one region. Take, for example, this question:

Q) *So how do you tell a fake smile from a real one?*

A) In a fake smile, only the zygomatic major muscle, which runs from the cheekbone to the corner of the lips, moves. In a real smile, the eyebrows and the skin between the upper eyelid and the eyebrow come down very slightly. The muscle involved is the orbicularis oculi, pars lateralis. [12]

This quote reveals a common problem that is also seen in digital characters where a smile effects only the mouth region. The question is answered by Dr. Paul Ekman, a psychologist and expert on the intricacies of facial expressions and their relationship to our emotions and even our thoughts. Since the 1970s, Ekman has been working to break down and quantify facial expressions into discrete coded entities. This work is invaluable to our discussion of digital character faces and Ekman's "Facial Action Coding System" (FACS) has been increasingly used in animation productions to lay a foundation for the expressions that will be needed for a particular character. Ekman's system breaks down the facial behaviors based on the muscles that produce them. This reveals directly how muscular action is related to facial appearances. Ekman and his colleague W.V. Friesen developed the original FACS in the 1970s by determining how the contraction of each facial muscle, both individually and in combination with other muscles, changed the appearance of the face. Their goal was to create a reliable means for skilled human observers to determine the category or categories in which to fit each facial behavior.

Also from this research, which included the analysis of high-speed video of interviews, the notion of microexpressions emerged. The term microexpression denotes a brief facial expression that lasts less than a quarter of a second. They often occur involuntarily and can reveal emotions that are not deliberately expressed. These microexpressions generally occur right before the more voluntarily expression that the individual wants to convey. Take for example your reaction to someone's cooking. If something is grossly unappealing to you but you do not want to insult the cook, you may convey a split-second expression of disgust followed by something more concealing, but ultimately false. A person trained or inherently able to read microexpressions would be able to tell your true feelings about the experience. Microexpressions are presumably a pathway to an individuals real emotions and are critical knowledge for animators.

8.4 **FACE SHAPE LIBRARY**

In developing a character's face, it is critical to conceive and design the face shapes expected of that character. Character bibles, the document that described the overall design of the character, should include sketches of what the character is supposed to look like in different emotional states and may even

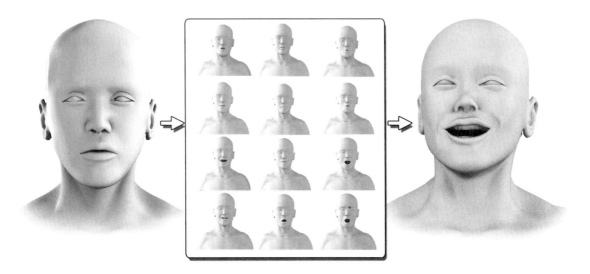

■ **FIGURE 8.2** Neutral face model with blend shape inputs results in an output face with a wide range of emotion. Original model by Lee Wolland.

go so far as to design the shapes related to speaking. Once approved, these sketches become the basis for the library of actions and controls that must be created for the face rig. With an eye on the future, our discussion of these shapes will be done regardless of the techniques used to create them. Suffice to say, these could be blend shape models, collections of controls for manipulating a joint system, or the animated tensions on a spring mesh to generate the shapes. No matter how they are made, the character setup artist will have to implement shapes associated with both emotions and speaking (Figure 8.2). The core functionality of a good facial setup is the ability to lip-sync to the dialog effectively and in tandem with existing expressions.

8.5 EMOTIONS THROUGH FACE SHAPES

Psychologists often say that emotions are most clear in human babies. Taking some basic emotions as a starting point, the shape descriptions for happiness, sadness, anger, fear, and disgust can be described. As with all face shapes, and blend shapes in general, the idea is to be able to build up complex shapes from smaller, more discreet ones. One must also keep in mind that an animator will rarely use the full shape and in most cases will only use a portion of it. Face shapes will also need to be asymmetrical, meaning that the left and right sides can be controlled independently but be designed to have a smoothly interpolated, seamless middle-region. All these generalizations will, course, vary based on the description and design of the character, but there are some core ideas that will transcend design. Figures 8.3–8.8 were generated using Ken Perlin's "Responsive Face" applet (http://www.mrl.nyu.edu/perlin/facedemo/).

Happiness

Happy expressions are universally recognized and are interpreted as conveying feelings related to enjoyment, pleasure, a positive outlook, and friendliness. It is said that one can train ourself to depict happy expressions, so these are often used to mask true emotions. Real or faked, the hallmark facial attributes of happiness include the following features:

- Corners of the mouth up
- Mouth slightly opened, teeth possibly showing
- Eyes partially closed
- Eyebrows up

Sadness

Sad expressions convey messages related to loss, bereavement, discomfort, pain, helplessness, and the like. Many psychologists contend that sad emotion faces are lower intensity forms of crying faces which can be observed early in newborns as both are related to distress.

- Corners of the mouth down
- Eyebrows down

Anger

Anger expressions convey messages about hostility, opposition, and potential attack.

- Eyes very nearly closed
- Eyebrows pointed down and inward
- Mouth corners in, teeth possibly showing

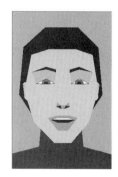

■ **FIGURE 8.3** Basic happy expression. Image created using Dr. Ken Perlin's "Responsive Face" applet.

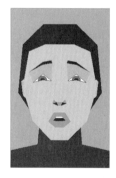

■ **FIGURE 8.4** Basic sad expression. Image created using Dr. Ken Perlin's "Responsive Face" applet.

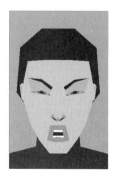

■ **FIGURE 8.5** Basic angry expression. Image created using Dr. Ken Perlin's "Responsive Face" applet.

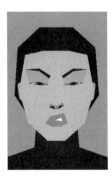

■ **FIGURE 8.6** Basic disgust expression. Image created using Dr. Ken Perlin's "Responsive Face" applet.

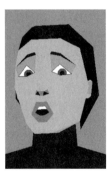

■ **FIGURE 8.7** Basic fear expression. Image created using Dr. Ken Perlin's "Responsive Face" applet.

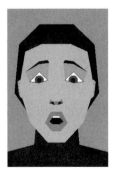

■ **FIGURE 8.8** Basic surprise expression. Image created using Dr. Ken Perlin's "Responsive Face" applet.

Disgust

Disgust expressions are often part of the body's response to objects that are revolting and nauseating. Obnoxious smells are effective in eliciting disgust reactions.

- Mouth asymmetrical and sneering (one corner up, the other slightly down)
- Eyebrows pointed down and inward
- Nostrils up

Fear

Fearful expressions can be described as a feeling of agitation and anxiety caused by the presence or imminence of danger, a feeling of disquiet or apprehension, such as a fear of looking foolish or extreme reverence or awe.

- Eyes wide
- Pupils dilated
- The upper lip raised
- Brows drawn together
- Lips stretched horizontally

Surprise

Surprise expressions are fleeting and difficult to detect or record without high-speed recording. They almost always occur in response to events that are unanticipated and convey messages about something being unexpected, sudden, novel, or amazing. A surprise seems to act like a reset switch that shifts our attention. Surprise can be neutral, pleasant, or unpleasant.

- Eyebrows raised, becoming curved and high
- Stretched skin below the eyebrows
- Horizontal wrinkles across the forehead
- Open eyelids, the upper lid is raised and the lower lid is drawn down, often exposing the white sclera above and below the iris
- Dropped jaw, lips and teeth are parted, with no tension around the mouth

There are many more subtle and complex emotions that we experience in life including contempt, shame, and startle. The basic ones described above should form a baseline that your character can achieve. These, plus the visemes for speaking described below, should start to produce a character that is capable of a basic facial performance.

8.6 **VISEMES AND LIP SYNCING**

In human language, a phoneme is the smallest unit of speech that distinguishes meaning. Phonemes are not the physical segments themselves but abstractions of these in the acoustic domain. An example of a phoneme would be the "t" found in words like tip, stand, writer, and cat. The shape set for desired arrangements are referred to as visemes. A viseme is a basic unit of speech in the visual domain that corresponds to the phoneme or the basic unit of speech in the acoustic domain. It describes the particular facial and oral movements that occur alongside the voicing of phonemes. Phonemes and visemes do not share a one-to-one correspondence; several phonemes will often share the same viseme. In other words, several phonemes look the same on the face when produced. For digital characters, it is essential to be able to create all the visemes.

There are some basic sounds that need visemes to do lip-sync.

- M, B, P
- EEE (long "E" sound as in "Sheep")
- Err (As in "Earth", "Fur", "Long-er" - also covers phonemes like "H" in "Hello")
- Eye, Ay (As in "Fly" and "Stay")
- i (Short "I" as in "it", "Fit")
- Oh (As in "Slow")
- OOO, W (As in "Moo" and "Went")
- Y, Ch, J ("You", "Chew", "Jalopy")
- F, V

8.7 **EYES**

The eyes are a portal to the mind. They reveal so much about what we are feeling when our spoken language may reveal

Table 8.1 Phoneme to Viseme Mapping

Phoneme	Viseme	Phoneme	Viseme
P		K	
B	/p/	G	
M		N	
EM		L	
F	/f/	NX	/k/
V		HH	
T		Y	
D		EL	
S		EN	
Z	/t/	IY	/iy/
TH		IH	
DH		AA	/aa/
DX		AH	
W		AX	/ah/
WH	/w/	AY	
R		ER	/er/
CH		AO	
JH	/ch/	OY	
SH		IX	
ZH		OW	
EH		UH	/uh/
EY		UW	

otherwise. For digital characters, the eyes have the same benefit and responsibility, while at the same time unfortunately pose one of the greatest challenges. We often encounter digital characters with "dead eyes." As we discussed previously in Section 8.1, when this occurs for realistic characters, the

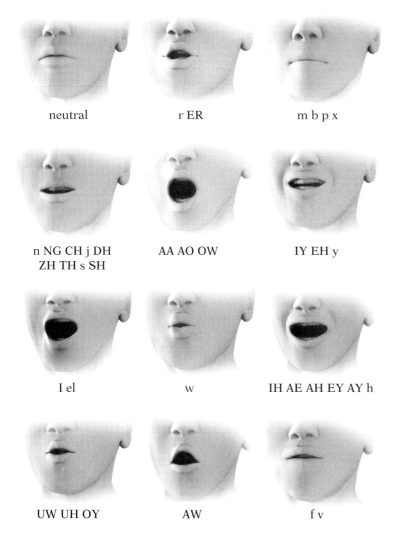

neutral

r ER

m b p x

n NG CH j DH
ZH TH s SH

AA AO OW

IY EH y

I el

w

IH AE AH EY AY h

UW UH OY

AW

f v

■ **FIGURE 8.9** Face visemes. Original model by Lee Wolland.

illusion is broken entirely. When it comes to stylized characters, it is often just the animation that is responsible for
characters eyes looking alive. For realistic characters, we need
to explore the small nuances that make eyes believable from
the point of view of both setup and motion. From the perspective of setup, the construction of the eye surface should
represent the iris, pupil, and eye ball (Figure 8.10). The iris

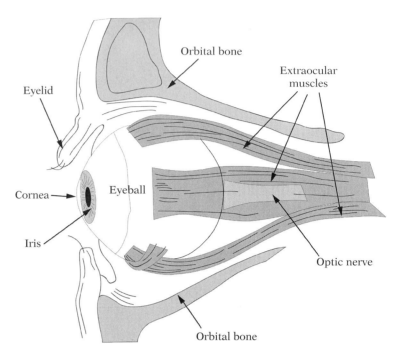

■ **FIGURE 8.10** Eye anatomy.

needs to be able to adjust and impact the radius of the pupil to dilate the eye. Keep in mind that the iris and pupil make up a lens that is slightly more convex than the general sphericity of the eye.

The shading and texture of the iris must communicate the color, the microstructures such as veins and capillaries and the eye must look wet (Figure 8.11). Often, artists will surround the eye, iris, and pupil surfaces with a larger semi-transparent surface that gives the impression of wetness and acts as a surface to render specular highlights and reflections. The area around the eye is also highly detailed and provides a lot of visual information to the viewer that is often over-looked. These details come from the micromotions that occur around the lids when the eye moves. Looking at someone closely or at yourself in the character setup artist's ever-present computer-side mirror will reveal that as the eye looks left the

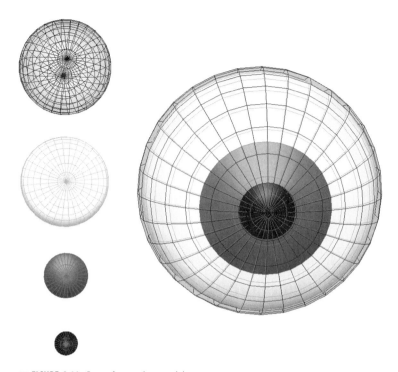

■ **FIGURE 8.11** Eye surfaces and eye model.

skin around the eye shifts slightly to the left. The same is true for the right and, of course, the lids react to the motion of the eyes looking up and down. These motions are critical to realistic characters as they provide a physical relationship between the eyes and the face, which for a long time were treated as separate unconnected entities. The motion of the lids and the area around the eye should be mostly automated so that the animator's control of the eye logically triggers the motion of the skin around the eye.

The motion of the eyes is complex. Rotational motion based on the direction of gaze causes the eyes to look at the object of interest. This is usually controlled via a constraint that causes the eyes to aim at an external object. This object, usually an animation controller, is normally parented to the head but can also be constrained to objects in the world. This is important so that character's eyes can be fixed as needed on animated objects. The setup usually involves each eye being controlled individually, each with their own goal, and those two goals are parented to a single controller. Independent eye movement is important for cheating the look of a character in a shot. A believable gaze is difficult to recreate for digital characters and must often be modified to look correct in the render and not necessarily what looks correct in the shot. This is sometimes due to the reflectivity of the eye surface and how the iris and pupil look at the time of rendering. Other times, it is just the camera angle and how the pupils read in the shot.

Eye blinks happen normally at regular intervals and are usually animated over a couple of frames. They also occur, as needed, as a reaction to a surprising moment and are used in animation often as a means of transitioning a character from one emotional state to another. In general, the weight of the eyelids is a prime vehicle for expressing a character's emotional state and is, of course, expressed in a heavy manner for a tired character. Blinks also occur during the start of a head turn motion. Lid motion is not linear, so setting up a proper eyelid requires that the geometry of the lid surface rotates around the eye geometry. Often, a spherical deformer of the same dimensions of the eye is constrained to the eye geometry and programmed to deflect lid geometry points so that the lid surface never penetrates it.

When humans are talking or thinking, our eyes look around the environment in quick bursts of motion. This motion is typically referred to as "eye darts" or saccades. Saccadic motion is an involuntary eye movement that occurs when your brain is trying to draw in more information. The information can be visually evident or not. Many people will produce eye darts when visualizing something imaginary from memory. "Look-at" constraints are a relationship between the character's eyes and the object that they are looking at. This is usually in the form of a controller sitting out in space in front of the eyes. It is usually composed of three objects: a master controller, two controllers, one for each eye which is a child of the master eye controller. The individual eye controls give the animator the ability to cheat the gaze direction to the camera. Sometimes, to keep both eyes on camera and look correct, they must be oriented in an unnatural direction (if viewed from another camera angle). Eye look-at controls are often implemented in a character's local space relative to the head controller so that the eyes move with the head as expected and do not need to be counter-animated with the motion of the head. There should also always be the option to global constrain the position of the eye look-at controller to something else in the scene.

The motion of the eyes is quick and loaded with meaning. The subtle motion of the pupils as they dilate can tell a whole story in an instant. Luckily, eyes and eye controls are typically very portable systems and can be moved from character to character. This means that lengthy research and development for one character will have benefits for all the characters in a production.

8.8 INTERFACES FOR FACIAL ANIMATION

Because the face is a small area to work in, mapping out the regions and the systems implemented is critical. In many cases, one of the most effective techniques is a mix of blend shapes and joint-based transformations. Blend shapes provide direct access to the desired poses via a sculptural interface, while a point-based offset allows for those shapes to be additionally modified. This ability to hit an art-directed expression through blend shapes and to offset the shape with a point-based method allows the animator to generate asymmetry quickly and to create interesting in-between shapes that the linear interpolation of geometry morphing will not account for. With this in mind, the notion of high- and low-level controls comes into play. High-level controls allow you to manipulate multiple attributes for a system at one time to reach a descriptive goal. This might include a control that ranges from "happy" to "sad" which triggers all the needed underlying controls to reach the pre-defined mark. These high-level controls are often the starting point for an animator to block out expressions. Since high-level controls are merely manipulating, or non-destructively modifying attributes, an animator can drill down to low-level controls to tune individual attributes as desired.

In the same manner that the motion system for the body has an interface for animation, facial controls need a combination of ease-of-use and direct control of the high- and low-level controls. Typically, a camera is fixed to the face or parented to the head joint so that animators always have easy access to a front view of the characters face, no matter what configuration or position the body is in. User access to the controls is the next step. Much of this is preference or historical depending on who you talk to, but there are many schools of thought when it comes to facial controls. Some artists prefer controllers which reside directly on the face surface so that selecting and manipulating them will affect the face. Imagine the corner of the mouth having a controller associated with it; its motion in an upward direction triggers blend shapes for the position of the mouth corner to move up accordingly. Better yet, the motion of that controller moves a joint that the face surface is weighted to. No matter how the face is deformed, face controllers need to be accessible and move with the deformations of the face so that they remain unobstructed by surface geometry and always reside in a logical place (Figure 8.12).

Another form of interface is the control panel which is a non-renderable set of handles, or curves representing the elements of the face being controlled, that contain all available options for the user. This control set is often parented to the head but exists just beside it so that it can be easily seen in connection with the face geometry. The simplest form of interface is merely the attribute spreadsheet that lists all the controls associated with the face rig. While this is not the most intuitive control strategy, an experienced user can navigate an interface such as this quickly and efficiently. As the spreadsheet is the raw visualization of control attributes, it is usually accessible in tandem with other control systems.

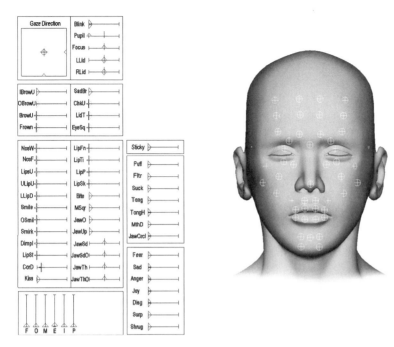

■ **FIGURE 8.12** Possible face interface. Model by Lee Wolland. Interface by Institute of Animation (Filmakademie Baden-Wuerttemberg).

8.9 **DYNAMICS AND SIMULATION**

The face goes through its contortions at a rapid rate and the anatomy of the face contains many regions that remain flexible. These two conditions result in a structure that jiggles, even slightly, as it goes through its motion. This secondary motion adds a subtle cue that the structure is alive and affected by forces in the world it inhabits. With this in mind, like deformations on the body, it is worthwhile to consider a dynamic simulation pass once animation is complete. Because the resulting face is geometry, all the same jiggle and post-animation spring dynamics developed for the body are possible and similar systems can be implemented. What is important to consider for the face is the ability to tone down simulated motion that interferes with the visemes for lip-sync or the general read of the emotions of the face. This involves mostly damping vibrations during moving holds where the character's motion is minimal. On the contrary, for a cartoon-styled character, the stretching and pulling of the face while in motion will need to be exaggerated for full effect.

8.10 REAL-TIME ENGINE CONCERNS

Facial animation shares the same limitations within a game engine as the body motion. Historically, facial animation has been the area most affected by the lack of support for deformers and, because of the fine detail required for effective facial motion, has been the area least developed for digital characters in games. Similarly, and possibly a consequence of this, games spend less time looking at faces with the player looking at the backs of their player's head as they run around. As we discussed with regard to deformations in real-time engines, there are a number of ways to work around this. It is entirely possible to have each vertex of the face mesh be attached to a joint. These joints could contain the motion required for each of the face shapes as triggered curves, thus baking the motion of the deformers to the motion of the joints. This essentially gives the game developers access to techniques such as blend shapes. When used in tandem with normal maps for wrinkles and other details, the quality of facial shapes can be very high.

8.11 CONCLUSION

For a character's face to fill a movie screen and convincingly convey emotion, it requires a sensitivity and understanding of all the factors going into that moment. For stylized characters, we have a chance to see into the mind of a fantastical character that is intended to make us laugh or cry (Figure 8.13). For realistic characters, we have the opportunity to travel to another place or time, that cannot be recreated in the real world, and feel through the emotions of a digital character. As has been stated repeatedly, human faces, as artists strive for realism, are one the hardest aspects of digital character technology to recreate, but there is positive direction with each research paper and production. It is inevitable that digital characters will eventually be visually indistinguishable from reality. Getting them to act right (and in real time) will be the hurdles beyond that.

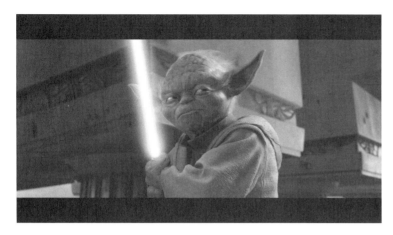

■ **FIGURE 8.13**   Yoda from "Star Wars Episode III - Revenge of the Sith" (2005). Courtesy of Lucasfilm Ltd. "Star Wars Episode III - Revenge of the Sith" copyright & trademark registered by 2005 Lucasfilm Ltd. All rights reserved. Used under authorization. Unauthorized duplication is a violation of applicable law.

The combination of motion systems, deformation systems, and the interplay of those components into facial setup all amount to a rigged character that is ready for animation. As we will see in the next part, there are many ways to create and attach motion to a rig depending on the type of project, production resources, and creator preference. What does not differ is that the time and effort that goes into the development of a digital character is nothing without the motion and acting that creates the performance.

8.12 **EXERCISE**

In this exercise, we go through the conceptual and technical process of creating a character facial setup. Split into groups of two or more. One of you is the animator, the other team members are the character setup artists. Follow the steps below.

8.1   Starting with the character you developed in the last section, sketch out a plan for the face shapes that the character needs to produce and your method for creating them.

8.2 List out the steps that need to be carried out to create the controls and deformations for the character's face.

8.3 The animator should find a piece of audio, break it down, and list out the shapes required to be created.

8.4 Implement the deformations, testing the results against your initial sketches from the first step.

8.5 The animator should begin lip-syncing the character's head to it. They should also provide feedback on the interface for animating and the shapes they are able to achieve or not.

8.6 Maintain this review/fix feedback loop until satisfied.

■ FURTHER READING

The controversial aspects of emotion classifying run the spectrum from Ekman's categorical model to Russell and Mehrabian's dimensional model:

Paul Ekman. An argument for basic emotions. In NL Stein and K Oatley, editor, *Basic Emotions*, pages 169–200. Lawrence Erlbaum, Hove, UK, 1992.

James A. Russell. Reading emotions from and into faces: Resurrecting a dimensional-contextual perspective. In James A. Russell and José M. Fernandez-Dols, editors, *The Psychology of Facial Expression*, pages 295–320, Cambridge University Press, Cambridge, 1997.

Albert Mehrabian and James A. Russell. *An Approach to Environmental Psychology*. MIT Press, Cambridge, MA, 1974.

A great practical overview into the theory and practice of face setup is Jason Osipa's "Stop Staring:"

Jason Osipa. *Stop Staring: Facial Modeling and Animation Done Right*. SYBEX Inc., Alameda, CA, 2007.

■ INTERVIEW: NICO SCAPEL, RIGGING SUPERVISOR, FRAMESTORE CFC

■ BIO

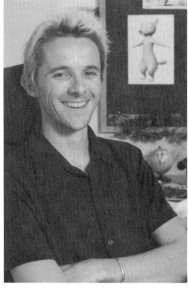

Nico Scapel, Rigging Supervisor, Framestore CFC

Nico Scapel works as Rigging Supervisor for Framestore, London, UK. Framestore is the largest visual effects and computer animation studio in Europe. Since 2001, he has worked for PDI/DreamWorks and DreamWorks Animation SKG, first as Character TD, then as Lead Character TD. His film credits include the Academy Award nominated "Shrek 2," "Madagascar," "Over the Hedge," and "The Chronicles of Narnia: Prince Caspian." In 2004, he received a DreamWorks Technical Achievement Award for developing the "Wig System." This patent-pending hair animation and simulation system has been used on five feature films and thousands of shots. Nico was also one of the driving forces in creating Dream-Works' next generation integrated rigging environment and supporting technologies. In his current role, Nico supervises a team of 20 Technical Directors. He and his group are set to deliver over a hundred creatures as well as all hair and cloth simulations for "The Tale of Despereaux," an animated feature based on the novel by Kate DiCamillo. In his free time, Nico is also an accomplished oil painter and percussionist.

■ Q&A

Q) *The components of character technology are diverse and span the artistic and technical spectrum. How did you get your start in the industry? Based on where you see the field heading what experience/training do you recommend people have?*

A) There is still no typical background for a Character Technical Director. Some universities are starting to provide a few specialized courses, but there is no specific degree yet and when I started, there were no courses at all covering rigging. However, there are specific skills that are probably the most useful in this case.

My background is in mathematics and graphics, which has proved very helpful. I have three Masters Degrees, starting in Engineering at Ecole Centrale in Paris, then Image Processing and Artificial Intelligence from Ecole Normale Superieure, and finally Computer Science and Graphics from Stanford University. I have always been equally attracted by technical and artistic fields, but it is still hard to find that mix in one university.

During my two years at Stanford, I was able to get that interdisciplinary mix that is, to myself, invaluable in working with digital characters. While studying programming and graphics, I was taking life drawing, sculpting, and animation classes and even took part in a 3D archeological reconstruction research project. My last project there was a 3D short film done with a team of ten students.

I still think there is a big value in getting a solid and eclectic technical foundation to be able to make a difference in the field of character technology. A lot of great ideas coming to this new field come from other disciplines. Rigging is slowly becoming more of an established craft, but the core ideas behind the most successful digital creatures are not software-specific and can be boiled down and recreated in any software environment. Having enough technical knowledge to make that step and extract ideas from various sources is a key advantage.

Q) *Creating compelling digital characters is part art and part science. What is the greatest challenge you encounter on a daily basis? What aspect of character technology keeps you up thinking at night?*

A) To me, the biggest challenge in rigging is to understand the animators' needs and boil it down to the most intuitive, efficient, and reliable rig possible. A rig must work in layers, and if the fundamentals do not work very well, a few cool features are not going to save the rig. At the end of the day, a rig is a piece of software, and the goal is to polish it so that animators can focus on the acting, not on bugs, workarounds, or performance limitations. In other words, you have to make the science work, so they can create some art.

As far as the technology, we are still far from being on solid ground, as we discover new techniques every day. The way to go forward is to always question whether you are using the best tools for the job you are trying to accomplish. Are you spending your time working around the software limitations, or are you spending it to define and improve the unique look and performance of the character? For example, the standard skinning approach, which is the most widespread for character deformations, is very unintuitive and does not offer a way to represent the elasticity of the skin, bone versus fat, volume preservation, etc. Most big studios have their own muscle and skin systems, but we still have two different approaches, inside-out (bones, muscles, skin) or outside-in (stretchy skin with different properties and influences). No matter what the approach is, the goal is to develop techniques where decisions are more visual (e.g., paint a map of where the skin is sliding, bony landmarks, fat jiggle, etc.) and less of a black box, like painting multiple bone influences one by one and deciding on relative percentages. And, this applies to photoreal as well as cartoony characters, as they all need physicality.

Q) *What are the ingredients for a successful digital character?*

A) An interesting backstory and key objectives, carried by a strong design. That is the recipe, but I think the secret to get a really good character is to break the rules somewhere by giving the character a truly exaggerated trait, a defining weakness, a sweet design flaw, some unresolved sadness. That leaves interesting room to develop the character arc. But, most importantly, the viewers react to it and develop feelings towards it. The last thing you want is indifference, and an all too-perfect hero can be easily forgotten.

Q) *While the industry is competitive, it is ultimately respectful of great work., Outside of the work you have been personally involved in the production of what animated characters have you been impressed or inspired by? What is the historical high-bar?*

A) Short films are raising the bar every year, and they are extremely impressive to me, especially knowing that they have been produced in very small teams. On top of my list would be "Ryan," the Oscar winning short film from Chris Landreth, which was done in collaboration with the University of Toronto. It is highly original and is particularly successful at portraying a complex and fragmented personality using visual metaphors.

Q) *Where do you see digital characters in ten years? Where are animated characters for film and games heading?*

A) In ten years, we will see a more established set of tools and techniques, and the most advanced tools will be in everyone's hands, similar to what has been happening in the realm of rendering. With advances in performance, we will be very close to have real-time, fully believable creatures with hair, fur, layers of clothing, skin dynamics, and the ability to interact with the environment and other creatures.

Actors will be available for hire in flesh and blood or as a 3D asset (with freedom to change their apparent age) and will be in even higher demand. Digital creatures will become completely ubiquitous, as game characters, avatars, brand representations, and film celebrities. They will also become an affordable tool for independent content producers willing to explore the boundaries of imagination. Digital creatures will have reached a stage where people will focus on their appeal and performance rather than their technical achievements, which means that they will be more established as an art medium and less as a novelty.

Chapter 9

Rig Synthesis

9.1 **INTRODUCTION**

Once the motion system, deformation system, and face have been designed and architected, there is a necessary step of combining all these interrelated aspects into a unified digital character rig. These systems should already be working well together, but this last stage is really about polishing and double-checking all the details. The synthesis of the rig also allows for the testing of all aspects of the character by the character setup artist and animators before it is released into production. This process of quality assurance allows minor and major bugs to be identified and fixed before any animation is tied to the state of the rig.

9.2 **THE RIG IN A SCENE**

If at all we forget all the functionality discussed thus far, the most basic function of the rig is to successfully load a character into a scene. The character must exist properly in the scene as dictated by the production guidelines or the established character pipeline. Whether by referencing or importing, the character must be able to be loaded into a scene and have keys set upon its controls and stored. At the rig import stage, it is critical to think about optimization in terms of rig interaction speed, as we have mentioned previously, and general file size.

Deleting stray nodes in the rig that have no functionality or purpose will help decrease file size and speedup load time. For one character this may not seem like a big deal, but one can imagine the benefits for a scene with many characters. Each node in the rig should be accounted for and uniquely named.

A character should exist in a scene inventory as a single node and all of the rig and model components should be children of this node. This "master," "all," or "god" node lives at the origin ($x = 0$, $y = 0$, $z = 0$). It is not only the hierarchical parent for the character but also acts as the inventory node that can be used to query that characters are in a scene. Attributes about the character and the character's name are often stored on this node. Within any animation system, the character's name must be unique. Therefore, it is a good idea to have the top-level node of the character along the lines of name_char so that the character is identified and noted as a character. Just the character's name will suffice. Often times, characters will have special attributes on their top-level node that define them as type "character." To create an inventory of characters that populate a scene, all top-level nodes with this character attribute can also be queried. Not only the character's name but also the nodes that make it up should be unique, so as to avoid any potential conflict with other characters or objects in the scene. Making sure that all of the nodes have meaningful names will make maintenance much easier down the line. As such, pre-pending the character's name to all of the nodes that make it up is an easy step to achieve uniqueness. Scripts are often written which analyze a rig to look for node names that repeat and potentially clash with nodes in other characters or itself. Utilities such as this are good to run at fixed intervals in character rig development.

Since this master node contains all the nodes of the character, and some of the nodes may have multiple influences on them, moving it may have unwanted effects on the rig, and therefore it is typically not moved. If the model is moved by the same node that the rig is moved by, then there is a double transform in cases where skinning is used as a method to attach a model to a rig. The skin is moved once by the transformation of its parent world space node and again by moving the joints that it is bound to. Other deformation models, including layered surface deformations, can have the same issue. Usually there is a world space node and coincident to this node and used to position the character in world space. This is often called "body," "world," or "root" and is the most top-level animation control (Figure 9.1). As such, models that are deformed by the rig are stored under the "all" node, but in a sibling group, its transformations are unaffected. Once a character rig is under a world space node, it is critical that the rig be tested away from the origin and rotated about all three axes. Doing this will quickly reveal hierarchy issues and even deformation issues that were not obvious when the character was at the origin. With regard to the motion system, if a node is not under the world space node, it will obviously be left behind, but sometimes less obviously, constraints that are not calculating the position of nodes properly will be revealed when the space they exist in has changed. Similarly, for deformations, points not weighted to a joint or other objects in the rig will remain about the origin as the character is moved away from it. It is a common practice for a rigger to include off-origin testing in the evaluation of the rig.

Another factor that a world space node figures into is the ability of the rig and character to scale uniformly in the scene. In many situations, a character will need to change size to

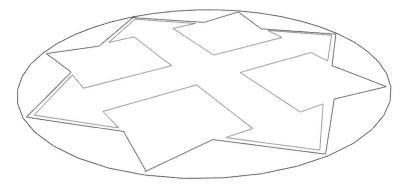

■ **FIGURE 9.1**   Top-level nodes are often visualized as a series of curves that can be selected.

play to the camera for shot composition, and as a result the rig should be able to scale. There are many reasons why a rig may not be able to scale properly, from the misplacement of nodes in the hierarchy and either inheriting the scale twice or not at all, or the composition of the rig may have elements which cannot scale. Some dynamic systems do not have the ability to scale uniformly or accurately because of the functions associated with them. In other cases, geometry which is used to attach joints might need to be specially placed in the hierarchy to scale appropriately. All efforts should be made to allow a rig to scale, and this functionality should be tested with the introduction of each system. This is one of those scenarios which can be very hard to fix without major changes to the rig architecture after the rig is finished. In a worst case scenario, the geometry cache for the rig is output and the resultant models are scaled as needed while the rig itself is not scaled. This is far from an ideal solution, but if the character does not need to make physical contact with other elements in the scene, it can be used to fix the lack of scale.

The control which moves the rig in world space is also the one used to attach the character to other objects in the scene. This is generically called "character parenting." For example, a moving prop, vehicle, or even another character can become a temporary parent of this node so that the character inherits its motion. Vehicles are an obvious example where the world space transformation of the character is carried out by another entity as the vehicle moves with the character on it. This basic principle of computer graphics can oftentimes lead to issues for complicated character rigs, and so it is necessary to test the functionality of a rig when parented to another object in the scene.

All aspects of the rig are fed into these top-level nodes. As such, they can also contain controls for rig visibility, character resolution display, or read/write status. Once the protocol for this node is established, all characters can share its functionality with each having its own set. As we will see in the next section, the functionality of all the systems that make up the rig should be tested as they become ready for animation.

9.3 **MOTION SYSTEM INVENTORY**

As we discussed previously, a motion system is a collection of interconnected elements that define the kinematics of a character rig. Each element is a system in its own right which must connect and interact with its adjoining systems. A humanoid motion system requires systems to control the arms, hands, legs, feet, spine (including the hips), neck, and head. A quadruped would include four leg systems structured to represent the type of leg required. Other anatomical elements such as wings and specialized feet or hands may be augmented on either standard humanoid bipeds or as building blocks for other animals. A tail-and-neck system might also need to be implemented. Returning to the subject of comparative anatomy, all mammals have legs with five major segments articulating at five major joints. Legs typically have a mirror image from front to back with corresponding joints bending opposite to each other. Certain animals like horses have an extended foot that gives them a lower leg segment similar in length to the other segments that gives them the appearance of walking on their tiptoes with their heels held high. These ideas are revisited to drive home the idea that no matter what the character is, the same rules apply and much of what we understand about our own kinematics can be ported to non-human or partial human characters. Whether they are biped, quadruped, or something different all together, the functionality of the rig should be consistent with more traditional characters, isolating idiosyncracy to where it is needed and relying on the familiar where possible.

These systems can be simple FK hierarchies with controls all the way up to complex multi-chain hierarchies controlled by custom constraints and multiple states of interaction. No matter how they are constructed, they need to be attached to other systems to function normally. As the pieces of the rig are combined into an integrated whole, switches that modify the space that elements exist in can be implemented. For example, an animator might want the shoulder of a character to be in the space of the hips for certain parts of the shot and the torso (as it would be normally) in other parts of the shot. This influences the space that the object operates in. Hand controls that are controlling IK are also good examples of this. Often these will be most beneficial in the space of the shoulders, and other times world space.

Control objects and the attributes they contain (Table 9.1) related to the position, rotation, and rig-specific attributes need to be keyed individually and often times together. An animator may want to key all the attributes of a control, those with the default values changed, or an entire system. This allows them to key the system they are positioning without needing to key all the specific attributes they may have to move unconsciously to achieve the pose. When multiple characters must be animated to interact, it is often useful to be able to key the controls for both characters at the same time. Thus, as the character contact is animated, such as in a fight scene, both characters can be posed simultaneously. Attributes are often collected into sets or bundles that can be keyed together. These collections of keyable controls are created by the character setup artist and are made to travel with the character rig into scenes. In an ideal scenario, giving the animators the ability to create their own collection of controls provides a lot of flexibility.

When the motion system is considered done, it should be sent to an animator to be tested. The animator should produce a short animation sequence that puts the rig through its paces. This gives the animator the opportunity to provide feedback as well as create a piece of animation that can be tested as rig modifications are made to see if the animation changes. An aspect that the animator should keep in mind is the rig consistency with other characters on the project. Is it intuitive and familiar? Are there any controls which do not work as expected? Do any of the controls not hold keys when the file is reopened? Another factor to test is the ability to export and import animation. This is something to be attempted using generic animation curves of a walk or run to see if generic cycle animation can be applied to the character. This is especially important for "variant" characters used in a crowd system.

Table 9.1 Sample Attributes on an Animation Control

r_hand_control	
Attribute	*Value*
TranslateX	5.6
TranslateY	3.2
TranslateZ	0.4
RotateX	6.5
RotateY	20
RotateZ	2.3
FKIK	1 (ik on)

Having a number of animated test shots is also necessary for testing and reviewing deformations.

9.4 **DEFORMATION SYSTEM INVENTORY**

Once the motion system is created, and while deformations are being architected, it is a good idea to build a test shot that includes your character going through a series of "exercises" that demonstrate the character transforming through a series of extreme poses. These poses should push the deformations to their limits and beyond and be used to iteratively develop the deformation system (Figure 9.2). With a consistent set of poses, progress can be reviewed and compared at intervals till completion. This test shot, in concert with any animation produced by an animator to test the motion system, can provide a good baseline for deformation review. The key features to look for when addressing deformations is volume preservation and the character staying "on-model."

Volume loss is common in areas of great deformations such as shoulders and hips that need to exhibit a wide range of motion. As points are rotated about a surface, they can be pulled inward and give the appearance that the area is deflating, especially when skinning is implemented as the deformation technique. In reality, the bone and muscle underlying the surface would prevent such things from happening and, as such, collision objects are often placed to stop these regions from collapsing and to preserve volume. With regard to staying "on-model," this is something to be analyzed at every frame of test animations when evaluating deformations. There can be no point, even in extreme motion, if deformations do not represent the designed character. If the character does not appear as itself, then a solution must be found to bring the character back "on-model."

Debugging deformations means looking for not only the loss of volume but also the smoothness of the deformations in motion. When collisions are used to preserve regions, there is a possibility of vertices popping from frame to frame as the collisions are calculated. This is, of course, visible in the

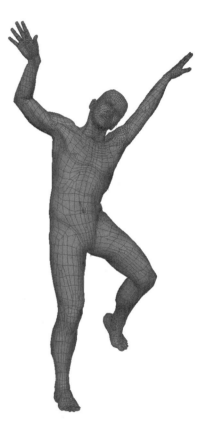

■ **FIGURE 9.2** Silly as they may look putting the rig through a series of extreme-pose exercises is an ideal way to test deformations while in development. Model by Lee Wolland.

animation of the character and may also impact other systems or elements informed by that surface. When collision-related popping occurs, the first thing to do is to check if that collision is actually giving you desirable results in general situations. This is always valuable to check as removing a collision calculation is a major optimization to the speed of a rig. If this is an isolated incident, then the calculating "pad" that surrounds the surface can be increased to provide a more gentle falloff for this specific shot. The pad is essentially an offset from the actual collision surface that can have an adjustable falloff distance. If the pad value is animatable, then if can be eased on around the time of popping and then eased off as needed. These per-shot fixes are unavoidable when collisions are part of the deformation system.

Since deformations are the end result of a series of systems and influences which start with the model, and run through the motion system and whatever tools are used to create the deformations, it is essential to be able to look at a region or single vertex of the deforming mesh and be able to follow its influences back to a non-deformed state. Being able to quickly isolate the influence or collection of influences that are impacting the region in question allows the solution to be reached more quickly. Being able to turn on and off special controls which might affect the deformations via the motion system, such as stretch, is also helpful. Since stretch is usually implemented as functions or connections on transform nodes or surfaces at the motion system level, these features can often be overlooked in the deformation debugging process.

Since part of the development of the motion system is the creation of stand-in geometry, it is important that this stand-in geometry reasonably matches the deformations when implementing them. Any model changes that were undertaken in response to the deformations and change in the shape of the model should be reflected in an update to the stand-in geometry that the animator sees.

As with body deformations and motion system, the character's face system must be reviewed and tested before it can go into production.

9.5 **FACE SYSTEM INVENTORY**

Depending on the way the character model was built, the synthesis step at the end may require some special work to attach the face system to the rest of the body. In the past, the head was treated as a separate model and the vertices at the border of the body and head needed to match up and seam perfectly. These vertices needed to be exactly coincident (existing at the same exact point in space), have the same normal direction, and be deformed by exactly the same influences. If any one of these factors were off, a seam would be evident in the deformation and the surfacing of the character model. This is still a valid way to work but the trend leads toward a fully integrated single mesh, or separate meshes that locally affect certain parts of a single mesh model. With the final model being a single mesh, the risk of a seam between the head and the body is eliminated. No matter what the solution is, care must still be taken in the neck region (Figure 9.3) which acts as an interface between the body deformation system and the face deformation system. Sometimes a layered surface at that region can act to smooth the effects between the systems. Other times, some

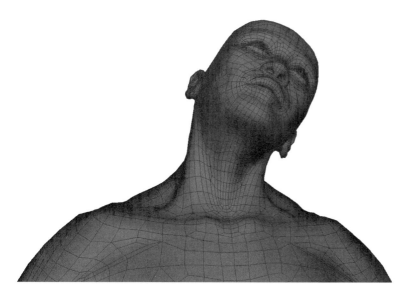

■ **FIGURE 9.3**   The neck is a complicated region at the boundary of the body deformation and face systems. Model by Lee Wolland.

careful weighting or a small deformation joint set driven by the respective systems can act as a blended result to insure that the neck benefits from both influences.

Once the face, neck, and body have been integrated, it is important to test that the effects of deformers that might carry over from the body onto the face do not impact them in a negative way. Due to the discrete nature of these systems, this is rarely an issue. For example, a relaxation algorithm that is applied to the body to smooth out deformations could be through the integration of systems propagated to the face. Relaxation algorithms iteratively smooth out regions by averaging the motion of vertices across their surrounding vertices. Because this changes the resultant shape, something of this nature could lessen the expected effect of blend shapes as it ends up being the target shape plus the effect of the relaxation.

If blend shapes have been implemented as part of a face system, it is paramount to have a plan to manage them through the pipeline. Because blend shapes are offsets from default vertex positions, they can be stored because these offset values as opposed to the models that were used to create them. In many animation systems, once the blend shapes have been added to the rig, the models that they were derived from can be deleted. The blend shapes still work, the file is now smaller and more lightweight as it moves through the pipeline, and the shapes are now protected from accidental modification. The original shapes can be stored in a "workshop" version of the file that the modelers and riggers have access to but not the published file that is shipped into production.

Testing the face rig is similar to testing body deformations. Test shots should be created to exercise a range of face shapes going through all the visemes, key emotional states, and that put the character through a short performance shot where they must lip-sync and emote at the same time. Eyes should be tested for tracking and expressiveness all the way through the surfacing and rendering stage as much of the communication of the eyes is affected by the materials applied to them. The interpolation of the face through extreme shapes will also test the interoperability of the controls making sure that they work together as expected. Again, as with a body, making sure that low-resolution animation control meshes reasonably match the high-resolution output is a noteworthy step. But thanks to the increases in processing speed, it is increasingly common for animators to pose with a high-resolution mesh, making an animation control mesh less important as compared to an intuitive control for the final mesh.

9.6 **DOCUMENTATION**

At larger facilities where many people will be using a rig and the work has the possibility of existing through multiple projects, documentation of the rig is critical. This can be as simple as a few notes about what makes this rig different from standard rigs at that facility to a detailed manual that can be modified by the community using the asset. Oftentimes, documentation is a spin-off of the initial specification that was developed for the creation of the rig. This document would have outlined the features and functionality that was desired for the motion system plus descriptions, ideally with images, of the key poses that the designers have envisioned for the character. As the specification evolves into documentation, it takes on the role of animator reference. Often incorporating short demonstration videos, images, and text descriptions to describe the functionality of the rig, the documentation should provide a clear and organized overview of the rig.

When implemented like a Wiki or other community-driven document, animators and character setup artists alike can modify it as needed. This then becomes a live and evolving document that is more up-to-date than static pages that might fall behind in the heat of production. These documents inevitably go out-of-date, but if maintained, they can be useful to new employees or team members and are often good augmentation for classes.

Whether it was built procedurally or through an existing animation system, a character rig is ultimately a piece of software. As such, like any piece of software, it will go through quality assurance (QA) and through all the stages of development, and at times rigs will be described as being in "alpha," "beta," or "release" stages with accompanying version numbers to keep track of revisions. As we described before, QA essentially is just the testing and revision cycle of the rig to make sure that it is working as expected and functions within the established or proposed animation pipeline and export if needed.

9.7 **REAL-TIME ENGINE CONCERNS**

Once the rig is synthesized into a complete package, it is time to test the elements needed to export it into the engine being used on the production. This usually involves developing a set of joints that the engine expects, constrained to the proper joints in the animation rig (Figure 9.4). The motion of these game export joints are then baked for the number of frames in the shot and exported to the appropriate format. Most game engines have detailed specs for what is expected or, more increasingly, provide export tools to go from established animation systems directly to the proper format. Because there are limits to the number of weights that can be applied to the skinning of any vertex of a polygonal model, it is mandatory to review that the animation and deformations are best represented at the moment of export. In addition, from a pipeline point of view, issues to watch out for include name conflicts in the engine for multiple characters. This should be addressed in the setup and export stage.

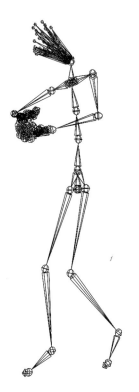

■ **FIGURE 9.4** The rig exported to the game engine includes a stripped-down set of joints representing the body and the face.

9.8 **CONCLUSION**

The synthesis of the rig into a unified whole brings us to the end of our discussion of pure character technology. As a high-level overview of all the concepts related to character setup, we have touched on the anatomical underpinnings of the character motion system, the various techniques possible in building the character deformation system, and the requirements behind a character facial setup. The challenges of first learning this material is understanding the relationship between all the systems and the cause and effect of all the component pieces. It is very easy to create your first rig with a few joint chains, some simple constraints to handle IK, bind the whole thing to the model, paint a few weights and call it done. This is the way most people start, and usually things go horribly wrong the first time. Those who want to understand how to make it better often get hooked on the subject of rigging, those who find it overly frustrating often look back on their initial rigging experience with the desire to never do it again. The advice I offer is to start over and try it again. Your second rig will be better than your first and they will keep getting better. As you work with animators to get feedback, demand more from your own rigs, or work with more experienced riggers, your rigs will develop more functionality, ease of use, and complexity. You will also gain more confidence in fixing issues that come up. As said previously, a large percentage of the character setup artist's job is maintenance of the rig as it moves through production.

With the rig in place and tested within a scene and with the production pipeline, it is time to apply animation to bring it to life. All this work leads up to animation in its many modern forms.

9.9 **EXERCISE**

In this exercise, we get a character ready for the production pipeline and go through the process of QA to make sure it is production-ready. Split into groups of two or more. One of you is the lead character setup artist, the other team members are the character setup artists who must work as a team to move this rig into production. If someone in the team can be designated as an animator, it is optimal. Follow the steps below.

9.1 Collect all the nodes in your scene under a single group that defines its position in world space. Create groups for the geometry, the rig, and possibly for other nodes that may or may not fall under the world transformation node of the rig. Move the rig off the origin and keep an eye out for objects that move away from the character. These have double transforms on them and this needs to be fixed.

9.2 Have one of the character setup artists (or the animator) run the rig through a series of exercises to test out the controls and to evaluate the deformations.

9.3 If time allows, the animator should also try to produce a short animation of the character in action doing something which might be typical of it.

9.4 Schedule two review meetings where the supervisor evaluates the performance of the rig in conjunction with the team. The supervisor prioritizes what needs to be fixed and what might not be clear about the rig interface and results. A list of fixes is produced.

9.5 With each iteration, emphasis should go on fixes that preserve the animation and test scenes produced. Notes about deformations and user interface should also be implemented.

9.6 Maintain this review/fix feedback loop until satisfied.

■ FURTHER READING

The references described in the previous chapters should still be a guide through this synthesis stage but it might also be helpful to wrap your head around some of the concepts behind software project management:

Jennifer Greene and Andrew Stellman. *Applied Software Project Management*. O'Reilly Media, Inc., Cambridge, MA, 2005.

This is also a good point to pause and take stock of the work that has been done on character technology. "Making of" featurettes on DVDs, books that document the creation or art of a film or game, and articles that might provide more in-depth coverage on the creation of digital characters in production are all good sources. In particular:

CG Channel is a great on-line resource for production articles geared more towards animation:

http://www.cgchannel.com

Gamasutra is another great on-line resource but is specific to video game production:

http://www.gamasutra.com

Cinefex Magazine is also an industry standard for deep coverage of the making of films and visual effects.

Part 3

Animation Technology

Introduction to Animation Technology

Complex digital characters and the architecture built to drive them would be meaningless without the ability to make them move. Animation breathes life into these systems, and whether it is driven by a talented animator, a motion-captured performer, or a procedural system, the skill required is formidable and the technology underlying these techniques is advancing rapidly. In this section, we explore the curves created by animators, capture of human performance, and code used to express complex motion for layering these techniques into the character performance required.

10.1 DEFINITIONS OF ANIMATION

As we stated earlier, the word "animation" at its most basic means "physically or graphically moving," and an animated character could be said to have had the divine or magic wind (animus) breathed into it. In this section, we cover the many aspects of introducing motion onto a character rig. All the techniques covered in this section are forms of animation. Types of digital animation:

Keyframe Animation The creation of character motion by means of hand-creating character poses from action to action and controlling the interpolation between those actions.

Motion Capture Also termed as "performance capture," it refers to the recording of motion data from live performance, which is then used to drive the character rig.

Procedural Animation The creation of character motion by means of code or simulation so that the animation system drives the frame-to-frame motion based on user-defined parameters.

Purists will argue that only traditional, hand-generated (even by computer) animation is real animation. Procedural animation, which is generated through the execution of code, is seen as a different entity altogether. Procedural motion should never be seen as a replacement for animation but as a complement or solution to issues of character volume in a scene. Motion capture, on the other hand, where a live performance is captured and applied to a character, is often thought of as something more imposing. Animators often fear that motion capture will put their jobs at risk. There is a belief that directors see the motion produced by a motion capture performer as providing them with instant results; thus, they direct their animated characters exactly like the way they direct live actors. Because motion capture records and injects reality into the character instantly, a digital character takes on hyper-real motion and behavior. Often times, the result is off-putting to people, likely inducing Mori's "Uncanny Valley" phenomenon. The truth is motion capture is a tool that is critical to realistic capturing of motion for characters intended to be integrated with live-action actors. It provides a baseline of motion that animators may build upon for realistic digital characters as in the case of Gollum from "The Lord of the Rings." As motion capture technology becomes more advanced, it will be possible to record more refined performances. Fine detail regions such as the face and hands will be captured with all the subtlety that we see in humans and make its way into our digital characters.

None of this will replace keyframe animation. While movies like "Beowulf" (2007) will push the art of performance-based animation, they are a very different animal from a movie like "Ratatouille" (2007). Motion capture, as it stands now, does not have the nuance of real motion nor does it have the caricature of keyframe animation. The embodiment of an animator in a digital character creates a very different, some would argue more subtle, performance than the application of motion capture. Where a motion capture performance manipulates parts of the rig, everything else must be controlled through triggered proceduralism or through the hand of the animator. This disconnect does not exist in fully keyframed animation which relies on the animator as actor from beginning to end of the character's performance. Many characters will require hand animation entirely, some could be a mix of motion capture and keys, others entirely procedural motion. The decision is based on project types, budget, time line, and aesthetics. One solution is to develop characters that take multiple streams of motion data and mixing and matching animation techniques to find ways of building up the desired performance from multiple sources.

10.2 **INTEGRATION OF ANIMATION TECHNIQUES**

Motion is created in a multitude of ways. Motion capture is often used as a reference for hand-keyed animation in the same way that animators would rotoscope film footage to capture the subtlety of human motion. This, however, is rare. What is more common, as we have discussed, is the layering of hand animation on top of motion capture data or procedural animation to create a blended performance. This notion of motion mixing and input blending is very similar to film editing where a scene is built up from the montage of shots to create a unified whole. The difference is that all of this editing is manifested as output on the character rig. This can be accomplished in the non-linear animation editing or on the rig itself.

In the non-linear animation editing stage, each control gets the result of the current edit of motion through the blending on animation curves for each region of the body. This is accomplished through a process of joint definition and characterization where rig controls are associated with like animation curves on all the incoming animation tracks. Once characterized and associated with each other, the motion of the arm, as controlled by animation, can be blended and edited with the action as derived from motion capture. This mixing and matching of tracks and clips of motion treats the character rig as the playback device performing the results of the editing operations. Similarly, the rig itself can be created with overrides and regions of blended output. Through the construction of an intelligent hierarchy of nodes, portions of the rig can be controlled by different streams of data or the weighted average of multiple streams at once. In this way, the animation all exists on the rig itself and streams are utilized, muted, or blended with other streams as needed. Both of these methods produce the same results and are really just work flow differences for getting multiple streams of animation data working synchronously on a character rig. They give the director and the animator choices when it comes time to finalize a shot. Often, motion capture data is too high frequency and needs to be dampened by more smoothly interpolated animation. The inverse is also possible. It is very rare that a shot will have a full motion capture performance and an animation performance, so, more often, if motion capture or procedurally generated motion does not hit the mark expected or desired, then it is animated on top to finalize the shot.

10.3 INTERFACES FOR ANIMATION

Animation is a time-intensive process and a grueling amount of work for the artist. The interface that an animator uses can be the bane of its existence. The animator's desk is very different today than in the past, when it contained an animator's light table with its pegs to register animation frames. These days, animators might still have those off to the side for use in preliminary pencil work for a shot, but the tools used in general production are similar to those used in any setting where a computer is in use. Digital animation, like so many activities undertaken by humans using computers, is usually created via a mouse and keyboard interface. Tablets and tablet PCs, with their gestural stylus interface and software to recreate natural media, are also making in roads as an interface for 3D animation and as a replacement for the traditional light table for hand drawn animation. Animators manipulate components of the rig and set keyframes on their transformations and attributes over time using these tried and true user interface devices. Keyframes are the starting or ending positions of an animated transition and adjusting the distance between them changes the timing with which they occur. As we will see later, there is, the possibility of live and recorded performance of a live performer through motion capture.

These tools will likely remain the standard for the immediate future. Looking forward, research is focusing on methods for providing animators with alternative interfaces to produce animation. Apparati, such as mixing board systems for facial animation and performance rigs like the ones used by the Jim Henson Company, provides a more tactile and real-time, performance-driven interface. While these are not ideal for all productions, they are, like motion capture, a way to bring real-time gesture to the animation production. Animators often miss the tactile gesture of drawing in 3D animation. Animators, and artists in general, traditionally create quick gesture drawings to capture the essence of a pose. A few prototype systems have been developed that allow an animator to sketch out the pose of a character and for the system to adjust the character articulations to propose a fit to match it. This is a difficult problem to solve because a 2D drawing can be ambiguous as to how it should result in a 3D articulation, but when implemented could be a boon to animators. A few examples have surfaced in which the artist draws a stick figure depiction and the 3D character fits itself to a pose. Much of the work in this area deals with the sketch-based posing of a human body. This is a good place to start as the rigid limbs of the human body once defined can be fit to the like-length portions of the sketch based on an analysis of the figure in the image. "3D Character Animation Synthesis from 2D Sketches" (2006) [24] by Yi Lin of University of Waterloo is a good example of work in this area. There is also research going on the animation of faces such as the case of "Sketching Articulation and Pose for Facial Animation" (2006) [6] where Edwin Chang and Odest Chadwicke Jenkins of Brown University implemented a system that converted sketched lines into poses for a rigged facial setup. While no commercial equivalent has emerged and no animation studio has formerly presented such interfaces in production, this is no doubt on the horizon. This is paradigm-shifting technology and a bridge between traditional techniques and modern interface.

■ FURTHER READING

Yi Lin. 3D character animation synthesis from 2D sketches. In *GRAPHITE '06: Proceedings of the 4th International Conference on Computer Graphics and Interactive Techniques in Australasia and Southeast Asia*, pages 93–96, ACM Press, New York, NY, 2006.

Edwin Chang and Odest C. Jenkins. Sketching articulation and pose for facial animation. In *SCA '06: Proceedings of the 2006 ACM SIGGRAPH/Eurographics Symposium on Computer Animation*, pages 271–280, Eurographics Association, Aire-la-Ville, Switzerland, 2006.

Chapter

Traditional Animation Techniques

Traditional animation refers to the means of creating moving images frame-by-frame without the assistance of a computer. This encompasses hand-drawn animation, stop-motion puppetry, and any imaginable technique that uses traditional media over time. In many ways, modern digital 3D animation has a lot in common with stop-motion animation. The processes of modeling, surfacing, rigging, cinematography, animation, and lighting are very analogous. Modeling may involve making a sculptural character out of clay. The model may actually be built around a metal armature that serves as the character rig. The model is painted and adorned with clothing and other accessories. The camera is placed along with the lights, and characters are animated. This all sounds remarkably like modern 3D animation.

The fundamentals of character animation, however, were devised on paper for the purposes of hand-drawn animated characters. While animation is surrounded by strong historical figures and its origins are diverse and worldwide, it is worth delving into Walt Disney Studios pioneering and defining work to set the stage for how motion is applied to digital characters.

11.1 CLASSIC PRINCIPLES OF ANIMATION

Animation was not a particularly new medium when Walt Disney introduced Mickey Mouse in 1928 with "Steamboat Willy" (1928), but his research and development on how to make characters emote was innovative. Disney and his early animators studied animals and people, used rotoscope and developed technology to take the art of animation to another level, and made it possible for them to produce animation on a large scale. As Disney collected motion and expression into a set of personality types, he and his animators defined these characters, no matter what form they took, for a generation. Along with these personality types, and even more important to modern animators, they outlined the definitive set of animation principles in "The Illusion of Life" [37]. As we look at the traditional principles of animation as an example, we can discuss the ways these principles are implemented for modern digital characters. In a 3D animation system, the gestures and arcs that Disney's Nine Old Men defined take a more controlled and calculated positioning of character elements than the gestures inherent with pencil on paper, but the principles apply equally. In fact, because of the inherent rigid nature of 3D animation, these rules play an even larger role. The application of traditional principles to modern 3D digital animation is a challenge for every 3D animator. John Lasseter [21] spent some of his early days at Pixar helping to develop tools that would allow himself and the other animators there to have the ability to apply these principles to their work. Since then, animators have added other steps to this process, and as character setups have become capable of performing difficult deformation procedures, such as squash and stretch, there is a decreasing discrepancy between what has been typically created in 2D and 3D with regard to formal character animation.

Squash and stretch is the notion that as an object moves, its shape changes reacting to the force of the movement. In doing so, it compresses and stretches, preserving the volume of the character shape. Both the axial body and the appendages react to the notion of squash and stretch and can be thought of as a scale along the axis that is aligned with the motion. For elements of a digital character, one can imagine that when something is scaled up in the y axis, it must be scaled down in the x and z axes to stretch. Conversely, scaling something down in y axis would require that the object be scaled up in x and z axes, giving the impression that the object is squashing. The setup for stretching characters varies and ranges from scaling joints, translating joints, or even a post-process on the model itself at the deformation level.

Anticipation is the announcement of an action before it happens. It is the wind-up before the pitch. It allows the viewer to get a sense of the flow of motions, with each motion anticipating the next and presenting a clear performance. A character rig should have the ability to bend and move in all directions equally. The arch of the spine should be flexible enough for the typical bend to be anticipated with a curve at the reverse angle even for a few frames. This often requires that the animator be able to do things that the character setup artist might not have anticipated. Of course, anticipation of an action happens at the pose level, but every control should be available to move a part of that character in the "broken" direction to some degree.

Staging is the most general principle that deals with the cinematography and framing of the action. The emphasis here is in making sure that the intended idea is clear to the viewer watching the scene. For digital characters, the position of the render camera has the same effect on the audience as it does for live-action actors in films. The position of the camera creates a relationship between the actors on screen and their relationship to each other, the set, and our view of them. The distance from the camera has direct impact on digital characters as well. A character that is at a substantial distance from the camera will not need the same amount of resolution as a character that is in the foreground of a shot. Model resolution, texture resolution, density of hair, and quality of cloth simulation are all issues related to the notion of distance-based level-of-detail (LOD). LOD is essentially an optimization step that attempts to minimize the weight of the scene and the length of rendering. It is particularly important in game engines where processing power is at a premium. Many of these decisions reside in the character setup as switches that can be automated based on the character's distance from the camera. This is especially important when it comes to crowd scenes where a large number of digital characters will fill the screen. Automated LOD allows those character to be optimized both with regard to screen presence and computational execution.

Straight ahead action and pose to pose are the two main approaches to animation from the point of view of production. Straight ahead action is produced frame-by-frame from the start by the animator deciding the motion as they go, always keeping the end goal in mind. Pose to pose is the laying out of key poses then working out the in-between poses that fall between them. It is more typical among modern digital animators because of the non-destructive, non-linear nature of animation systems, which lends itself to this work flow. Modern animation systems also inherently interpolate the transitions from pose to pose based on the curve associated with the keys. The spacing of those poses on the animation time line informs the timing of the action. As we will discuss later, the type of interpolation chosen for the keys will dictate the transition from key to key.

Follow through and overlapping action are complementary concepts. Follow through is the termination part of an action. In throwing a ball, the hand continues to move after the ball is released. In the movement of a complex object, different parts of the object move at different times and at different rates. In walking, for example, the hip leads, followed by the leg, and then the foot. As the lead part stops, the lagging parts continue in motion. Heavier parts lag farther and stop slower. Antennae of an insect will lag behind the body and then move quickly to indicate the lighter mass. Overlapping means to start a second action before the first action has completely finished. This is meant to keep the interest of the viewer since there is no dead time between actions. The ability to manipulate parts of the rig independently of others makes the addition of overlapping action easier to add to a shot. Typically an animator will, for example, want to be able to control the character's hips and not have them affect the upper body. This independent region control allows an animator to modify the motion of one region without impacting another so that motion can be overlapped.

Slow in and slow out refers to the spacing of the in-between frames at maximum positions. It is the second- and third-order continuity of motion of the object. Rather than having a uniform velocity for an object, it is more appealing, and sometimes more realistic, to have the velocity vary at the extremes. This is due to our expectations regarding physics and how an object moves, or appears to move, in the real world. For example, a bouncing ball moves faster as it approaches or leaves the ground and slower as it approaches or leaves its maximum position. The name comes from having the object or character "slow out" of one pose and "slow in" to the next pose. In traditional animation, the speed of actions was based on the number of drawings. In modern digital animation systems, the timing of poses can be shifted around easily and shots can be re-timed in a non-destructive manner.

Arcs are the visual path of action for natural movement. Even the fastest motion should happen in curves. In a digital system, as keys are laid out, the curves that represent the path of the action should be separate from the curve that defines the timing of the in-betweens. Spline-based interpolation naturally creates curves between a small number of keys. For non-character objects, curves can be drawn in the scene and objects can be attached to them so that the arcing path can be refined and tuned based on the timing desired.

Secondary action is an action that directly results from another action and can be used to increase the complexity and interest in a scene. It should always be subordinate to, and not compete with, the primary action in the scene. Secondary action is where modern animation systems make up for some of the challenges that they create as this motion can be computed automatically. Secondary motion usually includes all the accessory pieces to the main performance and often is contained in props and clothing. Elements such as clothes, tails, hats, swords and the like can be setup or programmed to move dynamically based on the actions of the main character. If simulation is too costly in terms of time and computation investment, then simple expressions can be created to move these objects based on the motion of other parts of the body or to lag behind these main motions.

Timing for an animator, as in comedy, is something that is part honing a skill and part innate talent. For animation, timing is the spacing between keyframes which sets the tempo of the action and speed of the movements. The more the in-betweens that exist within key poses, the slower the action will appear. One or two in-betweens results in almost immediate transitions between key poses. As stated earlier, the spacing of keys in an animation system is easily edited both at the pose and at the individual element level. This does not make the animator's natural sense of timing any less valuable, but it does make their jobs a little easier.

Exaggeration accentuates the essence of an idea via design and action. This is often what is meant when an action is "made bigger" or the moment is said to be "over-the-top." It applies to everything from a single movement, to the arc of a motion, to a sequence of events. Often, exaggeration is used to communicate a motion more clearly by amplifying it. Since exaggeration lies in the performance and the natural extension of the rig's potential, the setup artist should need to do very little to accommodate this principle. One aspect to keep in mind is the character's face. Most of the time, facial controls are created with the possibility of achieving more range than is exposed to the animator or set in the default range. By ensuring that values outside of the typical range for a character are reasonable and exposing them for use during moments of exaggeration or anticipation gives animators a lot more freedom.

Appeal is about creating a design or an action that the audience enjoys watching, in the same vein of an actor bringing charisma to their performance. While not strictly a motion principle, it is always important to question the appeal of a character's design and performance. Even villains need appeal and this comes down to original character design and the execution of the model. The implementation of an appealing set of shapes for the face to achieve is in the domain of the character rig, but much of this still relies on the design of the character and the appeal of the character's performance as determined by the animation.

11.2 **CURVES AND INTERPOLATION**

Animation is based on curves. A node's position or rotation in space over time creates a series of points in a cartesian space as it moves, forming a curve for each channel, usually defined by transformation axis such as translation z or rotation y of movement. During playback, that node travels from point to point based on the interpolation of that curve. The nature of the animation varies widely depending on this interpolation type, and therefore, the curve type selection is an imperative decision. Since curves are defined by points and interpolation, they are easily described, edited, and communicated through an animation system. Interpolation is the method of constructing new data points within the range of a discrete set of known data points (Figure 11.1). Thus depending on the interpolation, the curve will construct a different path to follow from one point to the next.

Each point on a curve has an in-tangent and an out-tangent. The in- and out-tangents define how the curve enters and leaves the point and are usually depicted graphically as two vectors originating at the point. The angle of these tangents will modify the direction of the curve based on interpolation. Often times, animators, when animating in the preferred pose-to-pose style, will plot out key frames with a stepped, non-interpolated curve so that they never rely on interpolation from one pose to the next. Poses are the foundation of animation and define the key moments in the course of the action of the shot. They are critical not only for composition but are also used to block out a shot and to work out

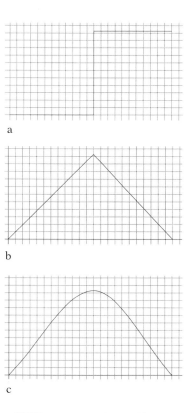

a

b

c

■ **FIGURE 11.1**   Curve with stepped, linear, and spline interpolation.

the timing based on the time between poses. The out-tangent of points on a stepped curve is flat; thus the curve segment is horizontal so that the values change at keyframes without gradation or interpolation from one to the next. This lets them focus on the silhouette of the poses and to "spline out" the motion later. Splining is akin to what traditional animators refer to as in-betweening or "tweening." Splining out an animation curve involves changing the interpolation type to a spline-based interpolation and plotting out the in-betweens that occur. Specifying a spline tangent creates an animation curve that is smooth between the key before and the key after the selected key. The tangents of the curve are colinear as both are at the same angle. This ensures that the animation curve smoothly enters and exits the key. If tangents are not colinear, a discontinuity will occur not in position but in velocity (the derivative of position), producing artificial-looking motion. A side effect of this interpolation is that the position of the object may overshoot the position of the key in order to smooth in and out of its position. This is detrimental for characters where an interpolation such as this could cause the feet to pass through the ground plane or miss hand contact with an object. Many studios will implement their own brand of curve interpolation to satisfy the demands of animation. For example, the Catmull-Rom spline is defined as a spline curve where the specified curve will pass through all the control points. Similarly, a clamped Bezier-spline curve passes through the first and the last control points but the others are not actually passed through unless the previous or successive control point is tangent to it.

11.3 DRIVING VERSUS DRIVEN MOTION

The determination of a character in a scene can be defined by how the motion is carried through the action. One way to break this down is to make a distinction between driving and driven motion. Driving motion is where the character is the one applying weight to the objects or other characters in the scene, while driven animation is defined by the character being influenced by the other elements in the scene.

This is not a scene description but is worth considering when thinking about animation and the selection of controls used in a scene. Driving motion typically comes from the root joints, thus driving the child joints as it moves, as in FK. Driven motion, on the other hand, comes from the manipulation of end effectors and can often have a spline interpolated look about it. A character walking, particularly the motion of the arms, is usually animated with FK as this motion is driving motion originating from the shoulders. IK, in this regard, has the appearance of looking "floaty" or without weight often requiring careful selection of the interpolation type, but more importantly, the timing of keys set on these goals.

11.4 CLIP-BASED ANIMATION

As is common for video games and for multi character animation systems used for crowds, animations are collected into clips which are stored in a library for reuse. A clip is a collection of curves describing a discrete character action stored on disk and triggered by the animation system as needed. It is a building block for a reusable library of motions. For example, generic motions such as clapping, waving, and cheering would be collected and maintained by a company making sports games. Small clips are often looped, such as walks and run cycles, while more specific motions must be blended into these loops. Loops are often used as a base to layer a unique performance on top of. An animator might start with a cycle then spin off a variation on it either to create a new loop or a discrete non-looping motion. A loop is simply a collection of discrete motions which start and end in the same pose. As mentioned previously, a walk cycle is one of the most common loops and is also an exercise that every animator does time and time again. Typically, these are done using local motions so that the character does not travel through space and thus remains in one spot. Translation is then applied to the character and the cycle is sped up or slowed down to match the rate of translation. This higher level translation is important for characters walking along unlevel or uneven ground so that they can be constrained to the ground and walk as needed. In scenarios such as this, constraints can be built which orient the body and feet to a natural position relative to the angle of the ground. Constraints can also be developed for attaching a particular motion to an object, such as a character climbing a ladder.

On top of cycles and constrained actions, the motion clip library can also have specific non-looping actions that can be applied. These actions would be blended into the existing motion. Blending involves creating an overlapping transition from one action to another. It is carried out on a joint-by-joint or control-by-control basis but is usually cataloged and managed on a character element or whole character level. Creating a normalized blend creates a bridge between motions so that each component of the motion is interpolated smoothly from one state to another (Figure 11.2). Smooth curves are created between the blend points and the blend value travels along those points to generate the transition. Interpolation is a simple process that cannot easily predict the interpenetration of character elements from pose to pose, like a character's arm passing through its body. Having body regions be "mutable" meaning that you can turn off clips on a per-region basis allows for edits to be made to

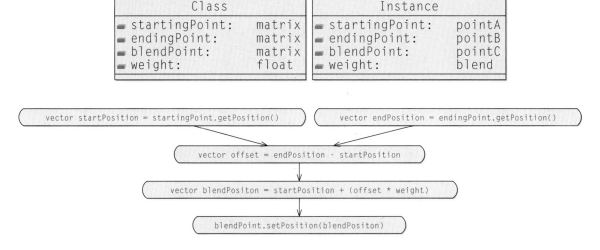

■ **FIGURE 11.2** Class, data, and method for a blending positions.

the animation of a subset of the character. For the most part, states to be blended must be fixed regionally, or clips must be carefully chosen so as to work smoothly together. At a lower level, poses can be stored as well. Poses are single frame snapshots of a character. In some cases, an animator may need to go in and manually adjust the transition to be more natural or add an in-between pose or clip if the motions are different enough that they cannot be naturally interpolated between each other.

11.5 **SOUND**

One component of production that has been tied to animation since the early days is sound. Although tied to all facets of modern animation and game production, since the production of Disney's "Steamboat Willie" (1928) animators have made particularly good use of sound. No matter how motion is produced, sound is a critical compliment and some would argue an essential component to animation. Lip-sync, of course, can not be undertaken until the voice actors work is complete. Taken a step further, sound effects help to accentuate and punctuate motion. Simple events such as a character walking benefit greatly from the synchronized sound of footsteps. In addition, sound helps to enhance the mood of the moment and the characterization of the actor. By creating theme music for a character or a moment in that character's story, we immediately communicate a richer emotional experience than can be achieved solely by performance.

The waveform (Figure 11.3) of digital audio can also be used as a base-line animating factor for basic characters. For example, the amplitude of the track can be used to control the amount that the mouth is opened. Thus, the opening and closing of the mouth is controlled by the amplitude of the

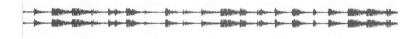

■ **FIGURE 11.3** Audio waveform.

audio track. When the track is silent, the mouth is closed. This can almost be thought of as automatic viseme triggering but on a more binary scale. An animator might cringe at such a technique, but in a pinch, for low-resolution characters, this can be a production lifesaver and can often serve as the staring point for more elaborate lip-sync.

Sound has been used as a time-saver ever since it was available to animators. Even the masters at Warner-Brothers knew when they use the offscreen sound of a ruckus to stand-in for the complicated animated brawl that Bugs Bunny might have gotten himself into. Productions geared for the stage also use this convention frequently also. While it is also true that how we might imagine that fight could be funnier than actually seeing it, the time-saving aspect of having sound in its place is still a means of streamlining production. When it comes to games, the sound design must be intricately planned as sound must be programmed to coordinate with character event triggers in the game like individual footsteps or various styles of jumps. These coordinated sounds, when coupled with a strong music track, greatly enhance the immersive experience and selling the character interacting with environment.

11.6 REAL-TIME ENGINE CONCERNS

As mentioned earlier, the animation for games consists of animation that is stored in a library which is called up by user action and looped, blended, and constrained as needed. Only in cut scenes are characters given specific animation performances to play out that exist outside of the motion library. As we will see in the following sections, the creation of motion is most varied when it comes to game development as characters need to react to innumerable situations and almost infinite camera angles. This makes animation substantially more difficult for games than for films where motion only needs to work for one particular shot from one particular camera angle. Blending animation in real-time is also far more difficult as the system has little warning about user-triggered events. We discuss the challenges for real-time animation in more depth in Chapter 14.

11.7 **EXERCISE**

This exercise is all about timing and gesture. With the character that you have been designing, plan out a single action for it to carry out. The action should be simple and accomplished in about three seconds of animation (72 frames at 24 frames per second [fps], and 90 frames at 30 fps). You will need paper and a lack of fear of stepping away from the computer and drawing.

11.1 With the action in mind, plot out the poses for that action on paper, first as quick thumbnail drawings that capture the flow of action in a single line. Build up your drawings iteratively until the character is more clearly represented and you can visualize all the articulations you will need to manipulate on the rig.

11.2 Scan your sequential drawings and bring them into a video editing program (something like iMovie is fine) and start timing out the spacing between images.

11.3 Did you draw enough frames to represent the motion over time? Do you need more? Add in-between images as needed until the rough sequence adequately represents the motion of the character.

11.4 Get feedback and critique on the posing and timing. Does it work? Does it read in the time allowed?

11.5 These frames will help you start to layout the keys in your animation software.

11.6 From largest motion to smallest, start blocking out the action.

11.7 Refer to your image sequence as often as needed. Have you captured the nuance of the drawings? Do you wish you drew more often? We all do.

11.8 Render out the sequence with rough settings to play it back at speed. Compare it to the drawing sequence and be critical of the animation.

11.9 Maintain this review/fix feedback loop until satisfied.

■ FURTHER READING

Three critical resources for the animator or the technician who wants to know about animation (and they all should):

Frank Thomas and Ollie Johnston. *The Illusion of Life: Disney Animation*. Disney Editions; Rev Sub edition (October 5, 1995), New York, NY, 1981.

Ed Hooks. *Acting for Animators*. Heinemann Publishing, Portsmouth, NH, 2001.

Richard Williams. *The Animator's Survival Kit*. Faber and Faber, London, England, 2001.

Lasseter's paper that distills down the principles into modern terms for the animator working digitally:

John Lasseter. Principles of traditional animation applied to 3D computer animation. In *SIGGRAPH '87: Proceedings of the 14th Annual Conference on Computer Graphics and Interactive Techniques*, pages 35–44, ACM Press, New York, NY, 1987.

And a great modern text from Angie Jones and Jamie Oliff:

Angie Jones and Jamie Oliff. *Thinking Animation: Bridging the Gap Between 2D and CG*. Course Technology PTR, 2006.

◼ INTERVIEW: JASON SCHLEIFER, HEAD OF CHARACTER ANIMATION, PDI/DREAMWORKS ANIMATION

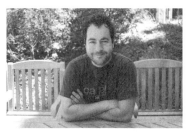

Jason Schleifer, Head of Character Animation, PDI/DreamWorks Animation

◼ BIO

Jason Schleifer is the Supervising Animator on Dream-Works Animations fall release "Madagascar: Escape 2 Africa." Recently, he was promoted to the Head of Character Animation on the studios next project "Master Mind." Since joining the studio in 2003, Schleifer has animated on the hit film "Madagascar," its spin-off short, "The Madagascar Penguins in a Christmas Caper," "Over the Hedge," and on the animated hit "Shrek the Third." During his off-hours away from the studio, Schleifer enjoys being a mentor for an online animation school, AnimationMentor.com.

Prior to his career at PDI/DreamWorks, Schleifer had extensive involvement at Weta Digital, beginning as a Creature Technical Director and later promoted to an Animation Lead while making "The Lord of the Rings" Trilogy. In addition to his film career, Schleifer has developed a couple of DVDs for Alias on creating animation rigs as well as being a co-author and co-presenter in a SIGGRAPH 2002 course on character rigging.

Schleifer has a BA in High Honors from the University of California, Santa Barbara. He also received an Honorary Doctorate of Animation from the Digital Media Arts College in Boca Raton, Florida.

◼ Q&A

Q) *The components of character technology are diverse and span the artistic and technical spectrum. How did you get your start in the industry? Based on where you see the field heading, what experience/training do you recommend people have?*

A) As long as I can remember, I have been fascinated and in love with animation. I remember writing a book report in

4th grade about animation, basically copying word for word Preston Blair's book "Animation: Learn to draw animated cartoons."

By the time I got to the University of California, Santa Barbara, I knew that my drafting skills were not quite up to the level of the Disney masters, so I focused on traditional art; painting, drawing, sculpture, etc. Luckily, we had a professor in the art department who was very interested in computer arts. She had contacts at Wavefront Technologies, a 3D software company, and was able to wrangle two SGI computers for our art lab and some copies of Wavefront animation software. I had already seen "Luxo Jr." by that point and knew that 3D animation was something I was interested in, so I convinced the teacher to let me go to Wavefront and learn how to use the software so I could help her teach it to the other students. She agreed and pretty soon I was sitting in a classroom with film artists from Disney, Dream Quest Images, and Sony Pictures Imageworks. I was over the moon!

After taking the training, I spent the next year teaching Wavefront software to the other students and completing an animated short film with a few other students. It was honestly nothing to write home about unless you like ten minutes of camera moves, wriggling meat torsos, and completely abstract music. At any rate, I had a taste of 3D animation and really loved it.

In the meantime, I was also producing quick little 2D animation tests at home using a package called Disney Animation Studio. They were not much to look at, but they were fun. One day, there was a notice up from a local illustrator who was in need of a student to help her produce 2D animation for a children's educational CD-ROM called "Kid Phonics." I gave her a call, and she came to my apartment to check out some of my work. I showed her some drawings and the animations, and she hired me on the spot. This was my first paid gig animating, and it was a blast. I worked with Karen quite a bit over the next few years on various projects and really enjoyed our collaboration.

As I reached the end of my college career, there was another notice posted at school about Wavefront needing interns to help them test a new 3D animation software called Maya. I applied and was hired just as Maya was getting off the ground floor. That was really my entry into the industry, from there it is just been onwards and upwards!

I highly recommend people focus on a variety of topics from math to art to architecture to psychology, but the main thing I would recommend is working on a sense of artistic appeal. No matter what aspect of character creation you enter, whether it is rigging, animation, surfacing, or modeling, in the end, we are creating an image that it supposed to speak to the audience. Without a sense of appeal, it is difficult to know what works and what does not.

Q) *Creating compelling digital characters is part art and part science. What is the greatest challenge you encounter on a daily basis? What aspect of character technology keeps you up thinking at night?*

A) The most challenging aspect of creating character animation at a studio is keeping the character "real" for the audience. Everything they do has to be motivated by an internal force; a thought process that is true and believable for that character. Remember, we act at 24 frames per second, so every gesture, every eye blink, every twitch of a finger has a purpose and is thought out. Making that look natural and motivated is incredibly difficult.

Technologically, I am constantly asking myself and others, "is this really the best way to do this?" Even though there is quite a lot of 3D character animation produced each year at all of the studios and certain techniques have become "standard," I still feel that we are really in the infancy of our craft. I have a strong desire to constantly re-evaluate our techniques to try and come up with the best way to really get our ideas across. I still feel like animators spend too much time thinking "technically" and not being able to let their acting just flow. My dream and goal would be for the animators to be able to see the final look of their frame while animating. The final lighting, texturing, fur, skin deformation, etc. Until we have that, until we can see the exact final image that the audience will see with all its complexity and detail in real time, I do not think we will be "finished." And, even then, I will bet someone's going to ask "but can we make it faster?"

Q) *What are the ingredients for a successful digital character?*

A) The main ingredient for a successful digital character performance is honesty. Everything the character does has to be based on an honest interpretation of how that specific character would act in that situation. There are no two characters that will light a candle in the exact same way. Each one has a different background, different physical abilities, light a match slightly differently. It is so important for the animator to really understand each character to the depth that any animation choices they make are true only for that character.

Of course, in order to achieve that performance, the tools have to enable and support the animator. So, it is imperative to have a close working relationship with the character TDs. Quite often, the incredible talent and work that goes into creating a quality animation rig is overlooked and it should not be. Their ability to provide intuitive and fast animation controls, deformations that suit the style, and tools that enhance the animators' workflow are imperative to creating a successful digital character performance.

Q) *While the industry is competitive, it is ultimately respectful of great work. Outside of the work you have been personally involved in the production of what animated characters have you been impressed or inspired by? What is the historical high-bar?*

A) There have been so many! One of my favorite characters recently is Bob from "The Incredibles." I thought that his acting was really fantastic. I am also a huge fan of the Valve character introduction videos that they have been producing for the game "Team Fortress 2." They are great examples of distinct and interesting characters that are totally unique and true to themselves.

Q) *Where do you see digital characters in ten years? Where are animated characters for film and games heading?*

A) I see the acting ability of characters increasing to the point of animated characters winning the award for "best actor." I cannot wait to see a team of 20 animators on stage thanking their parents. Films and games are converging and soon I do not imagine we will be thinking of them as separate "levels" of performance. They will just be different mediums, interactive, passive, and probably a combination of the two. At any rate, the experience will keep becoming more immersive and satisfying to the viewer and definitely more fun and interesting to produce.

Motion Capture

Performance capture is the recording of motion in the real world through various sampling means to drive the action of a digital character or representation of performer. Historically, motion capture is descended from rotoscoping where the motion of an animated character is derived from the frame-by-frame tracing of prerecorded video or film footage. Motion capture, often simply called mocap and often jokingly referred to as "The Devil's Rotoscope," is the sensor-based capture of performance motion to create a 3D representation of it. Sensors range from magnetic markers to video and essentially try to keep track of the motion of the performer over time. Motion capture is used for animation production, video games, and real-time interactive installations. For a variety of reasons, ranging from time constraints to budget to aesthetics, motion capture is a powerful and complex means of adding motion to digital characters.

12.1 MARKER-BASED MOTION CAPTURE

Motion capture is typically accomplished through the placement and tracking of physical markers attached to the performers body (Figure 12.1). Many technologies have been developed to capture marker motion ranging from magnetic, to optical, to electromechanical. Different markers are used for each of these methods. This is a thoroughly explored

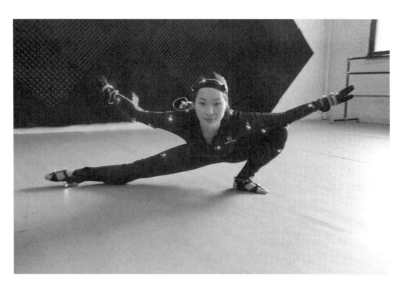

■ **FIGURE 12.1** Motion capture performer. Photo courtesy of Worleyworks, Brooklyn NY.

technique that is used to capture body and face motion with consistent results on human and non-human animals. Marker-based motion capture takes place in a calibrated space embedded with sensors. Sensor technology has evolved over time, ranging from magnetic to infrared, but the concept remains the same; markers are applied to the performer based on a specification for the system. Depending on the amount of resolution required, more or less markers are included in the set. Motion capture artists seek to resolve markers as consistently animated points over time. Marker positions are triangulated by the sensors in the space at a high frame rate. Occlusion of the sensors and environmental factors such as the composition of the floor or wall are all sources of noise that can affect the quality of the motion captured. For example, a magnetic system in a room with metal beams under the floor makes it difficult to resolve critical foot-to-floor contact. Many systems are optical and therefore the visibility of the markers by the sensors is essential. The motion of the performers and their position and orientation in the space can occlude a marker, and thus the marker's motion needs to be reconstructed for those frames. The issue of motion capture cleanup is covered in the next section.

There is a large amount of research going into capturing motion information from actors using markers through video in an non-calibrated space. For two of the "Pirates of the Caribbean" films, the team at ILM successfully implemented on-set motion capture to record the performances of the actors portraying Davey Jones' crew. This system used patterned markers, a few video cameras, rather than the array of fixed cameras flooding a volumetric space and computer vision algorithms to track the points through space during regular filming. Once back at the studio, the data was analyzed, turned into skeleton data, drove the character rig, and the rendered digital character replaced the performer in the shot. This is an oversimplification of the process but, as we will see later, there is research that takes some of these ideas even further and attempts to remove the markers altogether form the motion capture process.

The placement of the markers is an evolving topic, but basically markers are placed to capture the performers skeletal motion, body proportions, and the orientation of the body segment as a whole. Markers are placed at points of articulation in a symmetrical layout. In addition, asymmetrical markers are placed to capture performer orientation or sometimes just to distinguish between multiple performers (see Figure 12.2). Once captured, marker data is stored as a point cloud, representing each marker's motion over time for each take. This raw motion information usually needs to be cleaned up and then must be integrated into the production pipeline and attached to the rig.

12.2 **MOTION CAPTURE DATA CLEANUP**

The unfortunate downside of motion capture collection is the amount of noise that must be removed from the collected data in order to make the clip usable. Each type of motion capture apparatus is susceptible to noise and errors. These are as varied as physical marker drop-off, occluded markers, environmental interference, and camera or sensor calibration. Cleanup amounts to the reconstruction of a marker's path through space over time. Markers may have

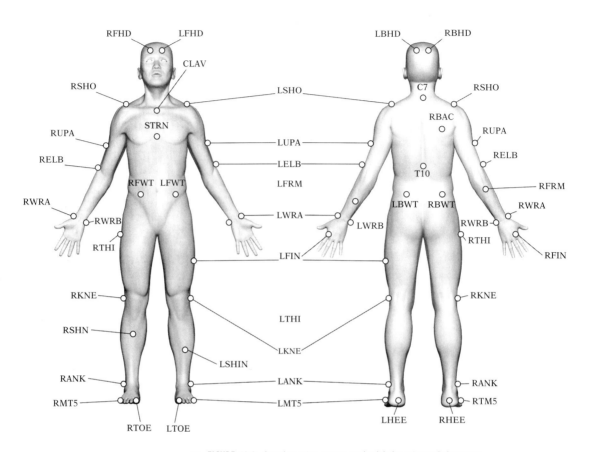

■ FIGURE 12.2 Sample motion capture marker label naming and placement.

disappeared or become switched with other existing markers. Typically, motion capture systems record at 60 frames per second while animation is produced at 30 or 24 frames per second. This difference allows the data to be down-sampled so that cleanup occurs at a lower resolution. This smoothing of the data will often help alleviate initial errors in the data.

The data, when it is looked at in its raw form, is a densely drawn curve for each marker in the three transformation dimensions. After a motion has been down-sampled, the curve shape can be reconstructed based on the sparser number of points. Once the motion is preserved and defined by the smaller number of points, an artist can adjust the curve as needed and apply function to further smooth curves or split and reattach curves created by markers that have become entangled or switched. When points disappear, if an interpolation does not work, then the point needs to be reconstructed based on the motion that exists, its relationship to other markers, and the eye of the artist cleaning up the data. Markers that flip positions with each other are endemic to systems where the markers are optical objects with no memory of a distinct identification number. This is common for reflective markers and less so for pulsed light emitting diode (LED) markers. Reflective marker identities are guessed based on an initial setup of the marker set.

During fast occluding motion, marker identities may be switched in the system. This is common for shoulders and hips. These regions are, of course, crucial for correct motion and difficult to untangle. Each pulsed LED has a unique identification. This means that between times of occlusion and the marker becoming invisible to the system, and thus temporarily lost, there is no danger of markers re-emerging and being tagged as another marker. When a marker is occluded, the position for that marker is set to zero, and the interpolation for these points has them appear to head back to the origin. This interpolation is usually performed by the motion capture data management software as the recording software will only store the raw data stream. The cleanup process can also involve editing together portions of different takes into one cleaner master take. However, because of the performative nature of motion capture, the overall position and action of the performer may be drastically different numerically between two takes of the same directed action. This may result in the clips being unable to be blended together if an overall global transformation to adjust performer position or orientation cannot be performed. Motion capture cleanup can be a costly and time-consuming process, so every effort should be made to get the best capture possible using the most noise-free system and environment.

12.3 **SKELETAL SOLVERS**

Fitting the data collected to a skeleton is an evolving process and directly related to cleanup. Algorithms are applied to reference skeletons to recover motion from the data set. There are a variety of solvers published, each with their own strengths and weaknesses. Many productions develop their own algorithms based on the needs of the pipeline or the production. The basic idea is that the external markers positioned on the performer need to be reconstructed to create the internal skeleton required for animation production. For example, the head is usually represented by at least four markers positioned at the front, back, and sides of the performer's head. From these four points, the goal is to reconstruct the the correct position and orientation of the single or multiple head joints over time. Since the head is a rigid, non-deforming object, the reconstruction of this point is relatively straightforward. Complex regions like the shoulders are more difficult. As every region needs to resolve to form rigid chains of joints, complicated regions like the clavicle and scapula, for example, are hard to collapse down to a single point. More often this region is defined as two or three points starting from the origin of the clavicle near the medial plane to another point at the top of the lateral end of the clavicle which connects to the upper arm/shoulder point. The spine can be solved as a curve drawn through the points recovered from the hips, mid spine, and upper back, or base of the neck. The rigid chain of joints is usually created in advance of the solving so skeletal solvers have more to do with mapping motion from markers to joint elements. It can be assumed that the lengths between joints are fixed and rigid. As such, dependant markers will need to be moved (through rotation and some translation) to accommodate a "best-fit" solution for all the joints but not scale the length between the joints in an unrealistic manner to achieve this fit.

Some solvers use an IK chain which solves quickly with stable results, but the high-frequency information in human motion is often dampened or lost. Often, the joint chains for knees, for example, exhibit a popping artifact as they are moved beyond full extension. Other solvers implement a non-linear minimization algorithm to find the optimal position for all joints in the system as opposed to breaking the problem into individual chains as the IK solution does. The solution fits the skeleton to the markers by maintaining the relationship between the bones and the markers defined during initialization. Solvers must deal with the rotation order, degrees of freedom, joint orientation, and preferred angle of bending for each solved joint. They also often include functions for filtering noise and for constraining the motion of joints to each other through the usual constraints related to translation, orientation, and aiming. Aiming is the process of pointing a single axis of a node at another point in space by defining the axis to aim and the up vector which controls the orientation of the constrained object about the aim vector.

Whatever methods are used, the point of skeleton solvers is to transform the motion of the markers into the motion of the expected joint structure. This joint structure is defined early in the production and likely is the standard for the studio working with the data. Constraints can be applied to limit the motion of joints within certain ranges or areas. For example, the notion of the floor is often enforced at this point so that joints are limited to moving below the zero unit in the up/down direction (usually y). The "floor" then affects the other nodes affected by the length-preserving function and moves everything to a reasonable place with regard to the floor. When joints are effected by non-motion related solving such as collisions, they often introduce other problems due to the fact that these points do not have a means to represent the volume of the character. As a result, collision response often times will put the character into unnatural poses. Some solvers implement rigid-body dynamics where joints can have surfaces parented to them to represent the volumes of the body. Then, as they are solved, collisions can help keep joints from getting too close. This helps the issues inherent with constraining the motion, but of course, it increases the time required to solve a single take of motion capture performance. There are often many takes which must be compared before the best one, or part thereof, is selected for production.

12.4 PIPELINES FOR MOTION CAPTURE

While video games have been using motion capture on a much larger and more common scale, films are increasingly incorporating it as a source of character animation. Some of the most successful film animations are those which layer keyframe animation on top of motion capture. The pipeline for motion capture requires passing the data through whatever cleanup is needed, then mapping it to the rig. The motion can either drive the model directly, replacing the rigging process, or more effectively it can be an input to the rigging solution as either an alternate rig or an input on the existing controllers. This latter, blended solution is the ideal. A blended rig has input for dense motion capture data and has the ability to layer animator-created performance on top of or in lieu of the motion for regions or the whole character at different intervals. The selection of motion for a region should be weighted between the motion capture data and the animation data, allowing an animator to augment, say, 40% of the motion capture for the arm for a sequence of 40 frames and 100% of the animation for 60 frames. This allows the motion capture to act as a base that can be added to by the animator to make the shot work. The setup can be two parallel hierarchies, one for animation and one for motion capture, that are blended into a third hierarchy responsible for deformations. It can be a set of hierarchical nodes that exist in the setup so each node has an input for animation and motion capture data (Figure 12.3).

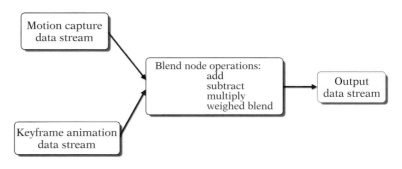

■ **FIGURE 12.3** Blended input on a node.

From an asset management perspective, motion capture data is usually large, requiring a sizeable amount of storage as well as the ability to access it quickly. The data should be accessed via a database through a front end that has descriptive information about the shot and each take, possibly even a low-resolution clip of the motion. Motion capture is accessed at the clip level and, like clip-based animation, can be blended and edited to suit the needs of the shot. The power of an organizational system like this is that animators have the ability to pick and choose animation and motion capture as needed. When dealing with many characters on a production, it is imperative to develop conventions that allow for motion to be shared across like characters. This requires that rig architecture and naming conventions be compatible and is key for humanoid characters where the ability to take a motion capture clip of a performer running can be offset, edited, and repurposed to a crowd of characters.

The decision-making tree for choosing motion capture clips is built into gameplay architecture. As a character is directed to move in different directions, perform specific actions, or encounter triggers in the environment, the necessary motion capture clip can be called and performed by the rig. So, if a character needs to run to the left, stop, and then lean over to pick something up, each of those discrete actions is pulled from the library and blended to create a reasonable chain of events. The blending between these actions is done on the fly and is generally just an overlapping interpolation from the ending state of one action to the beginning state of another.

12.5 **MOTION RETARGETING**

Motion capture data in the raw form is completely specific to the performer that it was captured from. Performers often do not match the proportions of the character they are portraying in the production. This is the case when the motion collected must be remapped to a control set with different proportions and, less ideally, different joint configurations than it was collected to represent. Much of this work involves overall character segment reorientations and the constraining of motion to reorient it against other directional planes. Scale is a major factor for retargeting both for the overall character and individual limb proportions. Characters might need to have slightly longer arm proportions or the overall scale of a human performer might need to be mapped to a creature with very non-human proportions. Because motion capture data is stored as an animated point cloud, once the relationships between markers are established and the skeleton is built, other information can be computed from the data. Most importantly, when rigid chains are created between the joints, their motion can be computed as rotations. These rotations are more portable to characters of other proportions as rotations can be applied to nodes regardless of position or scale. Constraints can be utilized to proceduralize the control of the data. For example, the feet need to be constrained to the floor when the character makes contact with it, so position-based code can be implemented that will not let the foot slip below the ground plane. Studios and animation systems have techniques for remapping motion to the required proportions and specifications for the character needed in production.

Motion retargeting is akin to comparative kinematics where biologists will compare the proportions of animal limb lengths, joint orientations, and scale to compare locomotive strategies and adaptations. By exploring the mechanical properties of motion of living animals, inferences can be made about extinct species. For example, because of the inherent morphological similarities between a Tyrannosaurus rex and the modern terrestrial birds like chickens and turkeys, researchers have made comparisons between them and even tried to remap motion captured turkey locomotion to come up with hypothetical kinematic models of the extinct carnivore. Dr. John Hutchinson of the University of London's Royal Veterinary College captures the motion of extant species, such as elephants and other large animals, and compares it to information collected from dinosaur anatomy. Of course, we do not have the benefit of using motion capture on dinosaurs, but this comparison is done to gauge what generalities about large animal stance and gait emerge from comparing these different lineages. Problems with motion retargeting, the transforming of one creature's proportions to those of another, and anatomy prevent a transfer of joint angles from elephants to dinosaurs, but the connections gleaned from traditional and emerging biomechanical analysis tools have shed an innovative light on the subject.

12.6 **MARKERLESS MOTION CAPTURE**

The limitations of marker-based motion capture and the rise of computer vision and image-based modeling have opened the door for markerless image-based motion capture. The idea behind markerless motion capture is that the performers can just walk into the calibrated stage and with little to no proportion registration, and their motion can be captured in real-time. "Stage™" by Organic Motion™ is an innovative example of this (Figure 12.4). Organic Motion's technique synthesizes the imagery from cameras positioned on the same object from multiple views. These views are compared and incorporated into data which can be used like traditional motion capture data or for volume filling operations. Behind the scenes of such systems is usually a jointed model that the volumes produced by the image analysis will fit into the computed position. Once the data is collected, it then works just like standard motion capture and can be integrated

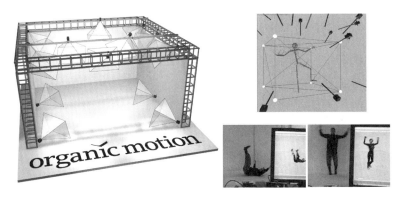

■ **FIGURE 12.4** Markerless motion capture by Organic Motion™.

into the production pipeline identically. Down the line, the data may be different as video-based systems have the potential of capturing surfaces with lighting and textures. These emerging systems, such as Stage and BioStage™ by Organic Motion, are the future of motion capture and will change the paradigm that we work with today. With these markerless systems, motion capture can be brought into the public arena for sports, entertainment, and medical applications for the general public.

12.7 **EXERCISE**

This exercise is intended to expose you to motion capture data. To start, you will need access to a sample motion capture file. A good source of this data is Carnegie Mellon University's Motion Capture Database (http://mocap.cs.cmu.edu). Since motion capture data comes in a variety of formats, you will need to find the one most convenient for you to open in your animation software of choice. Autodesk's Motion-Builder is quickly becoming the motion capture work horse in production.

12.1 Load the motion capture file into your animation software.

12.2 Select a single node and look at the translation animation curve associated with it. Notice how dense it is.

12.3 Attach primitive objects or joints and a simple polygonal mesh to the data points.

12.4 Use your application's curve editing tools to simplify the curve. Notice how the high-frequency noise disappears as you sparse the curve.

12.5 Create a simple rig that allows you to replace and/or offset the movement provided by the motion capture for one appendage. This can be done as simply as creating a mirror arm that rides along with (or hierarchically below) the motion capture arm.

12.6 Attempt to revise the action with that one appendage.

■ FURTHER READING

Two good resources for working with motion capture in production:

Alberto Menache. *Understanding Motion Capture for Computer Animation and Video Games*. Morgan Kaufmann Publishers Inc., San Francisco, CA, 1999.

Matthew Liverman. *The Animator's Motion Capture Guide: Organizing, Managing, and Editing*. Charles River Media, Inc., Rockland, MA, 2004.

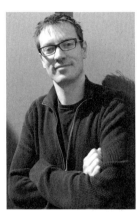

David Hunt-Bosch, Character Rigger, Bungie

■ INTERVIEW: DAVID HUNT-BOSCH, CHARACTER RIGGER, BUNGIE

■ BIO

David was never sure if it was a waste of time to spend countless all-nighters mapping out the dungeons of Norfair. All through childhood, he and the Brothers 306 made short films and pioneered special effects using barbecue sauce, Top Ramen, and stop, motion animation. He had no idea that gaming and indulging in collaborative imaginations would lead to a fulfilling career at Bungie, where he enjoys the privilege of working with some of the most talented and creative folks in the world. He is raising three brilliant young gamers of his own with his loving wife, Beata, and they are sure dungeon mapping is no waste of time.

■ Q&A

Q) *The components of character technology are diverse and span the artistic and technical spectrum. How did you get your start in the industry? Based on where you see the field heading, what experience/training do you recommend people have?*

A) Even if a student of digital character development is resolved to only practice art, they should gain at least a basic understanding of programming. This enables the person to collaborate effectively with people of different disciplines. An artist with an understanding of programming can think beyond the boundaries of their digital tools and get the best out of this intrinsically technical medium. They may even learn to develop tools of their own. Along with mastering the fundamentals of art, artists should learn to quickly adapt to new digital content creation tool environments as they will constantly be tasked to do so in the working world.

A programmer with an understanding of art has an appreciation for the visual nuances that create an illusion of life. A programmer who learns to draw will expand their perceptive skills and improve their ability to visually dissect images and talk about them with artistic people.

Artists of all disciplines should also try taking animation classes because animation is a hub of all content creation in a digital production. That will give the artist a holistic view of the production pipeline: how concept and modeling feeds into rigging, keyframing, and final presentation. The whole idea from idea to reality.

I was lucky to partake in an intense interdisciplinary production animation program at the University of Washington, where I earned my BA in Art in 2000. Even if an artist's job in production is only to paint the digital toenails on a character, they will do a better, more efficient job if they understand what their neighbors are working on and talking with them regularly.

Q) *Creating compelling digital characters is part art and part science. What is the greatest challenge you encounter on a daily basis? What aspect of character technology keeps you up thinking at night?*

A) My greatest challenge as Bungie's Character Rigger is maintaining the massive amount of data that flows through the animation pipeline. Bungie's games rely on a deep sandbox philosophy where characters are made to be compatible with a multitude of game objects such as vehicles, weapons, props, and interactive environments. This requires thousands of individual animations to be made for each character using the rigs I have developed. In pursuit of fun gameplay, Bungie iterates on game design constantly, which often calls for large-scale adjustments to be made across entire character libraries. I fully support this need to iterate and believe that it is critical to creating quality products! I sit up at night thinking of ways to build automated, data-driven pipeline tools to allow us to distribute changes and updates to character rigs while saving valuable animation data. Another benefit of this tool-based approach to rigging is that we are able to repurpose old animation data to apply as a base for future work. Using these distribution systems, I am also able to provide custom tools to our animators that help them work more efficiently.

Q) *What are the ingredients for a successful digital character?*

A) There are just too many to name here. I will focus on the particular aspect of animation: the creation of believable character motion. A character, whether simple or complex, must telegraph its thought process and emotional state to the viewer through animation. Successful animation suspends the viewer's disbelief and creates an imaginary world that they can feel. At any moment, this illusion can be broken by something even as small as an eye movement that is not perceived to be backed by believable motivation.

The eyes are especially important because we humans are all experts at interpreting the emotional meaning of millimeters worth of movement in an eyelid. While features like eyes say a lot, even a character with a hidden face like our own Master Chief can be fully believable as alive and thinking through animation. The tilt of the head in relation to the angle of the body and position of the legs, arms, and fingers all convey emotional meaning to the viewer. Good animation is when these members move from position to position in relationship to each other in a way that creates a sense of physicality, while also speaking the tacit body language that we all innately understand. This emotional content must be consistent with what the viewer believes the character's personality to be in relationship to the virtual world they live in.

Q) *While the industry is competitive, it is ultimately respectful of great work. Outside of the work you have been personally involved in the production of what animated characters have you been impressed or inspired by? What is the historical high-bar?*

A) The most compelling question in my mind right now related to digital character development is interactive character design. This is the intersection between making characters look good and feel responsive under player control so they can fit believably into their world. In recent generations, games have achieved a good visual bar in the areas of graphics, rendering, lighting, and resolution. So, still images in games are looking pretty good these days, but animation has a long way to go.

By far, the best recent example of good interactive animation that I have seen is Altair of "Assassins Creed" by Ubisoft Montreal. They really took it to a new level by making a character that truly has natural and beautiful movement through the urban environments in the game. He can climb just about any surface in the entire map and then take a graceful swan dive off the tallest building. I feel so immersed in that world because Altair's animation is so seamless and fluid. There is obviously a lot of smart tech going on under the hood of his animation system, and it is presented to the player in a simple, intuitive context.

One of the most amazing animated characters I have seen in film is Scrat by Blue Sky Studios. They take the concept of squash and stretch to a crazy new level with him. I can hardly believe how many ways they can push, pull, inflate, distort, smash, and bash that little guy and still put him back together again! As a Character Rigger, it makes me cringe to imagine the work behind Scrat.

Q) *Where do you see digital characters in ten years? Where are animated characters for film and games heading?*

A) In the near future, we will see interactive real-time characters grow beyond the borders of games. This will allow people to interact remotely through sophisticated digital avatars. The concept of the "ractor" in Neil Stephenson's book, "The Diamond Age," is an idea that extrapolates current day performance capture technology. In Stephenson's vision, a ractor is a human performer with a network of nanosite transmitters imbedded just under the surface of their epidermis. A scanner detects the nanosites and reads volumetric 3D motion of the performer. The motion drives a digital character that can interact in real time with other such avatars. Combine haptics hardware development of tactile force feedback with this idea, and it is not hard to imagine creating believable physical interaction between avatars and their virtual worlds. The entertainment industry will pioneer technology like this and use it to a great effect while opening doors to other industries such as its close sibling, the advertisement industry.

Most of all, it will be exciting for me to watch this technology branch into the field of education. There will be a renaissance of learning across the world when these advanced user interfaces catch up to the vast libraries of information we have access to now. Students will experience virtual remote locations as if they were there. They will be able to connect with learning on the same twitch/reflex feedback basis that magnetizes them toward interactive games.

13

Procedural Animation

Procedural animation is the application of algorithms to create motion. These algorithms can be intelligent manipulation of the character based on rules and constraints or the implementation of a physics engine to drive the character based on simulated forces in relation to the environment it exists in. The combination of the two is the direction that game engines and intelligent animation systems are headed. By combining smart procedural motion with the weight and reality created by a physics engine, results can be achieved quickly and which are highly believable.

13.1 **FUNCTIONS TO CONTROL MOVEMENT**

The use of math functions for controlling the motion of objects is a typical means of controlling movement. This method uses trigonometric functions to inform the motion of objects based on the position or orientation of other objects. Many animation systems refer to this type of code as "expressions." When simple functions are used, this motion has a tendency to look mechanical, which is why expression-based motion is very suitable for inorganic motion. With a little work, however, function-based motion can complement key-framed curves by adding secondary motion to objects already

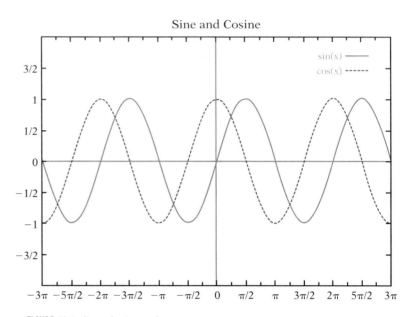

■ **FIGURE 13.1** Sine and cosine graph.

animated. Elements such as the tail of a dog, the trunk of an elephant, the feather in a cap, or even the tentacles of an octopus can be controlled through procedural functions. Expressions can be as simple as a direct relationship between multiple objects with an offset so that as, for example, a character's hips rotate, its tail moves in the opposite direction as counter motion. Sinusoidal motion can be attached to objects so that they oscillate along a curve function (Figure 13.1). These wave functions are useful as they are inherently arcing curves that easily add appealing visual motion to objects. When described as a function of time (t):

$$y(t) = A \cdot sin(wt + \theta),$$

where A = amplitude, w = radians per second, and θ = phase.

Basic procedural animation in games typically involves head and eye tracking to allow characters to look at the appropriate object in the scene and IK for hands and feet to be placed in the right position based on goals.

13.2 SCRIPTED ANIMATION AND PROCEDURAL ACTORS

Taken a step further, using expression-based transformations, entire motions can be procedurally scripted and incorporated into the animation system. These discrete motions can be built up modularly so that motion elements can be moved from character to character and mixed and matched as needed or combined with function-based motion. The movement can also be animated cycles that are called upon at the right moment from a database of actions which are then strung together by an animator or by a procedural system. With scripted motion, we delve into the notion that, in these scenarios, the animator acts like a director of a live-action film telling characters how to act out a series of motions. "Walk into the room, drop your bag on the floor, and open the window." The individual scripted motions can be thought of as actions in a database which have specific in and out points, but that must be blended into each other. This blending is a difficult prospect as the motions on each end of the blend may be drastically different from each other. Situations such as this may require hand-animated blend segments to look right.

Character motion is difficult to distill down to discrete procedural motion, but researchers such as Dr. Ken Perlin at New York University are leading the way in the creation of fully procedural characters. By offsetting and blending trigonometric curve functions, such as sine and cosine, with noise, Dr. Perlin has been able to achieve body and facial motion which is both pleasing to view and completely interactive. This work can be seen in the software "Actor Machine" that Dr. Perlin is helping to develop. On the simplest level, a character controlled by the "Actor Machine" software can be directed to walk across a room and everything regarding the animation is taken care of. The feet hit their marks on the floor based on the pace of the walk and the arms and torso move appropriately based on some basic tunable parameters. The user, who in this case is acting like the director of the shot, has access to many types of "emotional dials" that they

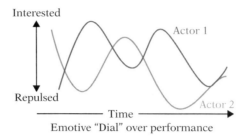

FIGURE 13.2 Emotional curves for a procedural system by Actor Machine™.

might choose to use. For example, they could turn up or down how tired, sad, happy, or arrogant a character is and all the combinations in-between. Similarly, the user can direct the level and type of emotional relationships in a scene between the characters such as their respective mutual interest, love, or fear of each other. Moods and relationships can be changed over time within a scene to reflect the "inner thoughts" of the digital actors. As emotional curves, these high-level directives can affect a suite of underlying parameters over time (Figure 13.2).

These directions would affect the body language, glancing motions, hand gestures, facial expressions, or other appropriate expressions, which physically describe the directions conveyed. Unlike blended animation, all motion is procedurally generated, so the engine never produces the repetitiveness seen in game engines that call the same mocap clips over and over. The small amount of performance randomness gives the character more of a sense of being alive, in that the same action will be performed differently every time. Social interactions, meaning expressive interactions between two or more characters, are a challenge to procedural actors as characters need to have a sense of history with their social partner and also must be able to see into the future of the scene to avoid any emotional latency that may arise from actions needing to be processed by the counterpart. Many of these issues are solved by the notion of a procedural actor script. Like a live actor's script, a procedural actor's script will have their dialog and information about their emotional state and the setting in which the scenario occurs. A procedural actor's script might contain more detailed information about a character's relationship to the other characters in the scene. These details would set the appropriate attributes, allowing the script to be baked into the inner workings of that character. The following actions for that character would build upon those settings and modify them as needed.

The emotions applied to the character act like surface shaders. Shaders in computer graphics rendering are programs that define the visual properties of a surface with regard to color, texture, how light reacts to it, and how it appears to the camera and ultimately the renderer. Shaders have inputs and outputs to connect them to the results of other operations and can be layered together to create more visually complex results. In the same way, emotional shaders can be strung together and layered atop each other to replicate complex behaviors and emotional states. One can imagine a situation where a character is scared, but putting on a brave face, where you would apply a "scared" shader with a layer of "bravery" with partial opacity on top of it. In this case, the animation input has a semantic quality with regard to mood, emotion, and intent that is resolved by the procedural animation subsystem. For example , the game's AI system and/or game cinematographers will be able to have the engine communicate to the emotion-based system with tokens like "set tired to 80%" and the actor engine will be translate that into the appropriate animation. This is as opposed to telling it which exact clips to blend in.

The Actor Machine software (Figure 13.3) is an evolution of the "Improv" project that Dr. Perlin helped develop in the late 1990s [30]. This earlier work deals with the understanding and recreation of motion from the perspective of algorithmic functions. Part of this is the analysis of motion created by animators and through motion capture. Once these performances are captured, the expression and animation curves associated with the performance are analyzed in an attempt to distill them down into procedures. This work attempts to convert motion into procedural functions that can be reused by the character or mapped to others. In many ways, the data

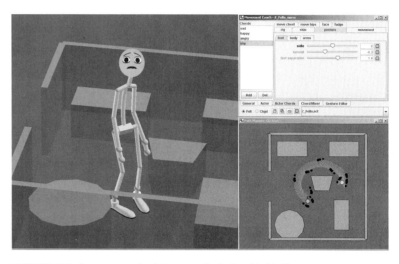

■ **FIGURE 13.3** Prototype procedural character engine by Actor Machine™.

produced by procedural systems looks remarkably like motion capture as it ends up being absolute matrix positions for character nodes per frame. As such, the integration of motion capture data into a procedural system is another way to teach a digital character how to move. The proceduralization or the replacement of motion capture data with procedural motion is also a form of compression. As stated in the motion capture section, the data captured and needed to be maintained is voluminous. Once established, the amount of data required to create a procedural performance is negligible as it is the only animated parameter to a system and not the raw per-control, per-frame positions that swell mocap data. This paradigm shifting mode of motion production is like mocap-in-a-box and stands to be a valuable tool for previsualization, background characters for film, and machinima, to name some initial applications.

13.3 PHYSICS TO CONTROL MOVEMENT

Rigid-body or "ragdoll" physics is being increasingly implemented for both film and game characters and is usually combined with motion capture data. The combination of these techniques requires the use of simulation to solve a scenario. A simulation is an imitation of a real event, system state, or evolving process and involves the algorithmic representation of the characteristics or behaviors of physical or abstract systems. Objects in a simulated scenario may start as animated entities or exist as purely simulated entities. The motion of animated objects is controlled by keyframes or motion capture data, while the simulated objects depend on the representation of physical processes, such as forces and collisions in the environment, to drive motion. All of this needs to be controlled by a physical dynamics engine that calculates the position of each of the elements in the character on a per-frame basis with regard to the forces in the world and the collision objects in the environment. Rigid bodies are defined as non-deforming objects whose position is defined by linear and angular vectors representing position and orientation. The rigid body is ascribed a mass value as a scalar, and its angular mass, or moment of inertia, is calculated by its size. The moment of inertia of an object about a given axis describes how difficult it is to rotate about that axis. As the object is affected by the forces in the world and reacts to collisions, its linear and angular velocity and acceleration are calculated and used to place the object from frame to frame. Velocity is the rate of change of position defined by speed and direction from frame to frame, and acceleration is the rate of change of velocity.

For example, a character can be defined and then attached to a piece of motion capture data to have it walk, then run. In the middle of its running path can be placed a low obstacle. Depending on the shape and size of that object, the character will collide with it as chain of rigid objects that connect to match the proportions of a human. Limits and constraints can be placed on all the character joints so that the impact and subsequent reaction of the character will happen within the limits of human motion. These rotational limits are a range of values with the extremes softened so that high-velocity motion can push a joint toward extreme motion but be dampened as it reaches the extreme limits. Simulated characters need to be represented by polygonal surfaces, which are representative of the character volume so that collisions and interactions with objects in the world can be calculated with the lowest amount of surface resolution possible. These surfaces also have mass properties so that forces such as gravity produce predictable results. Characters in dynamic systems are never solved in their highest resolution state, so characters in these systems are representations of the production character. Once the system has solved the position of all the rigid links from frame to frame, this data can be written to disk and stored as a cache of the simulation. This acts like dense keyframes for the character preserving the results of the simulation but now playable in real-time without the need to solve it again. Now that the simulated motion is stored as essentially animation data, characters can be blended into or out of existing animation as needed as described previously (Figure 11.2). This combination of keyframed animation, motion capture, and procedural motion allows an animator to mix and match motion sources to create the final performance in that shot.

13.4 BEHAVIORAL ANIMATION

Behaviorial animation is a form of procedural animation whereby an autonomous character determines its own actions based on a set of rules. As an example, flocking is one of the most widely explored behavioral animation systems. In this system, a layer of rules is added on top of a group of agents which gives them a framework with which to behave in relation to one another. Craig Reynolds [33] described flocking with regard to computer graphics by outlining the behaviors, on what he called "boids," that needed to be implemented to recreate the phenomenon. The basic flocking model consists of three simple steering behaviors to describe how an individual member of the flock should maneuver based on the positions and velocities of its flock neighbors:

1. Separation: steer to avoid crowding local flock mates.
2. Alignment: steer toward the average heading of local flock mates.
3. Cohesion: steer to move toward the average position of local flock mates.

This model of simple rules that, when combined, create the possibility for emergent behavior is the foundation for behavioral animation. Emergence is the scenario where complex global behavior arises from the interaction of simple local rules. On top of this, an individual's understanding of the world around them through means of virtual sensing opens up even more complex behavior. Virtual sensing is the application of senses, such as sight, proprioception, or even bound-box-based positional collision detection, to nodes in a scene. Once enabled with these abilities, they can avoid other characters and objects in their environment. Similarly, action-on objects are functions used to perform a specific action upon a certain object. This could be actions related to what to do when a character encounters a door. As characters interact within complex scenes and navigate within a dynamic environment, the requirements for collision detection, collision response, and on-the-fly decision-making increase. Once obstacles are included in a scene, characters must be able to anticipate their path in order to avoid them. This notion of pathfinding, sometimes referred to as path-planning, is critical to crowd simulation, which will be introduced subsequently. Historically, algorithms such as A* (pronounced A-star) have been the default pathfinding implementation (Figure 13.4). A* is a best-first graph search algorithm that finds the most economical path from an initial position to a goal node. Best-first search algorithms explore a graph of choice by exploring the most promising node chosen according to a defined rule. A* iteratively searches all possible routes leading from the starting point until it finds the shortest path to a goal. Like all informed search algorithms, it searches first the routes that appear to be most likely to lead toward the goal. There are usually secondary functions that deal with terrain constraining and obstacle avoidance but these too can be incorporated into A*. The cost of each tile in the grid is calculated as the cost of getting there from the starting location (in unit steps) plus an estimate of the cost of getting from the tile in question to the goal.

Pathfinding is a form of iterative 2D or 3D search over time. Other algorithms like A* have been developed as have

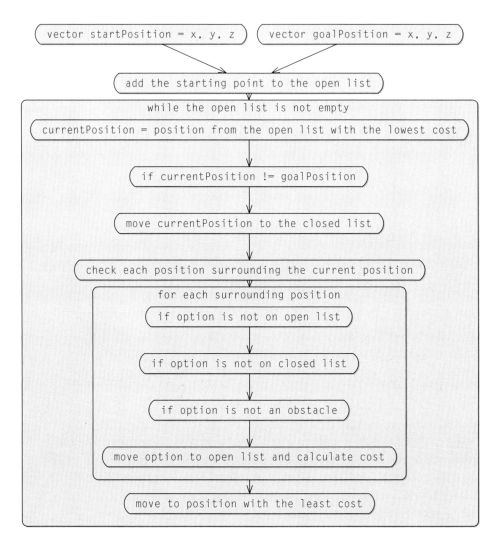

■ **FIGURE 13.4** Method for a A* pathfinding.

the notion of heat dispersion maps which flood a volume with values and attempt to map the most efficient, or coolest, path through them (See also [29]). Although real-time methods have been implemented into game engines, off-line pathfinding used for films requires longer computation time and is ultimately more accurate, while at the same time, opens the door for many more characters. Non-real-time processing also allows for collisions and avoidance of arbitrarily shaped obstacles and higher resolution terrain processing.

While behavioral animation is more than path-planning, this is a major consideration. The goal of behavioral animation is to imbue characters with enough rules to build up emergent life-like actions. Reynolds has stated that this behavior takes the form of "unpredictability over moderate time scales." It is impossible to predict which direction boids in his flocking system will be moving five minutes from the time you are watching them. On the contrary, within short time intervals, the motion is relatively predictable. This is a distinguishing characteristic of complex systems. Chaotic systems, on the other hand, have neither short- nor long-term predictability. Reynolds cites Chris Langton with the observation that "life-like phenomena exist poised at the edge of chaos."

13.5 **ARTIFICIAL INTELLIGENCE**

Combining scripted animation sequences with notions of algorithmic decision-making lays the foundation for building an artificially intelligent system that makes decisions based on a rule-based model. A series of requirements are presented to the system, along with a database of motions or procedural motion events. Once goals and behaviors are added as inputs to the system, AI is allowed to make decisions about where the characters are and what they are doing, pulling motion from the database. As Matt Elson [11] postulated, this is a major evolutionary step for digital characters and opens a huge realm of possibility with regard to crowd systems, and it is the core of behavioral animation.

AI attempts to put the decision-making in the hands of the character. The ability to reason based on knowledge of the world and the system the character is contained within is a step above rule-based procedural motion. Techniques for AI for digital characters typically comes in two varieties: deterministic and non-deterministic. Deterministic is behavior which is defined and generally predictable. Basic chasing algorithms are a good example, where the behavior is clear from the beginning and the result is evident from the behavior. A character moves toward a goal. Non-deterministic behavior, on the contrary, is unpredictable, and its results are uncertain. This is due to the notion of behavior adaptation whereby the character's behavior is enhanced by learning the player's tactics or evolving new strategies. This makes the results unpredictable and gives rise to emergent behavior which develops without specific instruction. Of course, deterministic AI is easier to code and debug, while non-deterministic AI is more complicated to implement and essentially results in a system of unlimited possibility, making it very hard to test and tune. Most game engines incorporate some notion of deterministic AI, while non-deterministic AI is usually implemented as a module created by a third-party engine developer. As a subset of AI research, intelligent agents are defined by their ability to adapt and learn. Within a crowd system in animation production, they are the node-based embodiment of non-deterministic AI on a per-character level within a scene. At times, the word agent merely implies an individual character in a crowd but we will reserve the term for autonomous adaptive entity. Adaptation implies sensing the environment and reconfiguring behavior in response. This can be achieved through the choice of alternative problem-solving rules or algorithms or through the discovery of problem-solving strategies. Learning may proceed through trial and error, implying a capability for analysis of behavior and success. Alternatively, learning may proceed by example and generalization. In this case, it implies a capacity to abstract and generalize the information presented (See [7] as an example).

AI is often ascribed to nodes which act as agents in a system. This guides the agents based on functions related to environmental awareness and animatable attributes. The entities are given goals and then interact with each other as members of a real crowd would. Agents are the base unit character in a multicharacter environment usually termed a crowd system.

13.6 **CROWDS AND VARIATION SYSTEMS**

Once artists were able to produce one digital character well, the impetus was to create many, and before long many turned into full crowds. Crowd systems have at their core frameworks for creating character variations and applying animation to them at a group behavior level. "Massive™" developed by Massive Software is the most well-known commercial software specific for producing crowds and was developed in parallel with the production of "The Lord of the Rings" trilogy. The motion of crowd individuals is typically either particle-based or agent-based. When controlled by a particle system, characters are driven via simulation using forces such as wind or gravity and by establishing attractors, goals, and defining collisions. Most animation systems have these functions built-in, so implementation of a particle-based crowd is fast to implement and does not require specialized software. As with all simulations, this method is extremely difficult to art direct and the actions of a single individual's motion is almost impossible to control. Agent-based systems utilize AI to drive motion, and although more expensive to compute and often requiring specialized software, it provides much more accurate results and more compelling and life-like character behavior.

Crowd systems are usually computed using generic representations of the final characters. These are stand-in rigs that are computationally lightweight and representative of the final group. Because crowd systems implement many of the techniques we have discussed thus far, it is no surprise these are complex systems that require a large amount of planning to integrate into the production pipeline. All aspects of rigging, deformations, animation, motion capture, procedural motion, and behaviorial animation are tied up in to the processing of these systems. Therefore, they are computationally optimized to process large amount of data per frame and can run the simulations at multiple levels of resolutions for fast iterations. Most important is the choreography of group character motion. A simplified walk-through of the inner workings of a crowd system is described below (see [36] for a more complete overview) .

1. Define environment topology and boundaries
2. Define number of agents and initial positions
3. Define agent properties: motion library, relationships, variations
4. Define agent goals and obstacles
5. Simulate: pathfinding, character steering, and AI
6. Output agent data to animation system or renderer

Building on the AI we discussed earlier, crowd systems synchronize multiple actors applying principles similar to flocking to implement group behavior. The AI involved with crowds is in many ways far less complex than that associated with the single individual, the pair, or the small group. Crowd behavior is ultimately not very complex and due to the large-scale number of characters, the problem is as much a graphics problem as it is an AI problem. Once agents and goals are defined, even if goals are just to mill about in a specified area, character pathfinding is implemented so that the characters build an internal map to their goal. This is a dynamic process because, although environmental obstacles are static, other characters are not, and therefore path-planning needs to be executed as one of the first processes. Iterations of the character path-planning are run until a functional solution is found. Character steering, which is the planning and execution of body positioning related to the results of pathfinding is the second step. From this point, character collisions trigger responses based on character attributes. Often times, it is these character interactions that define the action required of the scene, such as the warring crowds in "The Lord of the Rings" trilogy. It is these moments of interaction or character collision that become action-on scenarios, which trigger a sequence of events, and subsequently calling clips from the motion library, to carry out hand-to-hand combat. This is all based on a decision tree (Figure 13.5) where probabilities are assigned to actions and the outcomes of actions trigger other responses, all building up to the point where one character perseveres against another. All these actions can have an overarching weighted curve associated with them

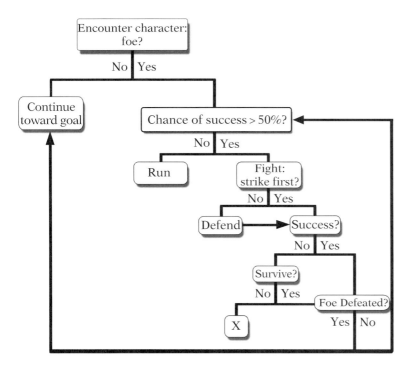

■ **FIGURE 13.5** Basic decision tree for a crowd character engaging in a fight sequence.

that shifts the balance of the action toward one outcome or another.

Variation systems are those which allow an artist to create a series of characters based on a core model or character database. Variations can be as simple as a change of clothing or as complex as an entirely different species. Variation systems are basically high-level controls for switching attributes on a character. For a small amount of minor variations, the attributes to select different variations on a character may just control the visibility of different objects. A good example of this is a character who sometimes wears a hat and other times does not. This basic variation of the main character is essentially a prop switch, but the principle can be applied to crowd characters that may have minor variations.

For more complex variations, we get into the realm of procedurally built characters which are created on-the-fly when the scene is loaded. These systems can take many forms. One configuration is that a file is associated with the scene that contains all the variation details for the specific characters in the scene. When that scene is loaded for simulation, each character is loaded and the variation file tells the system what variations are associated with it. The creation of this file is manual (can be done through a graphical user interface), but the art director has specific control over the amount of character variation in the scene. Crowd builders can be more automated, whereby the system is loaded with all the possible variation choices and allowed to build the characters at random. Often times, there is internal logic associated with these variations so that the system can make accurate decisions related to the fit between variations. For example, certain body types may not fit with certain clothing variations or certain hair styles must be associated with certain hats. By being able to include exceptions for certain variations, the user can minimize the number of simulations that need to be rerun later to eliminate incorrectly assembled characters. Variations can also encompass body types which has an impact on the locomotion of the character, particularly body height modifications which change limb lengths. If a piece of raw motion capture data is applied to a character whose legs are longer than the captured character, the stride will not look appropriate for that character. If there is no possibility of using a procedural motion solution, then the system must scale the mocap data to fit the character. If the data has been attached to constraints like IK, then the position of the feet is controlled by two points, which can be scaled to offset the base position and look right for this new taller or shorter character. This is akin to retargetting, which was discussed earlier.

13.7 **EXERCISE**

In this exercise, we go through the conceptual process of designing a decision tree for a group of procedural characters. Split into groups of two or more. Split evenly between programmers and art/animation directors. Follow the steps below.

13.1 Sketch out an environment for the character to exist in along with a descriptive goal that they are trying to reach or accomplish.

13.2 Based on the spec, develop the relationships between the characters. Are they enemies that must battle? Are they allies that must co-operate to succeed?

13.3 Implemented on a digital grid or on paper, run characters step-by-step to their respective goals.

13.4 When character comes in contact with another character, obstacle, or the goal, diagram out the decisions that they must make for those scenarios. Be as detailed as possible as procedural systems must deal with these situations by making many microdecisions as opposed to one one complex overarching decision.

13.5 Trade rule-sets with another group. Does their rule-set and decision tree work for your scenario?

13.6 Maintain this review/fix feedback loop until you find a common language and start building more complex scenarios that the rule-sets satisfy.

■ FURTHER READING

A good introduction to AI for programmers and non-programmers alike:

David M. Bourg and Glenn Seemann. *AI for Game Developers*. O'Reilly Media, Inc., Cambridge, MA, 2004.

Perlin noise as it relates to textures and to characters:

Ken Perlin. An image synthesizer. *SIGGRAPH Computer Graphics*, 19(3):287–296, ACM Press, Newyork, NY, 1985.

Ken Perlin and Athomas Goldberg. Improv: A system for scripting interactive actors in virtual worlds. In *SIGGRAPH '96: Proceedings of the 23rd Annual Conference on Computer Graphics and Interactive Techniques*, pages 205–216, ACM Press, New York, NY, 1996.

http://www.actormachine.com/

Craig Reynolds' seminal paper on flocking and the introduction of his "boids":

Craig W. Reynolds. Flocks, herds, and schools: A distributed behavioral model. *Computer Graphics*, 21(4):25–34, 1987.

Crowds as implemented for various media platforms from Massive Software:

http://www.massivesoftware.com/

The almost legendary (even before it is released) game "Spore" from Will Wright has already revolutionized people's thinking about procedural characters and procedural character animation:

http://www.spore.com

INTERVIEW: KEN PERLIN, PROFESSOR, MEDIA RESEARCH LABORATORY, COURANT INSTITUTE OF MATHEMATICAL SCIENCES, NEW YORK UNIVERSITY

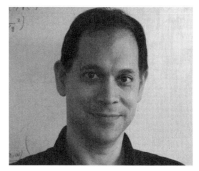

Ken Perlin, Professor, Media Research Laboratory, Courant Institute of Mathematical Sciences, New York University

BIO

Ken Perlin is a professor in the Department of Computer Science at New York University, He was founding director of the Media Research Laboratory and also directed the NYU Center for Advanced Technology. His research interests include graphics, animation, user interfaces, science education, and multimedia. He received an Academy Award for Technical Achievement from the Academy of Motion Picture Arts and Sciences for his noise and turbulence procedural texturing techniques, which are widely used in feature films and television, as well as the 2008 ACM/SIGGRAPH Computer Graphics Achievement Award, the TrapCode Award for achievement in computer graphics research, the NYC Mayor's Award for excellence in Science and Technology and the Sokol Award for outstanding Science faculty at NYU, and a Presidential Young Investigator Award from the National Science Foundation. He has also been a featured artist at the Whitney Museum of American Art.

Dr. Perlin received his PhD in Computer Science from New York University and a BA in theoretical mathematics from Harvard University. Before working at NYU, he was Head of Software Development at R/GREENBERG Associates in New York, NY. Prior to that he was the System Architect for computer-generated animation at Mathematical Applications Group, Inc. He has served on the Board of Directors of the New York chapter of ACM/SIGGRAPH and currently serves on the Board of Directors of the New York Software Industry Association.

Q&A

Q) *The components of character technology are diverse and span the artistic and technical spectrum. How did you get your start* *in the industry? Based on where you see the field heading, what experience/training do you recommend people have?*

A) I got my start in this area several decades ago, in an unusual way. I had been working on using procedural stochastic methods for creating surface textures, and I was curious to see whether I could apply those techniques to human movement and gesture. That led to a broader exploration of synthetic acting.

I think the most important experience/training is understanding acting itself; how people move and why, what motivates gesture and body movement. This is a set of skills that good trained linear animators already have.

Q) *Creating compelling digital characters is part art and part science. What is the greatest challenge you encounter on a daily basis? What aspect of character technology keeps you up thinking at night?*

A) There are two problems: realism and character motivation. The tricky thing is that when you are trying to do both, you are serving different masters. Realism asks you to pay attention to balance, physics, muscle, and joint constraints, whereas motivation asks you to understand what the character is thinking, feeling, why this character is looking at that one in a certain way, why somebody stands up from a chair or walks in a particular way that suggests surprise or weariness, etc. Making these different levels work well together is the most challenging problem I think.

Q) *What are the ingredients for a successful digital character?*

A) By far the most important thing is that they need to be able to sell an emotion; you must believe that the character actually cares about what is going on and that they are conveying a consistent personality – even better if that personality is conflicted and contains layers and contradictions. In the physical world, no actor merely picks up an apple. They pick up an apple angrily or absentmindedly or tentatively. The movement only exists to advance the story and reveal character.

Q) *While the industry is competitive, it is ultimately respectful of great work. Outside of the work you have been personally involved in the production of what animated characters have you been impressed or inspired by? What is the historical high-bar?*

A) There are plenty of great examples in linear animation, and I think that is where the great inspiration comes from so far. There are many examples there. Highlights for me in US animation are the Warner Brothers characters (Bugs Bunny, Daffy Duck, etc.) and the recent work by Brad Bird, such as "The Incredibles" and "Ratatouille." Looking more globally, I am particularly inspired by Miyazaki.

I do not think we have yet gotten to the point where we could place any interactive character side by side with these masters. But, I think we will get progressively closer if we keep at it.

Q) *Where do you see digital characters in ten years? Where are animated characters for film and games heading?*

A) In ten years, we will take for granted that interactive actors will be able to take direction and that the skills and training they need to do so will be built into them, having been incorporated beforehand through a kind of training process (although not at all like the training process that real actors go through, the results might be roughly analogous).

We might also see a merging of acting in these different media. Just as Gollum was a great early example of a fusing of many different techniques – capture of a live-action actor's movements, hand-crafted animation, procedural animation, and so forth, I think the industry will gradually learn to fuse these elements in a seamless way until in many cases, it will no longer be possible to draw a clear line between live-action actors, animated characters, and game characters.

Chapter 14

Case Studies in Character Interactivity

Much of what we have been discussing fits neatly into the realm of digital characters for animation and video games. That being said, the implementation of AI in the system allows for more advanced interaction and opens a field of research and design in character interactivity. There is currently much promise for practical "virtual interviewers" and other avatars who interact with us to serve various functions and to be a familiar life-like interface for interacting with digital systems. There is another possibility in the form of gallery-based work that demonstrates research, aesthetics, or tools for filmmaking for a new medium. This is a direct descendent of work in video games but with a focus more fixed on user interaction for artistic expression and social relationships between characters for research. It is worth making the distinction between animation created for linear animation and that which is produced for interactive products. While there are many similarities between these two outputs, there are also distinct differences. Both linear and interactive animations share a common goal which is the creation of an engaging experience for the viewer/player. Table 14.1, adapted from UC Irvine's Bill Tomlinson's paper [38], outlines the major differences between linear and interactive animation. The brief descriptions below are generalizations. There are exceptions to each of these topics, and active research is ongoing in all of these areas.

Table 14.1 Summary of Five Major Differences Between Linear and Interactive Animation

Topic	Linear animation	Interactive animation
Intelligence	The intelligence and behavior of characters are determined by screenwriters, storyboarders, and animators prior to the audience experiencing the work.	The intelligence and behavior of characters are generated by a computer program in real-time.
Emotional expressiveness	Animator controls emotional state exhibited by characters in each shot. Each action a character takes is inextricably tied to an emotion.	Animator creates dynamic emotional ranges explored during gameplay based on a range of factors. Emotions may be layered on top of actions and controlled independently.
Navigation collision avoidance	Characters only run into things when the animator wants them to.	Characters may accidentally collide with others and with objects in their world. Characters need a mechanism for avoiding collisions dynamically and coping if they occur.
Transitions	Since sequence of events is fixed, transitions between small chunks of animation are controlled by the animator, and may be long or short.	Since the sequence of events is variable, cycles must be kept short or they cause a character to take too long to switch to a different action. (If this is solved by animations not running to completion, characters may exhibit discontinuous motion.)
Multicharacter interaction	Two characters may be animated simultaneously.	Enabling two characters to robustly engage in expressive close contact (fighting, affection, etc.) is an unsolved problem.

When it comes to intelligence in linear animation, the behavioral modeling of the character happens in the mind of the human artist. Animators, writers, and directors define and execute the behavior that the characters should undertake. In interactive animation, the modeling of character intelligence that will be seen by an audience happens instead inside the animation system itself. The creative team designs the behavior, and this interactive system acts as an intermediary between the artists and the audience. During an interactive animation production process, like those we have discussed for procedural animation, animators and programmers produce the raw material for believable behaviors and the rules for connecting them, while linear animators produce the behaviors themselves. This distinction can be frustrating to a linear animator and often requires that they only produce "cycles" or discrete motions. It is also more difficult to document the work that has been done by a single artist. It can be an interesting new undertaking to think through a character in sufficient depth to determine all possible actions and reactions that the character could take, but this is a very different prospect than working through a complete performance by a character over the course of a moment in a film. Another frustration for animators transitioning from linear production to interactive work is that, when animating for interactive products, it is not possible to see the final form that the animation will take in every possible situation. The animator can play-test the game and get a broad sense for the way an animation will look when it is finally rendered and make revisions based on that process. For linear animation, animators typically animate "to the camera," meaning that the camera is placed first then the character is posed for the shot. The position, orientation, size, and other features of on-screen elements, including character components, may be adjusted (also know as "cheated") to the camera to make a scene look better. Often, when viewed from other angles, the character looks totally broken and off-camera elements may not even be animated. Digital characters for 3D interactive work must read in-the-round at all times, and due to the broad range of potential interactions among interactive characters and their environment, there can be no final round of hand-tweaking by the animator to make sure that every element of the scene works together.

In interactive animation, main characters often face away from the camera so that players are able to see where the characters are going rather than seeing the characters' face. This deemphasizes facial complexity in interactive systems, leaving cinematics and cut-scenes to use a different facial rig to emote through the narrative elements of the game. To create variety of motion and to ensure that motion is not repetitive, frequently multiple animations are created for each action to provide action variety. Rather than having just one animation for a given behavior, a character may have several subtly different alternating variants. Procedural noise, in particular Perlin noise, may also be added to the actions to give them a more life-like quality and to give the viewer/player the sense that the motion is unique at every instant. The process of interactive animation and the design of interactive systems require animators to more fully understand their character's behavior than in linear formats. In an animated film, if a character wanted to show disgust at a situation, the animator would just animate them reacting at the right moment with the facial and body cues that communicate the feeling of being disgusted, but in an interactive system, the animator might create a similar disgusted animation clip, but the conditions that should cause the behavior would have to be defined in the system.

The consensus is that animation created for interactive systems is more difficult than animation created for linear applications such as film. Linear animation has an established set of conventions and techniques on which to draw with numerous examples of well developed and compelling characters, while computer games and other interactive media are still working out many core questions on how to present believable and engaging characters in an interactive format. For example, in traditional linear animation, making a character that can smile requires a few strokes of a pencil but is a complex pursuit in an interactive domain.

In areas where linear animation has laid groundwork, interactive animation should be able to draw on the established forms of its linear predecessor but nothing can be taken for granted. Take for example, the point Tomlinson makes about comedy. He notes that in linear animation, comic timing is relatively easy to manipulate, while in interactive animation, it is much more challenging. Linear animation can be easily re-timed to achieve the desired effect. Any comedian will tell you how difficult comic timing is. The same rules and ability to make something funny apply to animators; there is no software that has the ability to encapsulate comic timing. In interactive animation, however, where users may impact the timing of events, certain kinds of comedy become very difficult. We can animate a character to tell a pre-recorded joke or pratfall, but this is simply a pre-recorded dialog or action and without the controlled timing of linear animation, these often fall flat. Comedy is a staple of linear animation, and most animation, from "Loony Tunes" to "South Park," has traditionally been based on humor; it is not nearly as prevalent in interactive animation. As John Lasseter, director of "Toy Story" and other Pixar films, offered in describing an early computer animation he had done, "It was not the software that gave life to the characters, it was these principles of animation, these tricks of the trade that animators had developed over 50 years ago" [21]. The similarities between linear and interactive animation lie in the principles of the traditional animation formulated by the Walt Disney Studio. An understanding of the differences between linear and interactive animation may help interactive animations exhibit the same appeal that has made traditional linear animation so successful to such a broad audience for its long history.

Three projects are introduced below that demonstrate interactive character technology outside of the conventional context of computer games. These projects provide a unique perspective on digital characters and lead us to speculations on the future of research and development on the subject.

14.1 "ALPHAWOLF" BY THE SYNTHETIC CHARACTERS GROUP AT THE MIT MEDIA LAB

"AlphaWolf" is an interactive installation in which people play the role of wolf pups in a pack of autonomous and semi-autonomous gray wolves (*Canis lupus*). Presented at SIG-GRAPH 2001, "AlphaWolf" allowed users to howl, growl, whine, or bark into a microphone. In turn, the vocal cues influenced how the participant's pup interacted with the other members of the pack. The focus of the project was on social learning, allowing the digital wolf pups to benefit from context preservation as they interacted in their environment (Figure 14.1). As such, in each successive inter-character inter-action, individuals were able to bring their interaction history to bear on their decision-making process. The computational model captured a subset of the social behavior of wild wolves underscored by two lines of inquiry: the relationship between social learning and emotion and development as it relates to

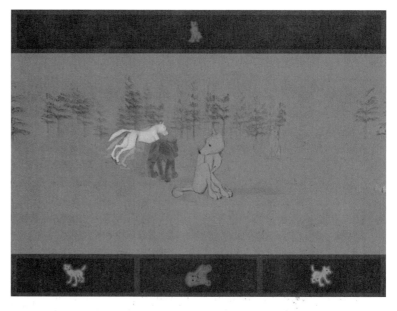

■ **FIGURE 14.1** "AlphaWolf" by the synthetic characters group at the MIT media lab.

social learning. The combination of these threads, as applied to digital characters, advanced the idea of character learning and the ramification of historical lessons on current behavior and reactions to stimulus. The applications of a project such as this are numerous, especially with regard to group dynamics. Just as individual animals provide good models for creating individual agents, populations of animals can inspire mechanisms by which those individual agents will interact. Social learning has huge ramifications for groups of agents both virtually, in animated crowd systems, and physically, in swarms or small groups of robots. Long-term applications such as computer interfaces that can interact more appropriately with humans by utilizing human social abilities are also possible.

The initial sketch was based primarily on the notion of dominance and submission between puppies. The intelligence is basic, everyday common sense that animals exhibit, including the ability to find food, to know who they like, and to build simple emotional relations with each other. The procedural wolves used blended animation clips to produce smart collections of behaviors, but in many ways, the motion of the characters was outweighed by the notion of learning and development in a digital character. The ramifications for this are tremendous and form the beginnings of a computational scaffolding for intelligent and learning digital characters. These autonomous and semi-autonomous wolves interacted with each other much as real wolves do.

"AlphaWolf" offers initial steps toward computational systems with social behavior, in hope of making interactions with them more functional and more inherently rewarding. The notion of character memory is monumental. This coupled with the idea that memory of behavior dictates current behavior is a level of character adaptation that has benefits to crowds that need to be able to share knowledge about their environment. The work is a stepping stone for character intelligence in the realms of interactive character research and associated industries (See [39] for more information).

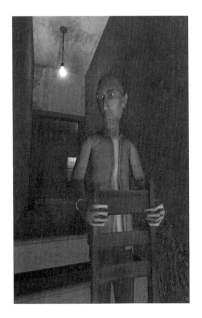

14.2 "TARTARUS" BY ALAN PRICE

"Tartarus" is a real-time 3D simulation in which the viewer interacts with a digital character (Figure 14.2). Traversing an infinite interior structure of dark rooms and dilapidated staircases, the "absurd man," as Price calls him, is destined to carry a wooden chair throughout the space, guided by the viewer's prompts. It is an exploration of an exercise in futility. As the viewer moves the character through the space, the perpetual replication of his environment is discovered. Iterations of the chair begin to accumulate, eventually building up to an impasse. At this critical point, the obstacles fade and the cycle repeats. The absurd man becomes a celebration of his fate as we rationalize the tormented plight of the individual in this world.

"Tartarus" incorporates real-time 3D graphics and game engine technology. Facial expressions are procedurally driven and respond to the location and prompting of the viewer's position in the scene. The virtual camera is in constant motion, programmed to follow the character and navigate within the confines of the architectural space. Over two dozen animation sequences are randomly accessed and blended to control the character in response to the viewer's interaction and to the geometry of the environment. High-Level Shading Language pixel shaders were utilized to render high-definition surface features on the character's skin and clothing. Open Dynamics Engine was implemented for dynamic interaction with the chairs that accumulate in the scene.

The real-time simulation involved the visitor engaging in an exercise in futility at the expense of a digital character. The viewer used a touch screen to guide a virtual figure carrying his burden in the form of a wooden chair through dilapidated staircases and dark rooms. Over the course of the installation, replications of the chair began to accumulate, eventually building an impasse within the space. At this critical point, the obstacles fade and the cycle repeats. Real-time 3D graphics and game engine technology put the viewer in control of this representation of the individual's daily burden. "Tartarus" won the Prix Ars Electronica, Honorary

Mention Interactive Art, at Ars Electronica in Linz, Austria in 2006. The write-up by the curators of the exhibition was as follows:

> *"Alan Price's Tartarus utilizes real-time graphics and game engine technology to create the unlikely virtual character of an emotional old man in a nihilistic and absurd environment. The user accompanies the old man whose burden is a single chair. As you adventure through this world of naked stairways, and unwelcome rooms, more and more chairs begin to accumulate in a metaphoric homage to the Sisyphean task of being an individual."*

Price is working on a follow-up to "Tartarus," a series called "Empire of Sleep," which includes similar touch screen technology for user interaction, but follows a group of characters (Figure 14.3). "Empire of Sleep" is an experiment in the application of the traditional narrative and temporal structure of cinema to the medium of real time rendered graphics and user interaction. A touch screen installation displays interactive real time 3D renderings of surreal landscapes depicting events haunted by calamity on massive scales, and a protagonist's attempts at evading the impending consequences. By incorporating the immediacy, immersive, and non-linear characteristics of real time rendering with temporal and narrative structure of traditional cinema, this work explores the combination of real time and traditional animation. The intent is to find a balance between these modes of representation, attempting to make the viewer aware of the issues being examined while engaging in a narrative sequence that simultaneously depicts the perspectives, and fates, of the digital characters as they strive to comprehend their own relationship to their simulated environment.

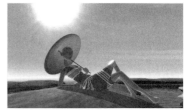

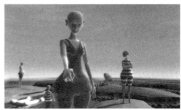

■ **FIGURE 14.3**　"Empire" by Alan Price.

14.3 **"MOVIESANDBOX" BY FRIEDRICH KIRSCHNER**

Friedrich Kirschner develops tools to support creating films using game engines. His film "The Journey" (2004) (Figure 14.4) was screened at film festivals and available

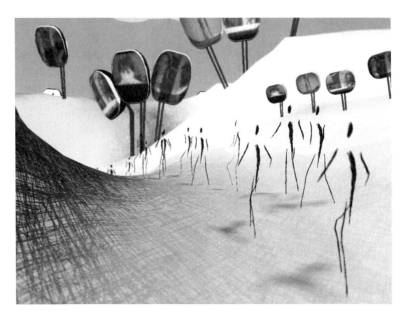

■ **FIGURE 14.4** "The Journey" (2004) by Friedrich Kirschner.

as self-playing modification, often just called a "mod," for the popular game Unreal Tournament 2004. Mods are customizations of existing games ranging in scale from custom characters or elements, to brand new games developed within the framework of the game.

With the creation of this film and others following the same machinima paradigm, Kirschner began developing an authoring tool for others to create films within game engines. The current incarnation of this toolkit is "MovieSandbox" (Figure 14.5). "MovieSandbox" is a graphical scripting tool that enables users to script their own gameplay elements. "MovieSandbox" does not use a linear time line but rather is designed to string together actions in a procedural node-network where you can create relationships between nodes and trigger actions and commands. It allows you to easily create your own characters, sets, and poses and direct them in a quick and modifiable manner.

While the initial implementation of Kirschner's "Movie-Sandbox" was implemented as a toolkit within Unreal Tournament, it is now evolving as a stand-alone application. It is

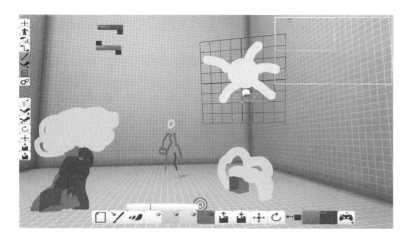

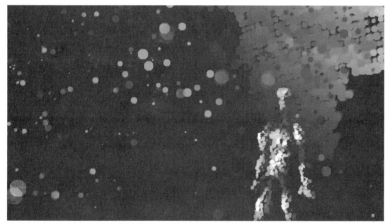

■ **FIGURE 14.5** "MovieSandbox" by Friedrich Kirschner.

an evolving toolkit that strives to put unique creative control in the hands of filmmakers who want to work in an interactive context. By incorporating do-it-yourself instructions for building a simple 3D scanner, fast tools for rigging models, and intuitive controls for puppeteering motion, the system opens the door to creative people who need an entry point into the great potential of machinima. The puppeteering controls often utilized physical interfaces giving the artist a tactile response which has a shallow learning curve by limiting the controls. Kirschner utilizes the pupeteering analogy because most people have probably played with a marionette in their life at some point. As such, it is quickly evident that even though the initial mechanical construction might seem complicated, the act of pulling a string and seeing the puppet react to it in a physically comprehensive way is comforting and demystifying of the process. This is in sharp contrast to typical digital animation where complicated rigs and animator controls often do not have a direct relationship.

The toolkit also attempts to transition the aesthetics of game engines from vertex-based computer games to a more artistic and organic style based on particle-based pointillism. Kirschner believes that today's computer game engines have all the technical prerequisites to offer a wide variety of art directions and visual styles, but they are too often utilized in a very traditional way. A performance entitled "Puppet Play," created using an early version of "MovieSandbox," moved away from the traditional computer game look and feel, demonstrating alternatives not only to the naturalistic trend in computer game graphics but also showing new usage scenarios for computer game engines that are closer to animated filmmaking and puppetry. By advancing this new art form, "MovieSandbox" gets the technology out of the way of the artistry and is a stepping stone into a new realm of aesthetics for the interactive industry.

■ FURTHER READING

For more information on AlphaWolf and Bill Tomlinson's more recent work refer to his web site:

http://www.ics.uci.edu/~wmt/

His article on the difference between animating character for film and interactive applications is very insightful:

Bill Tomlinson. From linear to interactive animation: How autonomous characters change the process and product of animating. *Computers in Entertainment*, 3(1):5, 2005.

More information on Alan Price's "Tartarus" and his recent work can be found on his web site:

http://accad.osu.edu/~aprice/

Information and the latest news on Friedrich Kirschner's "MovieSandbox" can be found on the project web site:

http://moviesandbox.com/

More information about Kirschner's films and other projects can be found on his personal web site:

http://www.zeitbrand.net

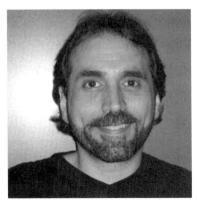

Paul Marino, Executive Director, Academy of Machinima Arts and Sciences, Lead Cinematic Designer, BioWare

◼ INTERVIEW: PAUL MARINO, EXECUTIVE DIRECTOR, ACADEMY OF MACHINIMA ARTS & SCIENCES, LEAD CINEMATIC DESIGNER, BIOWARE

◼ BIO

Paul Marino is Lead Cinematic Designer for game developer BioWare, working on the Mass Effect series of games. In addition to his work at BioWare, Marino is also a pioneer in the field of Machinima: using game technology to create films. He authored the first book about Machinima ("The Art of Machinima," Paraglyph Press) as well as co-founded the Academy of Machinima Arts and Sciences in New York. He has presented at a variety of events including the Austin Game Developers Conference, Edinburgh Interactive Entertainment Festival, USC School of Cinematic Arts, Harvard Law School and the Sundance Film Festival. Earlier in his career, Marino was a broadcast animator and designer with a number of industry recognitions, including an Emmy Award for his work with Turner Broadcasting.

◼ Q&A

Q) *The components of character technology are diverse and span the artistic and technical spectrum. How did you get your start in the industry? Based on where you see the field heading, what experience/training do you recommend people have?*

A) My path into animation was kick-started in high school. My school had a progressive internship program which allowed me to work at a small animation and visual effects studio for one term. From there, I continued my studies but also continued to work doing small animation tasks there until I was eventually hired full time.

To state the overtly obvious, the fundamentals of character animation are paramount to anyone forging a career in digital characters. However, as technology around digital characters evolves, it is the application of this knowledge that will gradually shift. Rather than implement the understandings of character movement and emotion at the keyframe level, directors and animators will be able to layer more complex performance work onto intelligent character rigs. Relatedly, I also recommend acting studies as well. Learning how to embody your character's posturing and performance will make recreating them digitally that much easier. Ancillary workshops in dance are also helpful, focusing on the body's freedoms/constraints temporally and spatially.

Technology knowledge is very important, but it is equally important to keep a good part of your character studies technology-agnostic.

Q) *Creating compelling digital characters is part art and part science. What is the greatest challenge you encounter on a daily basis? What aspect of character technology keeps you up thinking at night?*

A) My greatest challenge in the day-to-day is striking that balance between believability and realism. As we are handling characters that are designed with an eye towards realism, imbuing them with life is usually a give-and-take of what works best for the digital character and/or what works best for the audience. As a result, crafting a realistic performance can feel staged if the character's visual fidelity does not support the performance. Conversely, a less-than-realistic, nee stylized performance can make the character feel grotesque. With each digital character, their associated vocal work and animation in the mix, the full definition of performance is invoked – a larger work created from the contributing ones – and usually it is never the same mix twice.

The area of character technology that keeps me awake is object transference. While there are strides being made, it is still challenging to have a character pick up a heavy object (with appropriate weight shifting) and hand it to another character (with equal weight displacement). I am sure there are evolving solutions to address, but it is one that consistently causes me to cringe.

Q) *What are the ingredients for a successful digital character?*

A) Of equal parts (though not in any particular order):

Technically

1. Solid, yet simple rigging
2. Good system of facial bones
3. Support for a variety of control mechanisms (FK, IK, Rag doll, etc.)

Performative

1. To be spatially and self-aware
2. To channel inner thought
3. To have purpose

Aesthetic

1. Visually expressive
2. Designed with flexibility in mind
3. Carries an air of simplicity

Q) *While the industry is competitive, it is ultimately respectful of great work. Outside of the work you have been personally involved in the production of what animated characters have you been impressed or inspired by? What is the historical high-bar?*

A) I am going to go for relative safe ground here and say Bugs Bunny, but specifically Robert McKimson's Bugs. Some are critical of McKimson's work at Warner Bros (better animator than director more are fans of Jones or Freleng), but I always felt that McKimson's Bugs was the quintessential character. Hammy, yet nuanced; purposeful yet subversive. He made Bugs live beyond the frame, something that I feel many of the today's characters lack. There is much to learn from the way McKimson animated Bugs. Each time I watch one of his toons, I catch something new in his work.

Q) *Where do you see digital characters in ten years? Where are animated characters for film and games heading?*

A) I believe digital characters will begin to embrace additional support systems such as spatial, intellectual, and emotional rigs. To this, the medium will drive which systems are necessary when characters for a film project may not need strong intellectual support, but emotional support will be key. Once digital characters reach this level of autonomy, we can layer behaviors onto the base canvas of a character giving us the freedom to focus on the character's acting while rudimentary systems handle the non-performance-related tasks. This work is already being pioneered by Dr. Ken Perlin, who has been breaking ground in developing smart actor systems for digital characters.

Part **4**

Conclusions

The Future of Digital Characters

In exploring the theory and practice of digital character technology, we are constantly reminded of the many advances that have been achieved and also the many challenges that are dealt with everyday. Most productions require the need for innovation to both make the process more efficient and to overcome the seemingly impossible expectation of bringing the unimaginable to life. It is this need for innovation that drives not only the art and technology of digital characters but also the character technical directors who create them. While we have achieved near realism in film characters and responsive interaction in game characters, the ability to merge these two hallmarks is the challenge faced by future artists.

The practical challenges in the near future for digital characters fall mainly in the realm of rig interactivity with regard to the manipulation speed and efficiency while processing complicated constraints and deformations. Performance capture, as a means for artists to breathe life into digital characters, is another challenge. While character animation is consistently successful in bringing characters to life, we still have many hurdles when it comes to translating a motion capture performance into something where the actor inhabits the character on screen. Many solutions to these concerns are at hand and under active development, but of course, there are

291

long-term issues to think about. In this section, we discuss briefly some current character technology research threads and the potential impact of this work on the future of the field.

Innovation, within the many disciplines contained by computer graphics, comes from multiple sources. Research from the academic world has established the core ideas relating to the theory and technology behind techniques and our understanding of digital characters. These core ideas range from computer graphics concepts related to more stable joint rotations, to new ways of deforming surfaces, to the psychology of using digital characters as interviewers and avatars in our daily lives. Studios engaged in the production of animation and video games often take these ideas and implement them directly into their production pipelines. The innovation in studios often comes from the optimization of, and interface for, techniques gleaned directly from academic research, but much original research also comes directly from project pre-production at studios. It is at this stage that studios are engaged with finding answers to the questions that the upcoming production poses. With regard to character technology, this will involve defining the conventions of character setup for the project and the general character pipeline, as well as solving character-specific issues such as simulated elements and unique deformation situations. Whole new techniques are often developed during this pre-production phase that may end up being global to every character, such as a new technique for hair simulation, or discreetly specific to the intricacies of a single character. While academic work is often published in journals and at conferences, studio research (often times carried out by research and development staff with advanced academic degrees) is also presented at conferences and published in journals, but finds its home in the output of the project either in consumers homes or in the movie theater. While the goal of academic research is to publish and document new knowledge, studio research often remains proprietary to that studio and controlled by patents. In most cases, however, there is a lot of overlap between academia and production, with production artists teaching the next generation of artists in the university setting and academic researchers acting as consultants on production challenges.

Character technology advances exponentially from year to year and production to production. Starting at the base level of a digital character, with motion systems, the trend is toward auto rigging. When a studio develops a rig that is production tested, animator approved, and satisfies the production requirements, it is often turned into a system that can be used to generate instances of that rig for characters of any proportion. This is most common for humanoid characters. These systems are usually procedural where the rig is built via code based on interactive input parameters. For example, limb lengths are defined based on specified points of articulation and variable options such as the number of joints define a character's spine. The rig can also be built with a smart architecture that can be refitted to a character of any proportion without the use of code. Either way, systems such as these are critical for creating multiple rigs and these instantiated rigs result in characters that have the same functionality and naming conventions; every character has the same rig so that maintenance and upgrading is simple and standardized.

Along these lines, and because many characters are not strictly humanoid in configuration, studios will often develop a modularized rigging system that allows a character setup artist to build the character in scriptable, or proportionally malleable, pieces that are then connected together to form the full character rig. This building block approach infuses company knowledge into the modules so that, no matter what the character is, the approved arm rig with all its functionality and naming conventions is in place. If a unique element must be built, for example a mermaid's tail, then that module can be built in a way that it can become part of the character module library and reused by other artists. Thinking and tools such as these make the tedious tasks easier and allow character setup artists to focus on the innovative technical challenges that do not fit neatly into an existing tool set. These also allow a single artist to setup many more characters which fit with the trend of crowd and variation systems. Automation of repetitive tasks minimizes user error as well which, in turn, minimizes character fixes, a tremendous part of the character setup artist's job. In the near future, one can imagine simpler and more intuitive character rigs so that an arm is a single chain of joints and a couple of controllers without the need for blending between IK and FK using a multitude of nodes.

Since the purpose of the motion system is to define the architecture of the character and to provide an interface for animators, one can imagine that these two functions will become abstracted from each other. Character architecture is one of the most complicated pieces of character development, and the intention of animator interface is to be intuitive and simple. Placing both these responsibilities on the same system, in fact, makes achieving both well more difficult. Animator interface should be a layer above all this; as a whole other system that plugs into the motion system can be tailored to the animator's preference. This way animators define the interface the way they prefer and all characters follow those conventions. A system that does this and interfaces with whatever motion system it is manipulating will create happy animators and free character setup artists from needing to be user interface developers as well.

As we have discussed throughout this book, the influence of anatomy has greatly advanced the art of character rigging. For motion systems, there is still a need for intuitive tools to build anatomically accurate rig elements and systems. Much of this knowledge remains in the minds of experts and is difficult to port from project to project. Character setup artists, working under the advisement of anatomists and experts in locomotion, are well poised to develop such tools for artists seeking to develop anatomically rigorous characters.

The trend in deformation systems lies primarily in calculation speed. There are a number of existing techniques that cannot be performed interactively by the artist in real time. Solutions which cause muscle jiggle across the character in response to motion are typically simulated after the fact. Simulated solutions produce good results but are notoriously difficult to art direct. While the paradigm for simulation often involves computational knowledge of the state of the system in the past and thus caching large amounts of data, we can expect advances in computing power to make this intense operation faster. Physics research will likely also develop faster ways of computing dynamically deforming surfaces. A rethinking of character deformation from the algorithmic level can also be expected. Drawing on biological models for muscle contraction and skin deformations, much research is going into the elasticity of modeled surfaces and systems of implementation. In a hypothetical world, a truly biological model could be developed that took animation direction and triggered the correct muscles to carry that out, which in turn would manipulate the motion system to move the character element into the correct position per frame. We have a long way to go before naturalistic functioning such as this enters our workflow, but it is interesting to consider.

In the nearer future, we can expect smart algorithms that produce better deformation results with less manual labor. Building layered deformations or painting weights is an incredibly time-consuming task. The desired end result for a deformation system is visually pleasing surface deformations based on the aesthetics and technical limitations of the project. While additive techniques such as skinning, blend shapes, and surface layers allow an artist to get to that point, the time and investment is large and often the character mobility is still limited. What artists crave is a single technique that gets the combined results of these techniques but is fast to setup and easy to maintain. By creating relationships between the vertices of a polygonal mesh, tension and relaxation methods can be implemented to move the vertices based on a surface-derived method and not based on direct response to the underlying driver. Generating a local coordinate system and a knowledge of a base pose, the surface will react to the driving joints (for example), but the surface will attempt to maintain the per-vertex relationships created in the default bind pose or another specified pose. This drives the surface to maintain its original proportions and prevent common issues with loss of volume and collapsing regions. Combined with simple collision functionality to add underlying surfaces, a system such as this could maximize the results of skinning without the need to manually paint weights or define pose-space fixes. While there is no substitute for true multilayered anatomical-derived deformations for creating the sense of surfaces moving over each other, this system combined with underlying colliding surfaces would produce anatomically convincing digital characters.

Where great innovation may come from in the future is in the rethinking of how we build characters and the way we collaborate in doing the work. The modular workflow we have described for character technology development has glossed over the back and forth that often happens when one person sets up a character motion system, another the deformation system, and yet another the face. These are all complicated, interconnected systems that influence each other during development and in running the character. Since the task is huge and the details voluminous, working collaboratively with experts in each system simultaneously is often a necessity.

One can imagine a technology that integrates all these systems more seamlessly and proceduralizes the work to integrate them. This will likely fall into methods of abstracting the relationships and dependencies between systems so that the deformation system can be tuned regardless of changes to the motion system and vice versa. Algorithmically thinking, by defining the systems as a series of inputs and outputs, small bits of code can be defined to sew together the layers. At first, this would happen within strict limits of robustness, but over time, one can foresee that this sewing process could be smarter and able to deal with larger modifications between stages. For example, consider the motion system step as a single procedure with its input being the collection of joints, controls, and constraints and its output being simply the position of a subset of joints that the deformation system is dependant on.

If these joints are procedurally placed and relatively transparent to the motion system developer and the deformation system is defined to accept a collection of joints and output a deformed model, then ideally the work done at this step is abstracted and isolated from the other stages in a modular and insulated manner. This also allows artists to be working on systems relatively concurrently. If the stages are relatively automated as well, then a change to the input data to a system can be procedurally handled and pave the way for any manual artistic decisions that may be needed. The point of all these steps is to get the technology out of the way of the artist so that they can get to their desired aesthetic result faster without worrying about the process. This ideology is clear within character setup but is even more relevant to animation technology where we are likely to see the most obvious advances.

If we were to follow Matt Elson's [11] thoughts on the subject, the future of digital characters is autonomy. Without a doubt, this is in the cards for digital characters. Expressiveness is in the hands of the skilled animator, but the challenge that remains is procedural emotion and this, coupled with autonomy, will produce some interesting results. Autonomy puts decision-making in the hands of the digital character at runtime. Once the system starts, the character does what they want. This will have a lot more relevance to interactive and real-time systems over pre-rendered animation projects. Film directors and animators producing shorts would likely be less interested in characters that did what they wanted in lieu of what was required of them for the scene. Even with live actors, directors give them limits and performance direction. While we have discussed procedural actors who work within those limits to create unique performances, an autonomous digital character with a mind of its own, so to speak, may be difficult to get the desired performance out of.

Autonomy really comes down to spontaneity and giving character the ability to create impromptu performances based on their knowledge of the world around them and their desires. Autonomy requires more than triggering canned motions smartly but actually generating those motions as needed based on a complex AI. This entails a higher level of sensing the world than we have seen thus far, possibly including variations on the human senses such as sight, touch, and hearing (maybe even taste and smell in the future), but even more basic functionality such as proprioception. Proprioception is the sense of the position of parts of the body. This provides feedback to the body internally and gives the organism a sense of where their limbs are in space and in relation to each other. As one would expect, spiders have a very keen internal system for proprioception. To illustrate the use of this sense, law enforcement often tests the functioning of one's proprioception to test sobriety. If a driver is unable to accurately touch his nose with his eyes closed, then he is suffering from an impaired sense of proprioception and is more than likely intoxicated. The introduction of the proprioceptive system to digital characters implies that by giving characters a system that controls the relationship between their limbs that they then can make smart decisions as to where those are at any moment with regard to balance, locomotion, and performance.

This local motion knowledge could be very powerful when applied to large numbers of characters. At the high level, crowd system agents often need to be "dumbed down" so that they behave heroically and not as a normal person would when confronted with the impossible or certain death. For films, local autonomy might be more appropriate where characters can make small decisions in an autonomous manner based on the direction of the system. Video games would be a completely different experience if the developers had no idea what the non-player characters would do after they released the game. This is where innovation in this realm would radically transform digital characters from puppets that we animate to entities that we need to contend with. What if a digital character in your system became better at building new games than the original designer? What games would digital characters build? What characters would a digital character design? This all, of course, gets fuzzy and intangible, sounding in many ways like cyberpunk fiction.

I would like to think that we get to see these questions unfold over time.

As psychologists unravel more about emotion and how the human mind operates, we may start to see models which can be implemented into our autonomous character systems. While AI often deals with the notion of thinking, when we discuss emotion, we are strictly dealing with feeling. While thinking can often be distilled down into logical blocks that can be envisioned by a programmer, feeling resides very much in the illogical and is intrinsically wrapped up with personality. These are difficult notions to implement into the logical structure of programming and why AI research is often tied to ideas of machine learning and large databases of questions and answers that a system can "learn" from. Modeling AI and autonomous characters as a replica of how the human mind works may not be the answer, especially when our knowledge of that subject is still evolving. So far the best means we have to give a digital character emotion is to put an actor, in the form of an animator, in its shoes. It is hard to top these results. As such, the development of autonomous characters has to be informed by animators and actors. For digital characters to be truly autonomous, they need to have the mind of an actor and, for stylization, the eye of an animator. No doubt a tough challenge. As we have mentioned, this is all runtime behavior that is dictated by the state of the system that the character exists within. What about a system that never starts or stops? As computing systems make their way into every aspect of our lives and network communication moves our data from a local hard drive to some easily accessible centralized network space, digital characters have the ability to exist on multiple platforms at once. This is a question that leads us into the notion of digital character ubiquity.

Parallel with improvements in character rigging and motion will be the growing ubiquity of digital characters in our lives. Digital characters will find their way into our homes. In the same way that voice-enabled driving direction systems have been implemented in cars, familiar avatars will assist us with the setup of new electronics, act as home messaging systems, and answer our questions. Would advertising agencies jump on the chance to send you product endorsements through a life-like system? Could movie trailers come to life in your living room? Have we scratched the surface of the notion of immersion in games? We have already seen attempts at personalizing help systems both in fictional scenarios and research into human-computer interaction. Pop culture has given us a number of visions of how something like this could look. Is it a realistic projection that appears life-like in our homes? A high-end version of the little paperclip in Microsoft Office products? A hologram straight out of the world of "Star Wars" emerging from our mobile device or coffee table? Likely, it is something completely novel. The jury is still out as to whether a human face is an effective front end for a ubiquitous information system, but there is little doubt that we will be seeing digital characters more often and in more places.

As we move from the future back to the present, we are obliged to recall the past and to remember the analog precursors of digital characters and the lessons that they still have to teach us.

■ FURTHER READING

It is interesting to think how the future of digital characters overlaps and relates to puppeteering particularly the work of late Hollywood special effects wizard Stan Winston and his studio. Cynthia Breazeal, Director of MIT's Personal Robots Group recently collaborated with Winston in the creation of Leonardo, a compelling animatronic character which was used as a test bed for state of the art research in autonomy and socially intelligent robots.

http://web.media.mit.edu/~cynthiab/

Similarly, Hanson Robotics recently partnered with Massive Software (mentioned in the previous section) and use their crowd simulation software "Massive" as part of the brain for their robot Zeno. Using Massive, Zeno was able to analyze a 3D image of his environment to determine and control physical action and reactions. Massive Software's vision and decision-making components gave Zeno the ability to navigate, make facial expressions, and move his body based on what he saw in the physical environment. The video feed coming in from Zeno's eye camera is fed into the Massive part of his brain so that he can move appropriately and respond emotionally to what is going on around him.

http://www.hansonrobotics.com/

Some interesting work from MotionPortrait creates 3D avatars for use on various platforms from a single photograph:

http://www.motionportrait.com/

Conclusion

As we have traversed through the concepts and code that bring digital characters to life, we are reminded by how quickly this has all come together. Moore's Law stipulates that the transistor density of semiconductor chips would double roughly every eighteen months, meaning that the chip complexity would also be proportional to this rate. While digital characters and their interactive potential are somewhat tied to the speed of the underlying system, the rate at which this technology advances is expected to improve the performance and potential expressiveness of digital characters not only related to the core functioning of the character but also with regard to all the accessory aspects, such as real-time hair and clothing. Production has conquered anatomy; realistic characters can be created, animated, and rendered to be almost indistinguishable from their live counterparts. What remains, as we discussed previously, is the spirit and heart of the character.

When the original "King Kong" (1933) was released, it was a monumental event in cinema that ushered in a new era of filmmaking and audience expectation. At the same time, it was the first big monster on the screen as well as the first film in which the main character in the film was animated (Figure 16.1). This required that the character rise to the challenge of being viewed center-stage, and the creators knew that

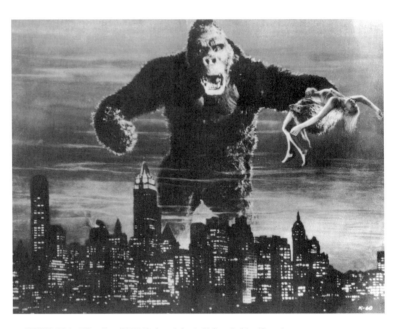

■ **FIGURE 16.1** "King Kong" (1933). Copyright © Hulton Archive/Getty Images.

Kong would have to have an emotional impact on the audience. They wanted him to be fierce and sensitive at the same time. They wanted the audience to be terrified of him in the beginning and sobbing at his demise at the end. They achieved these benchmarks. We feel sympathy for Kong, and he has stood the test of time as a film icon. This legacy was founded heavily in the technology developed to produce the film and the planning and care taken with the animation of Kong himself. After the grueling manual process of animating the Kong puppets (a few rigs were produced), the character transcended the eighteen inch metal frame, the foam and rubber padding and skin, and the rabbit fur exterior to become a living, breathing character that the audience could relate to. The design and construction was deeply informed by anatomy. When director Merian C. Cooper saw effects artist Willis O'Brien's first and second concepts for Kong, he was greatly disappointed. He felt it looked too much like a cross between a man and a monkey. Cooper wired New York's American Museum of Natural History for the correct gorilla specifications and had

O'Brien base his next concepts on them. The construction of the mechanical armature that Kong was animated with is very reminiscent of gorilla skeletal anatomy, and much emphasis was placed on making sure the proportions, anatomy, and motion were entirely based on a real gorilla.

All the techniques that, pioneering motion picture special effects artist, O'Brien developed for the production ushered in the concepts that are still in place for visual effects today including optics, composites, and miniatures. We live and work with modern analogies today, much of which are digital replacements of O'Brien's sophisticated analog solutions. Kong's creation, like that of most stop-motion puppets, has many analogies to digital character development. The manipulatable metal armature provides the points of articulation and the limits of rotation of all the joints. This metal structure is ostensibly the motion system. Covered over this was a filling of foam covered with rubber that created the skin of the character which was deformed, muscles even seeming to bulge, by the motion of the armature as the animators posed it. This is akin to the deformation system. Atop the rubber skin was a short-trimmed layer of rabbit fur. While the modern analogy here would be a character effect like fur, hair, or dynamic clothing, our long computing modern equivalents were lacking the one thing that Kong's fur had: fingerprints. As the animators posed Kong from frame to frame, they had no choice but to affect the fur as they touched it. Studio executives initially saw this as sloppy work until reviews of the film discussed the fur appearing to be blowing in the wind, and the executives decided they loved it.

The production of "King Kong" was kept a secret. The intention was to preserve the magic so that audiences would have no choice but to believe it was real. O'Brien was no stranger to magic. The dinosaurs he created and animated for Arthur Conan Doyle's "The Lost World" (1925) were presented by Doyle at a meeting of the Society of American Magicians in 1922. Magicians in the audience, including the great Harry Houdini and even the press, were astonished and tricked into believing that what they had seen at the meeting was real footage of live dinosaurs. Doyle explained the trick the next day, and the magic of Willis O'Brien gained appreciation from an elite group.

Through the use of technology and character performance, O'Brien had tricked the professional illusionists and sceptics alike. While modern filmgoers have seen the impossible on a regular basis in the theaters, we continue to strive to astonish with modern digital characters. The classic quote from the author Arthur C. Clarke states that "Any sufficiently advanced technology is indistinguishable from magic." With regard to digital characters, the technology behind it is increasingly magical, but the true magic comes from the performance and the life breathed into characters by talented artists.

■ FURTHER READING

There are many books and video documentaries with accounts of the creation of the original "King Kong," but a good recent article by Tom Huntington for American Heritage: Invention and Technology magazine, entitled "King Kong: How the Greatest Special-Effects Movie Was Made With the Simplest Technology," is a good overview of the technology behind the production.

Tom Huntington. King kong: How the greatest special-effects movie was made with the simplest technology. *American Heritage: Invention and Technology*, Volume 21, Winter, 2006.

Bibliography

[1] Vanity Fair (February) 1999.

[2] Irene Albrecht, Jörg Haber, and Hans-Peter Seidel. Construction and animation of anatomically based human hand models. In *SCA '03: Proceedings of the 2003 ACM SIGGRAPH/Eurographics Symposium on Computer Animation*, pages 98–109, Eurographics Association, Aire-la-Ville, Switzerland, 2003.

[3] Jim Bloom. Tippett studio muscle system and skin solver on "Hellboy". In *SIGGRAPH '04: ACM SIGGRAPH 2004 Computer Animation Festival*, page 250, ACM Press, New York, NY, 2004.

[4] Winslow Burleson. *Affective Learning Companions: Strategies for Empathetic Agents with Real-Time Multimodal Affective Sensing to Foster Meta-Cognitive and Meta-Affective Approaches to Learning, Motivation, and Perseverance.* PhD thesis, Cambridge, MA, 2006 (Adviser-Rosalind W. Picard).

[5] Steve Capell, Matthew Burkhart, Brian Curless, Tom Duchamp, and Zoran Popović. Physically based rigging for deformable characters. In *SCA '05: Proceedings of the 2005 ACM SIGGRAPH/Eurographics Symposium on Computer Animation*, pages 301–310, ACM Press, New York, NY, 2005.

[6] Edwin Chang and Odest C. Jenkins. Sketching articulation and pose for facial animation. In *SCA '06: Proceedings of the 2006 ACM SIGGRAPH/Eurographics Symposium on Computer Animation*, pages 271–280, Eurographics Association, Aire-la-Ville, Switzerland, 2006.

[7] Toni Conde and Daniel Thalmann. Autonomous virtual agents learning a cognitive model and evolving. *Lecture Notes in Computer Science*, pages 88–98, Springer-Verlag, London, UK, 2005.

[8] Frederick G. Conrad. Animated agents and user performance in interactive systems (research description). Avalilable at *http://www.psc.isr.umich.edu/research/project-detail.html?ID=33983*.

[9] Frederick G. Conrad and Michael F. Schober. *Envisioning the Survey Interview of the Future (Wiley Series in Survey Methodology)*. Wiley-Interscience, Hoboken, NJ, 2007.

[10] Roger Ebert. Final fantasy: The spirits within. *Chicago Sun Times*, July, 2001.

[11] Matt Elson. The evolution of digital characters. *Computer Graphics World*, 22(9):23–24, September, 1999.

[12] Judy Foreman. A conversation with Paul Ekman: The 43 facial muscles that reveal even the most fleeting emotions. *New York Times*, August, 2003.

[13] Yoram Gutfreund, Tamar Flash, Yosef Yarom, Graziano Fiorito, Idan Segev, and Binyamin Hochner. Organization of octopus arm movements: A model system for studying the control of flexible arms. *Journal of Neuroscience*, 16(22):7297–7307, 1996.

[14] Katherine Isbister. *Better Game Characters by Design: A Psychological Approach (The Morgan Kaufmann Series in Interactive 3D Technology)*. Morgan Kaufmann Publishers Inc., San Francisco, CA, 2006.

[15] David Jacka, Ashley Reid, Bruce Merry, and James Gain. A comparison of linear skinning techniques for character animation. In *AFRIGRAPH '07: Proceedings of the 5th International Conference on Computer Graphics, Virtual Reality, Visualisation and Interaction in Africa*, pages 177–186, ACM Press, New York, NY, 2007.

[16] Isaac V. Kerlow. *The Art of 3D Computer Animation and Effects*, 3rd edition. John Wiley and Sons Inc., Hoboken, NJ, 2004.

[17] Karim Biri, Kiaran Ritchie, and Jake Callery. *The Art of Rigging: Volume I*. CG Toolkit, San Rafael, CA, 2005.

[18] Karim Biri, Kiaran Ritchie, and Oleg Alexander. *The Art of Rigging: Volume II*. CG Toolkit, San Rafael, CA, 2005.

[19] Karim Biri, Kiaran Ritchie, and Oleg Alexander. *The Art of Rigging: Volume III*. CG Toolkit, San Rafael, CA, 2006.

[20] Linden Labs. Second life. Available at *http://secondlife.com*.

[21] John Lasseter. Principles of traditional animation applied to 3D computer animation. In *SIGGRAPH '87: Proceedings of the 14th Annual Conference on Computer Graphics and Interactive Techniques*, pages 35–44, ACM Press, New York, NY, 1987.

[22] James C. Lester, Charles B. Callaway, Joël P. Grégoire, Gary D. Stelling, Stuart G. Towns, and Luke S. Zettlemoyer. Animated pedagogical agents in knowledge-based learning environments. *Smart Machines in Education: The Coming Revolution in Educational Technology* pages 269–298, MIT Press, Cambridge, MA, 2001.

[23] James C. Lester, Sharolyn A. Converse, Susan E. Kahler, Barlow S. Todd, Brian A. Stone, and Ravinder S. Bhogal. The persona effect: Affective impact of animated pedagogical agents. In *CHI '97: Proceedings of the SIGCHI Conference on Human Factors in Computing Systems*, pages 359–366, ACM Press, New York, NY, 1997.

[24] Yi Lin. 3D character animation synthesis from 2D sketches. In *GRAPHITE '06: Proceedings of the 4th International Conference on Computer Graphics and Interactive Techniques in Australasia and Southeast Asia*, pages 93–96, ACM Press, New York, NY, 2006.

[25] Scott McCloud. *Understanding Comics: The Invisible Art*. Perennial Currents, New York, NY, 1994.

[26] Tim McLaughlin. Taxonomy of digital creatures: Interpreting character designs as computer graphics techniques. In *SIGGRAPH '05: ACM SIGGRAPH 2005 Courses*, page 1, ACM Press, New York, NY, 2005.

[27] Tim McLaughlin and Stuart S. Sumida. The morphology of digital creatures. In *SIGGRAPH '07: ACM SIGGRAPH 2007 Courses*, page 1, ACM Press, New York, NY, 2007.

[28] Masahiro Mori. Bukimi no tani (The uncanny valley). *Energy*, 7(4):33–35, 1970.

[29] Fiorenzo Morini, Barbara Yersin, Jonathan Maym, and Daniel Thalmann. Real-time scalable motion planning for crowds. In *CW '07: Proceedings of the 2007 International Conference on Cyberworlds*, pages 144–151, IEEE Computer Society, Washington, DC, 2007.

[30] Ken Perlin and Athomas Goldberg. Improv: A system for scripting interactive actors in virtual worlds. In *SIGGRAPH '96: Proceedings of the 23rd Annual Conference on Computer Graphics and Interactive Techniques*, pages 205–216, ACM Press, New York, NY, 1996.

[31] Michael Pratscher, Patrick Coleman, Joe Laszlo, and Karan Singh. Outside-in anatomy based character rigging. In *SCA '05: Proceedings of the 2005 ACM SIGGRAPH/Eurographics Symposium on Computer Animation*, pages 329–338, ACM Press, New York, NY, 2005.

[32] William T. Reeves. Inbetweening for computer animation utilizing moving point constraints. In *SIGGRAPH '81: Proceedings of the 8th Annual Conference on Computer Graphics and Interactive Techniques*, pages 263–269, ACM Press, New York, NY, 1981.

[33] Craig W. Reynolds. Flocks, herds, and schools: A distributed behavioral model. *Computer Graphics*, 21(4):25–34, 1987.

[34] Thomas W. Sederberg and Scott R. Parry. Free-form deformation of solid geometric models. In *SIGGRAPH '86: Proceedings of the 13th Annual Conference on Computer Graphics and Interactive Techniques*, pages 151–160, ACM Press, New York, NY, 1986.

[35] Alvy R. Smith. The making of Andre and Wally B. Available at *http://alvyray.com/Art/Andre&WallyB_TheMakingOf.pdf*, 1984.

[36] Daniel Thalmann, Christophe Hery, Seth Lippman, Hiromi Ono, Stephen Regelous, and Douglas Sutton. Crowd and group animation. In *GRAPH '04: Proceedings of the Conference on SIGGRAPH 2004 Course Notes*, page 34, ACM Press, New York, NY, 2004.

[37] Frank Thomas and Ollie Johnston. *The Illusion of Life: Disney Animation*. Disney Editions; Rev Sub edition (October 5, 1995), New York, NY, 1981.

[38] Bill Tomlinson. From linear to interactive animation: How autonomous characters change the process and product of animating. *Computers in Entertainment*, 3(1):5, 2005.

[39] Bill Tomlinson and Bruce Blumberg. Synthetic social relationships in animated virtual characters. In *ICSAB: Proceedings of the Seventh International Conference on Simulation of Adaptive Behavior on from Animals to Animats*, pages 401–402, MIT Press, Cambridge, MA, 2002.

[40] Guido van Rossum. Python. Available at *http://python.org*.

[41] Yoram Yekutieli, Roni Sagiv-Zohar, Ranit Aharonov, Yaakov Engel, Binyamin Hochner, and Tamar Flash. Dynamic model of the octopus arm. I. Biomechanics of the octopus reaching movement. *Journal of Neurophysiology*, 94(2):1443–1458, 2005.

[42] Victor Brian Zordan, Bhrigu Celly, Bill Chiu, and Paul C. DiLorenzo. Breathe easy: Model and control of simulated respiration for animation. In *SCA '04: Proceedings of the 2004 ACM SIGGRAPH/Eurographics Symposium on Computer Animation*, pages 29–37, Eurographics Association, Aire-la-Ville, Switzerland, 2004.

Index

311